# Welcome to the Homeland

# Welcome to the Homeland

## A Journey to the Rural
## Heart of America's
## Conservative Revolution

## BRIAN MANN

STEERFORTH PRESS
HANOVER, NEW HAMPSHIRE

*For Elaine Sunde, who raised a metro and*
*a homelander — and who thinks we're both right.*

For information about permission to reproduce
selections from this book, write to:
Steerforth Press L.C., 25 Lebanon Street,
Hanover, New Hampshire 03755

Library of Congress Cataloging-in-Publication Data

Mann, Brian, 1965–
   Welcome to the homeland : a journey to the rural heart of america's conservative revolution
/ Brian Mann. — 1st ed.
      p. cm.
   ISBN-13: 978-1-58642-111-3 (alk. paper)
   ISBN-10: 1-58642-111-5 (alk. paper)
   1. Conservatism — United States. 2. United States — Politics and government — 1989– 3.
Rural-urban relations — United States. 4. Politics and culture — United States. 5. Culture
conflict — United States. 6. Republican Party (U.S. : 1854– ) I. Title.

JC573.2.U6M344 2006
320.520973—dc22

                                                                    2006015279

FIRST EDITION
*Book design by Peter Holm, Sterling Hill Productions*

*Go back, go back, go back to the woods.*
*Your coach is a farmer and your team is no good.*
            — WENDELL BERRY

*Burn down your cities and leave our farms,*
*and your cities will spring up again as if by magic;*
*but destroy our farms, and the grass will grow*
*in the streets of every city in the country.*
            — WILLIAM JENNINGS BRYAN

# CONTENTS

# Two Brothers, Two Cultures

I've spent the past twenty years writing stories about small towns that are as true and honest as I can tell them. I'm old-fashioned in the sense that I believe in objectivity. I love arguing politics over a beer and a barbecue grill, but when I sit to the work of journalism, I generally keep my opinions to myself. I'll be honest: It feels a hell of a lot safer to at least pretend to be aloof and neutral — an observer and not a participant.

But the remarkable rise of rural America in our national politics, and the growing enmity that small-town folk feel toward urban culture, struck me as a tale that demanded an interested storyteller, someone who feels the passions and understands the night sweats of both sides. It's a tale told partly in statistics and voting trends and campaign strategies. But the clash between urban and rural values runs much deeper, dividing families as well as states.

In this simmering civil war, I consider myself a metro. Same-sex marriage seems like a no-brainer to me. It doesn't strike me as a political dodge when politicians say they're personally opposed to abortion but also pro-choice. As a lifelong Christian, it never occurred to me to believe that the Bible was literal truth. Modern creationism is an idea so muddled that it leaves me shaking my head.

But if many of my values are urban and progressive, I'm really sort of a half-breed, a straddler of the national fence. I grew up on the Kansas prairie, in Wichita and Augusta and Longton. I still love driving the chalky back roads of Elk County, smelling the wild garlic in the fields. There's no sight on earth more dramatic than the Flint Hills at night when the farmers are burning away the season's chaff.

The flame moves over the earth like mercury, like a force out of the Bible stories I studied as a child.

When I was a boy, my dad spent a good part of every year tending cattle ranches and hog farms. He even smuggled hogs for a while, until a local sheriff made him knock it off. One of my earliest memories is of my aunt trying to divine my future by randomly picking out passages from the Old Testament. I don't recall her predictions (I'm sure they were pretty dire; all her prognostications were tainted by fire and brimstone), only the sticky smell of Juicy Fruit gum on her breath and the nervous feeling that she and I were up to something impious.

My family settled for a couple of years on the outskirts of Owasso, Oklahoma, in a trailer park square against the railroad tracks. My brother, Allen, and I would find hobos in makeshift camps under the trestle, desperate men who would beg us to run up to the house and steal them cans of Campbell's soup or loaves of Wonder Bread. From the age of ten until I was a young man, we lived in Sitka, Alaska, a fishing-and-logging town perched on the edge of America. It's gone over to tourism now, catering to city folks who come for a taste of wildness; but in the 1970s the town was as blue collar as any factory burg in Michigan or Indiana. I was on the wrestling team with guys whose dads worked shifts out at the pulp mill and whose moms picked up extra cash baiting long-line hooks down on the docks.

Allen and I spent summers butchering salmon and drinking Rainier and flirting with girls in the cab of the pickup truck we shared. Like a lot of small-town kids, I thought sure we would eventually wind up in a city or maybe the suburbs. That was the real America we saw every night on TV. The schools were there — and the jobs and the excitement. Sitting on the cannery pier during cigarette breaks, rubber bibs smeared with halibut slime, I would turn the glossy pages of the *New Yorker* with a kind of yearning. The articles didn't fascinate me so much as the "Goings On About Town" column. New York City was a continent away, but the thumbnail sketches of metro life seemed like a personal invitation, a summons to a different and brighter existence.

It didn't turn out that way. I've worked assignments in plenty of American cities and spent a glorious season in Manhattan working for National Public Radio, but one accident after another kept nudging me back into small towns. I've cobbled together a career writing about mill strikes and factory closings and sagging dairy prices. I've sat through bingo night in the Alaskan bush, hunted whitetail deer in northern New York, and talked spiritual salvation with Mormons in southern Utah.

The good news is that I settled to it. T. S. Eliot — that displaced midwesterner — got it right when he talked about arriving back where you started and knowing the place for the first time. I have come to see small towns as complex places, vibrant and proud and full of twists. Driving through New York's Adirondack Mountains, where I live and work, I find people who are as thoughtful and creative as anyone I've met in cities. Not all are like that, of course, but I have been surprised more often than not by the intellectual rigor of rural folk and the vitality of their culture.

That's not how most Americans see it. In our increasingly urbanized society, small towns are viewed (when they're noticed at all) like Indian reservations. Their inhabitants are the last holdouts of a dying way of life. Their weird time-warp customs are made to look naively charming (think *Little House on the Prairie* or *Prairie Home Companion*) or laughable (*Dukes of Hazzard* or *Green Acres*) or downright menacing (*Deliverance* or *Texas Chainsaw Massacre*).

It's not just pop culture that paints this portrait. For a couple of generations, newspapers and television have barraged metros with images of rural life in decay. It's a rare month when the *New York Times* or the *Washington Post* doesn't publish an article about a fading prairie town, the death of a family farm, or another Tornado Alley trailer park swept away in the blink of an eye. In our collective imagination, small towns are places on the margin, overshadowed by our dense cities and sprawling suburbs.

But in the last few years, metros have awakened to a nervous new reality. Those folks living out beyond the urban beltway — out beyond the first dense ring of inner suburbia — have been making an unpleasant fuss, refusing to go quietly into the night. A new rural elite based in towns like Centralia, Washington; Lufkin, Texas; and Colorado Springs, Colorado, has emerged, wielding enormous power in Washington. These "homelanders" — as I've unceremoniously dubbed them — are demanding that we talk about things that most urban Americans thought were comfortably settled a long time ago, from abortion to the public role of Christianity to women in the workplace to evolution.

What's more, homelanders are winning more fights than they're losing. After George Bush was reelected in 2004, big-city newspapers ran baffling headlines proclaiming, "Rural Values Proved Pivotal" (*New York Times*), "Conservatives in Rural Ohio Big Key in Bush Victory" (Associated Press), and "GOP Won with Accent on Rural and Traditional" (*Washington Post*).

"I think the rise of what was called moral values in the polls on this election defined a group of people who in their family, faith, and work want to live and do live in what we would call an old-fashioned life," journalist and historian Richard Reeves told CBS's Dan Rather. "It's more *Father Knows Best* and less 'The Times They Are a-Changin'.'"

In 2005 the Senate overwhelmingly approved the appointment of John Roberts, a small-town conservative, as chief justice of the Supreme Court. In February 2006, South Dakota's legislature passed a draconian antiabortion law that bans reproductive choice, even in cases of incest and rape, and when a pregnancy endangers a woman's health. Activists in a state with half the population of urban Philadelphia are helping to roll back a freedom that two hundred million Americans support.

It doesn't seem to make sense. In a nation where 80 percent of the population lives in metropolitan areas, how can a bunch of rubes and Bible thumpers push the rest of us around?

As you've probably guessed, this isn't a *Blue Highways* sort of book. It's not about rural America's picket fences or colorful characters. A lot of interesting folks and places will be found in these pages, but if it were that sort of story, you wouldn't *need* to read it. The people described here wouldn't have any real impact on your life. The truth is that most of us don't live in small towns anymore. A rapidly growing number of immigrant families have no connection at all to America's rural heritage. Their roots are in Mexico City or New Delhi or London or Shanghai.

The main argument of *Welcome to the Homeland* is that home-landers do matter. Their influence is being felt with less and less sub-tlety in the heart of America's progressive cities and suburbs. When a Texas schoolbook committee demands a more conservative treat-ment of American history, your kids might wind up hearing that ver-sion in their high school class in Connecticut or New Jersey. When small-town voters in Oregon turn out in overwhelming numbers to reject gay marriage, same-sex couples in progressive Portland feel the cultural sand shifting beneath their feet. When Wal-Mart — the largest retailer in the United States, based in rural Bentonville, Arkansas — refuses to carry certain books or music (or contracep-tive pills) because they don't match the corporation's traditional values, the decision affects millions of urban Americans.

Washington, D.C., is ground zero in the clash between urban and rural culture. The Republican leadership has embraced homelander-style conservatism. Many of the most powerful men in America are themselves deeply rooted in small-town sensibility: George Bush (West Texas), Dick Cheney (Wyoming), Tom DeLay (the Houston exurbs), Bill Frist (Tennessee), Roy Blunt (rural Missouri), and Dennis Hastert (exurban Illinois). Their values, which the vast majority of us no longer share, are reshaping our laws and federal institutions.

It's not just Republicans. Leading rural Democrats are working aggressively to shift their party away from urban-progressive values. They supported President Bush's nominations to the Supreme Court, making any opposition by urban Democrats (or from metro activist groups like NARAL and NOW) strategically impossible. Part of this internal dissent reflects a basic political reality: Pro-choice Democrats who embrace gay civil rights are a vanishing breed in homelander states. Senator Tom Daschle's 2004 defeat in South Dakota showed just how dangerous progressivism can be, even for a powerful incumbent. But it's also true that many small-town Democrats simply don't share the values of urban party leaders such as San Francisco congresswoman Nancy Pelosi and New York senator Chuck Schumer. Go to Nebraska senator Ben Nelson's Web site and you'll find that the most prominent feature in his on-line biography is a testimonial from George W. Bush. According to Bush, Nelson "is willing to put partisanship aside to focus on what's right for America." "Nelson will never say he's a Democrat," University of Nebraska political scientist John Hibbing told a reporter, a claim that's not quite true. Deep within Nelson's Web content, buried in the fine print, there's a sheepish reference to Nelson as "the most centrist Democrat" in the Senate.

The rise of this rural elite confuses metros, who have long seen themselves as the nation's natural leaders and opinion makers. They're so used to seeing small towns portrayed as quaint or stagnant that the new reality has been slow to sink in. After the 2004 election, reporters with urban news organizations interviewed dozens of evangelical leaders and conservative activists, and the questions were nearly identical: "What payback do you expect for helping the president win reelection?" As if the conservative revolution were a smash-and-grab job, a furtive effort to steal a concession or two. Maybe overturning *Roe v. Wade*? Or same-sex marriage? Or how about school prayer and a couple of Supreme Court nominations?

But homelanders aren't robbing the store. To a remarkable degree, they *own* the store, and they plan a complete remodeling.

If metros see rural culture through a distorted lens, homelanders are just as guilty. They view the nation's cities as fallen places, Sodoms of secular indulgence, Gomorrahs of vice. They frown knowingly at the urban rabble they see on their televisions, whether it's a race riot in Los Angeles, looting in New Orleans, or an antiwar rally in Washington, D.C.

Sometimes this reaction runs to nutty extremes. My grandmother used to sit us kids down (this was in the early 1970s, in Augusta, Kansas) to explain how peaceniks and hippies were sinful, decadent blasphemers. The peace symbol, she warned, was really the Christian cross, broken and inverted as a sign of atheistic disdain.

Metros love this kind of stuff. They lavish attention on the Jerry Falwells and the Pat Robertsons, gobbling up every crazy pronouncement as if it epitomizes (and discredits) an entire culture. But my brother, who lives now in rural Missouri, is one of the sanest and most thoughtful men I've ever met. Allen, too, thinks city culture has gone awry, from the ethical lapses of Bill Clinton, to the plight of homeless people on the streets of St. Louis, to the soulless entertainment industry that pumps out five hundred channels of filth.

"I was watching a cop show on TV the other night with my boys," he told me one afternoon. "Suddenly the criminal plunged a needle into this guy who he had shackled to a chair and began to draw blood out of his carotid artery. The good guys broke in and one of the perpetrators took a knife and sliced his own throat, I guess for the entertainment of whoever was watching."

Allen shook his head, disgusted but also truly dismayed: "How the hell do you protect your kids from that sort of thing, short of removing them from it completely?"

Metros might say that Allen should just turn off his television or change the channel. And for a long time that's exactly what millions of homelanders did. They quietly dropped out. They turned away. They looked for new sources of news and ideas and leadership. When necessary, they created new institutions, launching their own television and radio networks (there are now more than fifteen hundred Christian radio stations in America) and bankrolling their own publishing houses and newspapers. They helped lift a new breed of

Christian rock bands, such as Third Day, into superstardom. They popularized writers like Jerry Jenkins and Tim LaHaye, who authored the bestselling *Left Behind* series.

They homeschooled their kids or started church-centered schools. They organized their own universities. They formed think tanks, newspapers, Web sites, museums, and movie studios. Last summer, my young niece and her husband showed up on our doorstep fresh from a Christian rock festival that included hardcore punk and metal bands. Conservative churches have linked up pastor networks designed to shuttle information from pulpit to pulpit, bypassing the urban media altogether.

Largely ignored by metro culture, tradition-minded Americans created a second, parallel culture. Tens of millions of Americans simply stepped out of the mainstream and watched the rest of the culture go roaring off.

These days, however, more and more homelanders are pushing their way back in. Allen and his neighbors (and their politicians) aren't satisfied with isolation. They don't want to wag their fingers from the sidelines. They want their moral and cultural compass to play a much bigger role, shaping the nation's culture and charting its political future. They believe sincerely that small towns deserve a leading place. To Allen's way of thinking, rural communities are inherently healthier, more virtuous, and decidedly more American than metro communities.

"The human body wants something that's much closer to a natural existence than what's available in the city," he says. "And I think that has ramifications that are pretty profound." He pauses for a moment, then adds a little skeptically: "There are certainly people who have good lives in cities. There are great people in cities. But I definitely think it slants your point of view a certain direction."

This widening chasm punches deeper than the next election cycle or the latest opinion poll. It cuts down into the bone of friendships and the muscle of families. Think of it as a divorce (or at least a trial separation) that gets messier every year. As homelanders claim more power, electing presidents, banning same-sex marriage, curtailing abortion rights, and confirming Supreme Court justices, I find myself watching with real trepidation, the way you eye a big tree that's grown up above your house. It's a pretty safe bet that the trunk is sound, but you never know when a good-sized limb might come crashing down and knock a hole in your roof.

Allen, on the other hand, is a ruralist to his core, so devoutly conservative that he thinks the word *treason* fits some urban Democrats pretty neatly. He's never happier than when he's out in the woods with his sons, Daniel and David, hunting turkeys or whitetail deer. Before you get the wrong idea, Allen's no survivalist and no John Bircher. He is certainly not a hick. He is an insightful teacher and administrator who heads an award-winning math department in a public high school.

But Allen also attends an evangelical Lutheran church, where the Bible-based theology is unbending. His pastor, a soft-spoken man named Mark Bangert, is convinced that the earth was created whole in exactly seven days, sometime in the last five or six thousand years, a view my brother and his family have accepted as literal scientific fact. The folks in Allen's community have deep reservations about the full menu of modernism and multiculturalism that frame much of city life, even questioning the merits of intellectual reason. "I believe that I have the truth," says Pastor Bangert, "and I believe that those who elevate their reason beyond the place where it is God-pleasing miss the truth."

This is awkward and dangerous territory, especially for people who are searching honestly for common ground. It's one thing to make fun of conservative Uncle Allen's dittohead rants or to mock Uncle Brian's Starbucks liberalism. It's something else entirely to sit down and really talk — and really listen. As I began work on this book, my brother agreed to help me navigate the enormous no-man's land between America's two tribes. He served as my guide and my interpreter through more than a year of research, travel, and often heated debate.

Thanks in large measure to his wisdom and patience and good humor, I have come to believe that conservative homelanders want good things for our country. Different things. Things that sometimes make me uncomfortable. Even a few things that I'll fight passionately to resist. Still, I'm convinced that the rural agenda isn't born out of malice or theocratic zaniness or despotism, but rather a desire to restore a way of life that small-town folks see as beautiful and blessed and besieged.

# The New Homelander Elite

This is the story of America's most powerful minority, the white rural conservatives who make up the base and the ideological anchor of the Republican Party. These fifty million homelanders aren't just huddled in the South or the Bible Belt. They're scattered in small towns and exurbs across the country, from the farm counties of California to the old mining towns of Pennsylvania.

The rural region in northern New York where I live voted for George Bush by breakaway margins in 2000 and again in 2004. In nearby Hamilton County, the most rural place in the state, folks gave Bush 80 percent of their ballots. My neighbors are mostly Christian, mostly white, and devoutly Republican. Drive the winding county roads through blink-and-you-miss-it towns like Ausable Forks and Upper Jay and you could easily be in the America that existed in the 1950s. Logging trucks outnumber Volvos.

After nearly a century of political and cultural irrelevance, people like these have managed to seize enormous control over the national dialogue. "Where Bush really won the election in 2000 was among rural voters," says top Democratic pollster and strategist Anna Greenberg. Al Gore was pummeled mercilessly in small towns — not just here, but nationwide. Thanks to the rural-exurban vote in Tennessee, he even failed to win his home state, a humiliation that cost him the White House.

Four years later, John Kerry and allied groups such as MoveOn.org and the Media Fund struggled to win back some of that ground, spending millions of dollars on rural marketing campaigns, deploying staff into the hinterlands, and even recruiting

John Edwards to bleed some of the red Republicanism out of rural counties. The effort was a dismal failure. Edwards's name on the ticket boosted Democratic support in his home state of North Carolina by a measly 1 percent. According to a 2005 study by *Congressional Quarterly*, 87 percent of the country's rural congressional districts swung for Bush.

"The belief was that if you could shrink Bush's rural margin somewhat, you might be able to turn the election the other way," Greenberg says. "In fact what happened was that Bush improved his margins significantly in rural states."

When the dust settled, homelanders accounted for one of every four ballots cast for George W. Bush, an astounding fifteen million ballots. In contrast, African Americans delivered only about twelve million votes to John Kerry, one of every five Democratic votes.

The Democratic Party with its largely urban agenda — supporting progressive economic policies, gay and lesbian rights, affirmative action, and a woman's right to choose an abortion — is a broken brand in small towns. It's not only that rural voters favor the Republican Party by wide margins; millions of homelanders feel they no longer have a choice. They vote for Republican candidates or they stay home. "I think this cultural divide is very, very real," says Republican strategist Bill Greener. "When John Kerry comes across as being more comfortable in Paris, France, than in Paris, Kentucky, that's a problem if you want to go get the rural vote."

Differences remain among rural attitudes in different parts of the country, but more and more, homelanders nationwide are acting and voting in unison, even in states that we usually think of as Democratic strongholds. Rural Texas is devoutly Republican, but so too are small towns in Michigan's upper peninsula and Washington state's eastern farm counties. In 2004 more than two dozen rural Connecticut townships broke away and voted for George Bush by margins approaching 60 percent — landslide numbers in American politics. In rural Illinois and Oregon, Republican support was even stronger, ranging between 70 and 80 percent.

Homelanders haven't just empowered George Bush. They have also helped to incubate a new cadre of tradition-minded politicians who have risen to dominate the Republican Party. Metros fume about fiery culture warriors like Tom DeLay and Tom Coburn, but even many Republican leaders who avoid open confrontation have embraced small-town social conservatism — that marriage should be defined as a union between one man and one woman to anti-environmentalism to gun rights and public Christianity — not as a political wedge issue but as a core ideology. House Speaker Dennis Hastert, whose rural-exurban district stretches from the outskirts of Chicago all the way to the Iowa border, has opened his office to evangelical crusaders.

"In the blue and gold elegance of the House Speaker's private dining room," wrote Stephanie Simon in a 2005 profile published in the *Los Angeles Times*, "Jeremy Bouma bowed his head before eight young men and women who hope one day to lead the nation. 'Thank you, Lord, for these students [Bouma prayed]. Build them up as your warriors and your ambassadors on Capitol Hill.'"

> Nearly every Monday for six months, as many as a dozen congressional aides — many of them aspiring politicians — have gathered over takeout dinners to mine the Bible for ancient wisdom on modern policy debates about tax rates, foreign aid, education, cloning and the Central American Free Trade Agreement. They learn to view every vote as a religious duty, and to consider compromise a sin. That puts them at the vanguard of a bold effort by evangelical conservatives to mold a new generation of leaders who will answer not to voters, but to God.

Until very recently, metro Americans have found it difficult to take the homelander movement seriously. The cognitive hurdles are set pretty high. Last year, I was sitting in a New York City hotel room, watching a rerun of Paris Hilton's "reality" show *The Simple Life*. If you've never seen it, count yourself lucky. The humor, such as it is, rises on the conceit that rural Americans are laughable, repressed, half-witted rubes, easy targets for the barbs of urban irony. Think minstrel show, with rednecks instead of poor hilarious "darkies."

In this particular episode, Paris and her God-awful sidekick Nicole turned up at a traditional quilting bee in Altus, Arkansas, population 817. The middle-aged and elderly women, with their *Far Side* hairdos and their Wal-Mart couture, looked warily at the young women, who were as impatient and fidgety as a pair of dolled-up toddlers. After a few minutes of gum cracking and coy glances at the camera, Paris and Nicole urged the women to discard the boring rituals of their art. "You should make it edgier," Nicole insisted.

When that failed to get a rise, the two asked bluntly about the sexual potential of Altus's menfolk, urging the women to pimp their sons and grandsons. I was disgusted but not really surprised. Here it was in a nutshell, the urban antipathy for all things rural, the adolescent glee that so many metros take from provoking the small-town natives.

A couple of years ago, CBS executives announced their own plans to create a rural-focused reality show based on the *Beverly Hillbillies*. The idea was for a real-life impoverished Appalachian family to be transplanted to Hollywood. The network bagged the idea after critics threatened protests. "It was going to present rural people as a foil for cheap laughs," Dee Davis, with the Center for Rural Strategies, told the *Kentucky Courier-Journal* newspaper. "We felt the rural experience was more important than that."

This sort of cultural disdain echoes frequently among urban political writers, and not a few Democratic strategists. Rural folk are too simpleminded to warrant serious scrutiny. If the homelander vote does matter, it must be because the hicks are being manipulated and tricked by wily Republicans. Slick operators like Karl Rove use family values to gin up outrage among poor and working-class whites, but they have no intention of ever changing abortion laws or purging gays from civil society.

"As culture war, the [rural] backlash was born to lose," wrote Thomas Frank in his influential bestseller, *What's the Matter with Kansas?* "Its goal is not to win cultural battles, but to take offense, conspicuously, vocally, even flamboyantly."

The idea that rural communities might be part of a coherent political movement, with their own cogent agenda, is dismissed out of hand. The metro linguist George Lakoff describes conservative culture as essentially infantile. "What is required of the child is obedience," he wrote in *Don't Think of an Elephant,* "because the strict father is a moral authority who knows right from wrong."

Like many progressives, Lakoff assumes that homelanders must be acting irrationally ("voting against their own interests" is the popular phrase) when they cast a ballot for George Bush or support rural-conservative organizations such as Focus on the Family and the Christian Coalition. The word *delusional* gets thrown around a lot. Metro politicians often describe social conservatives as ignorant barbarians. "We are under attack from the know nothings and the book burners and the people burners," fumed Bella Abzug, the Democratic congresswoman from New York City, in 1990.

We make fun of Tom DeLay's pomaded hair. We crack endlessly wise about George Bush's malapropisms. This urban political sneer is an old game. "Having lived both in great metropolitan centers of culture and in a small farming community," wrote the Kentucky essayist Wendell Berry, "I have seen few things dumber and tackier — or more provincial — than this half-scared, half-witted urban contempt for *provinciality.*"

But metro contempt for all things rural isn't just dumb or tacky, not anymore. These days, that kind of arrogance is dangerous.

Homelanders have made a sport of exploiting urban smugness. President Bush's career would have been well nigh impossible if Ann Richards, Al Gore, and John Kerry hadn't "misunderestimated" his political instincts.

The truth is the vast majority of homelanders aren't Klansmen or closet mullahs. They're not authority junkies or mindless puppets. Their vision for America doesn't look like George Orwell's *1984* or Margaret Atwood's *Handmaid's Tale*. Sure, there are fire-breathers and Bible-thumpers (the Left has its own loony fringe, after all), but there are also intellectuals and philosophers, businesspeople and teachers. They disagree with one another. They rebel against their own leaders. They debate and wrestle with complex ideas. For the most part they know what they want, and they've chosen the political party that seems most likely to give it to them.

Hard as it is for metros to grasp, tens of millions of rural conservatives believe that banning abortion and "defending" marriage are the moral equivalent of ending the Vietnam War or dismantling Jim Crow. In small towns, many people view gun rights as a civil liberty, just as important as freedom of speech. Telling folks like my brother that they're being delusional, or that they should "vote their wallets" instead of their consciences, just isn't going to fly. "Any time politicians start telling people they're wrong about what they should care about," says Republican strategist Bill Greener, "that's generally a recipe for disaster."

What's more — and here's a crucial point — many homelander values were once widely shared by progressive urbanites. Ranking civil order above freedom, propriety and restraint over self-expression, and faith over intellect were ideals that defined the broader American culture until quite recently. My mother is in her sixties, late middle age, as she would describe it. She grew up in an America where divorce, abortion, unwed mothers, homosexuality, integrated schools, and interracial dating were all simply unthinkable, well outside the pale of civilized behavior.

I am not suggesting that it's a good idea to go back to those days. But it's important to understand that we metros are the ones who have changed — and with remarkable speed. We leapfrogged in a single century from suffrage to civil rights to gender equality and rights for same-sex couples. And because urban Americans pay so little attention to their rural cousins, we assumed that homelanders were keeping up. Happily or unhappily, we didn't care, so long as they didn't cause a fuss.

But on a wide range of social questions, small-town folks have simply stayed put. They're not crazy or infantile; they've just refused to go along with our shifting sensibilities. And now they've come to believe that their way of life and their set of values offer a real alternative for the future.

In America's urban-rural culture war, the anger and intolerance flow both ways. In 2005, during the darkest days of the Hurricane Katrina debacle, African American looters were featured prominently on network news broadcasts. The same few minutes of terrifying footage echoed on television screens again and again, like an episode of *Cops* that had gotten jammed in the national consciousness. The day after the levees collapsed, I stumbled across this fairly typical diatribe posted on a *New York Times* reader forum:

> These are the "finest" examples of inner city black populations at their best. Representatives of a thug culture that glorifies every type of violence and immorality, a culture where 8 out of 10 babies are born to unwed mothers. The same lawlessness would happen in every American city with a large black population which suffered a New Orleans–style catastrophe.

Race is one of the fundamental boundaries separating metro and homelander society. One-third of urban Americans are black, Hispanic, or Asian. The tide of diversity is rising at a pace that can bewilder even the most multicultural-minded observer. One in ten legal American residents was born outside the United States; by the best estimates, there are another ten to eleven million illegal immigrants living inside our borders. The vast majority of these newcomers are heading for the cities and inner suburbs. The next big baby boom will come among Hispanic workers — legal as well as undocumented — whose children will be bona fide citizens. But here again, the American experience divides along urban and rural lines. In the course of an average day, metro Americans might encounter a Brazilian taxi driver, a Russian deli owner, a South African nanny, and a Haitian doorman.

As a consequence, metros have been forced to change and adapt. They cope with a thousand daily negotiations and compromises. This kind of churn and complexity changes a culture in ways that urbanites are still wrestling with, still trying to understand. From the vantage point of rural Nebraska or Wyoming, where more than 90 percent of Americans are still white, this multiculturalism looks like a politically correct fad, something cooked up at a Berkeley cocktail party. But in Chicago or New Orleans or San Francisco, it's a fact of life.

It's not just skin color, however, that sets the two cultures apart. One of the self-satisfied metro myths, which I hope this book will dislodge, holds that progressives lost rural America (especially in the South) for the simple reason that small-town folks are bigots. Democrats pushed through the Civil Rights Act and Republicans responded by adopting a cynical "southern strategy" that won over redneck voters — end of story.

Racism and intolerance are serious issues in small towns, to be sure, but it's more complicated than that. Millions of rural people have come to reject the larger framework of urban life. They despise the liberal modernism that shaped metro culture in the twentieth century and see it as an ideology that is every bit as foreign and threatening as communism. "New Yorkers don't really see themselves as a part of the rest of America," Ann Coulter told conservative radio host Al Rantel in 2005. "You've heard of Manhattan? I just think New Yorkers think of themselves as their own country."

This urban-rural culture gap isn't new. You find deep veins of urban-rural tension running back to the 1700s. Thomas Jefferson fully expected America to remain a homelander nation, dominated by yeoman farmers and enlightened plantation owners. "Those who labor in the earth are the chosen people of God," he wrote, "if ever he had a chosen people."

"We are a people of cultivators, scattered over an immense territory," wrote Crèvecoeur in his *Letters from an American Farmer*, published in 1782. "On a Sunday, [one] sees a congregation of respectable farmers and their wives, all clad in homespun, well mounted or riding in their own humble wagons."

Through America's first century of nationhood, that description held more or less true. Cities were few and far between and remarkably small by modern standards. Protestant Christian values were ubiquitous. But in the late nineteenth and early twentieth century, metropolitan culture exploded. Millions of immigrants arrived from overseas. At the same time, hundreds of thousands of Americans began to quit the farmsteads and hamlets of homelander country, flocking to the cities and the suburbs. In the course of a few generations, the centers of wealth, power, and population shifted inside the urban beltway.

Cities became strongholds for a new sort of society, one that was more racially and ethnically diverse, more cosmopolitan, and more secular. By the 1920s we were metro enough in our national sensibility that a genre of writing emerged that came to be known as the "revolt against the village." It wasn't just an ivory-tower phenomenon. Sinclair Lewis's novels, with their caustic repudiation of homelander life, made the top ten best-seller list five times in a single decade. "*Main Street* is the climax of our civilization," Sinclair wrote sarcastically, in his novel about Gopher Prairie, Minnesota.

That this Ford car might stand in front of the Bon Ton Store, Hannibal invaded Rome and Erasmus wrote in Oxford cloisters. What Ole Jenson the grocer says to Ezra Stowbody the banker is the new law for London, Prague, and the unprofitable isles of the sea; whatsoever Ezra does not know and sanction, that thing is heresy, worthless for knowing and wicked to consider. Such is the comfortable tradition and sure faith. Would he not betray himself as an alien cynic who would otherwise portray Main Street, or distress the citizens by speculating whether there may not be other faiths?

The journalist and provocateur H. L. Mencken described small-town life in terms that were frankly bigoted. "Neanderthal man is organizing in these forlorn backwaters of the land," he wrote. These days, liberal pundits describe Mencken's scornful view of the small-town intellect as scarily prescient: "On some great and glorious day," he wrote, "the plain folks of the land will reach their heart's desire at last and the White House will be adorned by a downright moron."

This simmering antagonism widened into full-blown opposition during the Roosevelt era. The first wave of truly modern policy-making — conceived by FDR's urban "brain trust" — began to reshape our society, over the fierce objections of rural leaders in both political parties. The rift took on a racial dimension after 1940, when millions of African Americans fled rural towns in the South for a new life in northern cities. It widened yet again during the social upheavals of the 1960s.

At the beginning of the twentieth century, cities were the most conservative places in the country, deliberately segregated by race and class; but by century's end, metros were the experimenters, the entrepreneurs, the mixers-and-matchers. They were willing to try new careers and new lifestyles. Urban culture has also drifted to the left politically. If you live in Manhattan or Seattle — or even Atlanta or Birmingham — it's possible to move in circles where no one voted for George Bush. John Kerry cleaned up in urban neighborhoods, not only in the Northeast and the coastal states, but deep in the South and the Midwest. In many cities the Republican vote plummeted below 25 percent in 2004.

In rural America, however, the dominant cultural force isn't change, it's tradition. From the homelander vantage point, much of the new relativism doesn't look like progress. My grandparents in August, Kansas, watched in the 1960s as our cities burned. They saw divorce rates skyrocket as families spun apart. They saw urban crime rates soar. Worst indignity of all, they saw their own communities begin to stagnate and fall behind.

Baffled and outraged, they pulled away. They began looking for different leadership, different ideas. They also looked to the past, to ideals and sensibilities that shaped American culture a century ago. America's new chief justice, John Roberts, is an eloquent symbol of this rural-traditional renaissance. Roberts is a conservative Roman Catholic who grew up in tiny Long Beach, Indiana, on the shore of Lake Michigan; the population is still 97 percent white.

Roberts isn't a sauntering cowboy, nor is he a rube or a hellfire evangelist. But his public writings show persuasively that like millions of tradition-minded Americans he is disenchanted with the rapid changes in American society that began with Franklin Delano Roosevelt's election in 1932. It's not just abortion or gay rights. It's the abrupt shift in women's roles within society. It's the idea that the federal government should play an activist role in improving people's lives. It's the dramatic expansion of civil liberties and personal freedom. It's the shift from a monolithic nation of white Christians to a complexly multicultural stew of ethnicities, languages, and faiths.

This divergence is the true frontier in our culture war, the Mason-Dixon line that weaves through every state in the nation. The two American tribes, homelander and metro, want and expect radically different things. They see their different values as uniquely legitimate and their own leaders as uniquely qualified and trustworthy. As a consequence, the disdain that each community feels toward the other is pronounced, and it grows sharper with each election cycle.

America is often described as a fifty-fifty nation, a land where elections and cultural debates split us right down the middle; but the truth is that most Americans don't share the homelander worldview, not anymore. For half a century the markers of our national sensibility — especially on social questions — have shifted steadily to the left. As more of us make our homes in cities and inner suburbs, our values (naturally enough) have grown more urban and progressive.

This trend is visible in a hundred different surveys taken over the last quarter century. Despite a thirty-year campaign by conservatives to discredit and overturn *Roe v. Wade,* two-thirds of us remain firmly pro-choice. Conservatives have succeeded in confirming pro-life justices to the Supreme Court, but it's telling that President Bush's nominees were at great pains to downplay and conceal their antiabortion beliefs.

When you push past opinion polls and look at the way we actually live, Americans appear even more liberal. From 1960 to 2000 the number of Americans living together without marrying increased tenfold, from roughly 440,000 to more than 5 million. "Men and women who moved in together used to raise eyebrows," wrote an essayist in *USA Today* in 2005. "Living together out of wedlock, once considered 'shacking up' or 'living in sin,' has lost its stigma as cohabitation has become mainstream. What a difference a few decades makes."

In the 1970s most women got married before they reached their twenty-first birthday. Now they typically wait until they're twenty-six and have begun their careers. Metros — who make up 80 percent of the population, remember — are having fewer kids, and they're also divorcing more often, at a rate that outstrips the godless Europeans by two to one. Interracial dating and marriage are increasingly commonplace, especially among young people. While a lot of Americans still have doubts about same-sex marriage, acceptance of gay and lesbian rights has grown dramatically since the 1970s.

There's growing evidence that even people who call themselves social conservatives are embracing lifestyle choices that were once considered downright progressive. A recent study conducted by the Barna Group found that the divorce rate among conservative Christians is equal to that of America's atheists. Hard-core Pentecostals are actually more likely to divorce than are godless heathens.

Our media is obsessed with conservative Christianity. Right-wing megachurches and rock-concert-sized revival meetings are often portrayed as the next big thing, evidence of a national spiritual awakening. But the fastest growing faith group in America isn't made up of evangelical Christians. That prize goes to people who profess no faith at all. Ten percent of the population now describes itself as atheist or agnostic, a figure that nearly doubled in a decade. The second fastest-growing group is made up of non-Christians, which includes everyone from Wiccans to Muslims to New Age spiritualists. The truth is that Protestants are actually declining rapidly as a percentage of the population.

"I do not believe that the majority of Americans share our values," acknowledged Paul Weyrich, one of the founders of the Moral Majority, in a public letter to his supporters. "I think it is fair to say that conservatives have learned to succeed in politics. That is, we got our people elected. But that did not result in the adoption of our agenda."

Perhaps the most powerful evidence of America's increasingly urban sensibility is the way we're voting with our feet. I mentioned that there are fifty million homelanders, not a bad foundation for a grassroots movement; but the population of rural whites is dwindling rapidly, while multicultural cities and dense, inner-suburban neighborhoods continue to swell with new immigrants.

The most common measuring stick for gauging "ruralness" —

known as the Beale Code — breaks communities into nine categories. On the most urbanized end of the scale are "central counties
of metro areas with one million population or more." At the opposite extreme are rural counties with "fewer than 2,500 [people] not
adjacent to any metro area." As you might imagine, the differences
between these two worlds can be profound.

Only a century ago, folk at the rural end of that scale made up two-
thirds of the American population. In the 1950s, when Dwight
Eisenhower occupied the White House, half of us still lived in small
towns. But in the course of a couple of generations, we evolved from
a republic of hamlets and villages — largely white and almost
entirely Christian — into a post-modern democracy made up of
crowded ghettos, vast suburbs, and dozens of mishmashed ethnicities and cultures. Over the past fifty years, fully 97 percent of the
country's population growth has occurred in cities and suburbs.
Rural communities now make up less than one-fifth of the population, and the demographic shift continues.

"The metropolitan United States is projected to grow by 12 percent
during the 2000–2010 decade, compared with 5 percent for small
towns and only 2 percent for rural communities," wrote researchers
Mark Mather and Jean D'Amico in a 2003 report published by the
Population Reference Bureau.

It's not just that cities are growing faster; thousands of small towns
are actually slipping backward. In the 1990s, one out of every four
rural counties in America lost population. "Many of these counties
are agricultural," wrote Calvin Beale, the researcher with the U.S.
Department of Agriculture who invented the code. "[M]any have
been losing population for decades, with no solution in sight."
Generally speaking, the more remote a county is, the more likely it is
to be shedding people.

The situation is especially dire in the Great Plains. Many of our
most conservative homelander states are suffering a massive exodus
of people. "The United States is in the midst of a major demographic

event: the depopulation of a significant portion of the nation's rural counties," writes Jeffrey Walser, a regional economist in Kansas City with the Federal Deposit Insurance Corporation (FDIC). In North Dakota, forty-seven of fifty-three counties are shedding people, a dangerous trend in a state where the average population density is roughly six persons per square mile.

"Many do not miss the irony that while the nation celebrates the bicentennial of the Lewis and Clark expedition, much of the northern plains they opened to European-American settlement is being abandoned," wrote Jack Coffman in the *Kansas City Star*. He quoted Robert Creighton, an attorney in Atwood, Kansas, another state where small towns are drying up: "If there's a solution to our population declines," Creighton says, "we have less than a generation to find it."

Other regions as well are experiencing this exodus. Alaska and Vermont have unveiled discounted college loan programs, designed to retain young people. In northern New York the brain drain has gutted small towns. Often, the cause of this out-migration is simple economics: It's hard to find good jobs in homelander communities. But according to Beale, a growing number of rural folk are leaving small towns for cultural and lifestyle reasons. The siren song of urban life — flashed over television screens and iPods — calls to young people, luring them away from their towns and villages.

"A recent survey of rural Nebraska raises questions as to whether a decline in economic opportunities is the only or even a major reason for population loss," Beale wrote in 2003. "When these residents were asked what type of place they would prefer, they tended to favor not their own type of setting, but a more densely populated setting."

If small towns are shrinking, how can they still be powerful or relevant? In any other democracy, this downward spiral would lead to permanent political marginalization. The fact that homelanders still play a potent role in American life is disorienting to metros and inexplicable to observers from other countries such as Canada, France, or Great

Britain, where political campaigns tend to be largely metropolitan affairs. A national leader in Germany makes a ritual nod to fishermen on the North Sea, then hustles back to court the urban vote.

"In most nations, cities are a big deal," wrote Joel Rogers in an essay for *The Nation* called "Cities: The Vital Core." "The mayor of Mexico City is likely to be his country's next president. But in America, cities are the neglected stepchildren, exploited and abused when not simply ignored."

America's lingering rural fixation is partly a cultural artifact. For all the lampooning in Hollywood, small-town life retains an iconic place in our national memory. Even a lot of metros still lean instinctively toward a guy who unbuttons his collar and has a little dirt under his nails. That idiom just feels more regular, more egalitarian, more down to earth.

Because of this conditioning, it rarely occurs to us to wonder why it's a political advantage for George Bush to own a ranch. We accept as a matter of course that presidential candidates will audition for the White House at county fairs in rural Iowa and country diners in New Hampshire, even though that way of life is foreign to most American voters.

Homelanders have capitalized on this cultural framing with an enormous amount of hard work and activism. It's a self-indulgent urban myth that social conservatives are anti-democratic, the stealers of elections and the stuffers of ballot boxes. You can mutter about Florida and Ohio all you want, but the fact is that rural folks have won thousands of contests the old-fashioned way, by getting organized and turning out the vote. They take to electoral politics the way Nebraska Cornhusker fans take to college football.

In the corner of rural New York where I live, yard signs thicker than weeds proliferate every autumn. Candidates for local office plot and scheme with real glee, fighting for the chance to spend evenings and weekends poring over school budgets and zoning plans. Small-town politicians also fight to win. Anyone baffled by the ugly tone of national Swift Boat–style politics should sample the smashmouth, take-no-prisoners fare of a village mayor's race.

In recent decades homelanders have also overcome some of their old prejudices, softening the racial and sectarian overtones that haunt the right-wing movement. The new tolerance is far from perfect. Indeed, many of the old animosities have been replaced by new fears aimed at Muslims, at secular Americans, and at gays and lesbians. But the shift has allowed rural Americans to forge a remarkable chain of alliances (with conservative Jewish, African American, and Roman Catholic groups, for example) that would have been impossible a generation ago.

These factors alone — cultural framing, grassroots organizing, and an improving track record on racial and religious tolerance — can't account for the homelander community's expanding influence. The other vital ingredient is a profound rural bias hard-wired into our political system.

Metros grumble about the stolen election in 2000 and rigged voting machines in 2004, but that's small-time stuff. In every presidential race, the electoral college reallocates huge amounts of voting clout, automatically boosting the influence of low-population rural states while penalizing the urban states, where most Americans live.

Alaskans see their per capita voting power tripled in presidential elections, as do folks in North and South Dakota, Vermont, and Wyoming. Meanwhile, one in every six ballots cast in California goes straight into the trash. That sounds outrageous, but it's literally true. California is home to 12 percent of America's population, but the state receives only 10 percent of the electoral college votes. The system quietly strips Californians of nine electoral votes, the political equivalent of disenfranchising the entire state of Colorado.

The rural tilt built into the U.S. Senate is even more profound. Each state receives two seats regardless of population. As a consequence, those lucky homelanders in Wyoming and Alaska receive seventy-two times more clout per capita than do California's metros. It's a startling fact that half of the American people live in just nine highly urbanized states — most of them staunchly Democratic — but they hold only 18 percent of the Senate's power. The lion's share of voting strength in the Senate is held by homelander states whose rural towns make up a tiny minority of the American population. "Senators from the 26 smallest states who represent 17.8 percent of the nation's population constitute a majority of the Senate," writes Sanford Levinson, a scholar at the University of Texas School of Law, "a reality which has aroused little interest or concern."

A quarter century ago the homelander tilt in our system didn't matter as much because rural voters split their ballots evenly between the two parties. If Republicans got a boost from one rural state, Democrats caught a break from another. Some of the most progressive Democrats of the twentieth century were elected in such places as Maine, Montana, Nebraska, and South Dakota. But beginning with the battle over the New Deal in the 1930s, small towns began a long drift toward the Republican Party. The rightward migration accelerated after Barry Goldwater's campaign in 1964, solidified during Ronald Reagan's reign in the 1980s, and culminated in 1994 with Newt Gingrich's Republican Revolution.

Rural Americans now channel their supersized political advantage almost exclusively to Republicans. The impact has been stunning. In a single decade, homelanders have reshaped our political culture, despite the opposition of a majority of American voters. In 2000, Americans chose Al Gore to be our president, but the system tilted the victory to George Bush. In 2002 and again in 2004, a majority of voters cast ballots for Democratic congressional candidates, but Republicans still gained seats in both the House and the Senate.

Thanks to their homelander base, Republicans have built a dominant eleven-seat majority in the Senate; but because they tend to get elected in low-population, rural states, GOP senators still represent 4.5 million fewer Americans than do their Democratic colleagues.

This fact is worth repeating: Even with eleven fewer seats, Democrats actually represent far more citizens than do Republicans — a disparity that's equivalent to the combined populations of Alaska, Idaho, Montana, North and South Dakota, and Wyoming.

Put bluntly, our political system is no longer a neutral playing field. In ways that our founding fathers could never have imagined, the electoral college and the Senate now favor one way of life, one set of cultural and political values, over another. Because those values are no longer shared by most Americans, the result is a growing disconnect between our political elites and the people they govern.

The deepening conservatism of rural voters isn't just skewing the balance of power between Republicans and Democrats. It's also changing the internal dynamics of the parties themselves. Homelander politicians have organized feverishly, leveraging their disproportionate clout to remake the Republican Party. The urban moderates who once controlled the GOP have been sidelined

In 2004, New Jersey's former Republican governor, Christie Whitman, published a political manifesto with the plaintive title *It's My Party Too*. "More than perhaps ever before in modern times, the Republican Party at the national level is controlled by extreme conservatives I call social fundamentalists," she wrote. "Unless you oppose abortion in every instance — including in cases of rape or incest — you're not a real Republican. Unless you think every environmental regulation is government overregulation, you're not a real Republican."

But the truth is it's not Whitman's party, not anymore. Rockefeller-style urban Republicans are welcome under the big tent, so long as they don't try to influence the national agenda or threaten the homelander wing's grip on power. Moderates who forget their place — Arizona's John McCain in 2000 or Pennsylvania's Arlen Specter in 2004 — are quickly humbled. (Homelander icon Grover Norquist has sworn to derail McCain's 2008 presidential bid at all costs, even if it means fielding a third-party candidate and ceding the White House to the Democrats.)

In 2004, Republican consultant Arthur Finkelstein, who has worked for New York's Alphonse D'Amato and North Carolina's Jesse Helms, gave an interview to the Israeli newspaper *Maariv*, describing the GOP as "the party of the Christian right."

> Bush's strategy [in the 2004 election] secures the power of the American Christian right not only for this term. In fact, it secures its ability to choose the next Republican president. Bush courted the evangelical vote and turned these elections, in fact, into a referendum on the religious and cultural nature of America.

More surprising is the fact that homelanders have also seized a significant amount of power within the Democratic Party. Senator Harry Reid, the minority leader from Nevada, grew up in the tiny town of Searchlight, where he attended a one-room schoolhouse until the eighth grade. "There in the desert, more than an hour away from the bright lights of Las Vegas," reads his official biography, "is where he was born and raised."

In a profile of Reid written for the *New Yorker*, Elsa Walsh noted that the most powerful Democrat in the country is a devout Mormon who disagrees with his colleagues — and with the vast majority of Democratic voters — on nearly every social issue. "He is opposed to abortion, gay marriage, and gun control, and supports the death penalty. He voted for both Gulf wars," Walsh wrote.

New Jersey Democratic senator Frank Lautenberg, in a 2004 interview with *USA Today*, questioned whether Reid was the right man to lead a movement that draws 90 percent of its support from metro voters: "Are the interests of the party served best by a leader who comes from a state that doesn't have the same urban flavor that we have in our industrial states?"

The pressure to tack the Democratic Party closer to homelander sensibilities is growing. After George Bush's reelection, Bill Clinton's former White House chief of staff, Leon Panetta, told the *Washington Post* that his party had to "take the time to understand the concerns of rural families and Christian families. The party of FDR has become the party of Michael Moore and *Fahrenheit 9/11* and it does not help in big parts of the country."

"We are too coastal," agreed Jim Jordan, a former Kerry campaign manager. "We are too urban. We are too secular."

This growing urban-rural tension within the Democratic Party has made unified opposition to the Bush administration's policies nearly impossible. Pundits often say Democrats need to grow a spine. In fact, the party has one spine too many, the urban wing that rose to power during Franklin Roosevelt's reign in the 1930s and an older rural faction that has its roots in the nineteenth-century Christian conservatism of William Jennings Bryan and Woodrow Wilson. In 2006, Democratic senators from metro states like California, Illinois, Massachusetts, and New York organized to block the confirmation of Samuel Alito, even trying to mount a filibuster. But Nevada's Harry Reid remained conspicuously silent, and the effort was derailed by homelander Democrats from Louisiana, Nebraska, and North Dakota who announced that they would vote in favor of president Bush's nominee.

Cultural friction within the Democratic Party isn't the only way that metro culture has left itself vulnerable. By the 1990s, Democrats had ruled Congress for nearly sixty years. They had accomplished monumental things, dismantling institutional racism, installing a system of social welfare programs that drastically reduced poverty, especially among the elderly, and helping smooth the way for women entering the workplace.

But by the time Newt Gingrich began delivering his midnight oratories on C-Span, the Left's big ideas seemed to have run their course.

Many of the Democratic Party's leaders were corrupt or distracted by self-indulgence. Bill Clinton was the consummate CEO, a brilliant political tactician, but his personal adventures with Monica Lewinsky and his lack of a clear political vision (the word that defines Clinton's administration, *triangulation*, suggests a kind of *fin de siècle* inertia) left the Democratic Party's various factions in disarray.

The mainstream urban media, meanwhile, was entering a period of turmoil that continues to deepen. Audiences are splintered by deregulation and by the proliferation of media. The industry's credibility has been chipped away by scandal and by attacks from the Right. News organizations have allowed themselves to be intimidated by the Bush administration and outflanked by conservative media outlets and personalities such as Fox News and Rush Limbaugh.

Meanwhile, urban reporters and editors overlooked or simply ignored the role that small-town America played in the Republican Revolution. In a way this blindness is understandable. Homelander society seems increasingly foreign and irrelevant to many metro pundits. "The news coverage isn't telling the big trend stories from a rural perspective," says the Kellogg Foundation's Ali Webb, who has surveyed media coverage of small-town life. "Rural America continues to be invisible to suburban and urban voters."

The major news organizations missed (or at least underestimated) the rise of the homelander insurgency for the better part of a decade. Many observers continue to downplay its significance, representing the culture war as a rehash of the old Democrat-Republican squabble, talking of pendulum swings and corrections. They suggest that the conservative movement will crumble when its latest figurehead (Ronald Reagan, Newt Gingrich, Tom DeLay, George Bush, Karl Rove — the list goes on) leaves the scene. They deploy their usual tools of irony and superiority, portraying their rural opponents as cynical snake-oil salesmen, deluded zealots, and simpletons.

This skewed portrait has misled millions of Americans. Until very recently, most metros were largely unaware that homelanders intend to reconfigure our society. It's not just a question of banning abortion or curtailing the "gay agenda" or returning Christian prayer to public schools. Homelanders and their allies hope to scrap much of the cultural change and innovation that revolutionized our culture after 1950: "To those who believe social trends are irreversible," wrote homelander sage and provocateur William Bennett, "our answer should be: no, it need not be so, and we will not allow it to happen."

Not so long ago this sort of thing sounded preposterous. But with more and greater power collecting in the hands of social conservatives, metros have begun to take notice. Urban culture has begun trying to see homelanders in more sophisticated and critical ways. It's telling that some of the most interesting and acclaimed films the past few years have taken as their subject the collision between small-town society and the urban sensibility.

In *Brokeback Mountain* sheepherders wrestle with their homosexuality. In *Million Dollar Baby* a square-jawed female boxer from southern Missouri breaks away from her trailer park family. In *Junebug* a wealthy, Europeanized metro ventures into rural America in search of a primitive artist and spends a baffling week with her homelander in-laws. In *Capote* a gay writer goes to Kansas to probe and exploit the raw brutality of a small-town serial killer. In *The Village* a group of modern metro expatriates creates an eighteenth-century paradise cloistered in the New England backwoods.

News organizations have also begun shifting gears, opening new lines of inquiry, thanks largely to the dynamics of George Bush's success at the ballot box. "Coverage of politics went up [after 2000]," Webb notes. "There were more stories about rural voting behavior. They saw that the rural vote mattered, that it was different."

NPR hired a rural reporter and created a rural issues desk. CNN enlisted a "faith and values" correspondent. The *New York Times* acknowledged publicly in May 2005 that its coverage of rural America was woefully inadequate. An internal review called for a "concerted effort by all of us to stretch beyond our predominantly urban, culturally liberal orientation, to cover the full range of our national conversation."

*Welcome to the Homeland* is meant as a contribution to that effort. I hope to answer a few of the questions that my urban friends have been asking with increasing urgency the last few years. Who are these people casting their votes on the basis of family values? How can they think like they do about issues such as same-sex marriage and abortion? How did they get to be so powerful so quickly? And perhaps most important: Where are they taking our country?

# No Man's Land

Highway 54 lies like a high-tension wire across Oklahoma's panhandle, an abstraction connecting two vanishing points. There's a steady whine of rubber and pavement, but the prairie is vast; it feels like the van is standing still. My brother's boy David is sprawled in the backseat with a pair of binoculars. He spots a mule deer grazing on a low hill off to the south and studies it eagerly. He shot his first buck last year.

"Hey, Uncle Brian," he calls. "Do you think that deer is a liberal? I think that might be the only liberal in Oklahoma!"

The kid loves to razz me about politics. He's a smart, gangly twelve-year-old and already a devout conservative like his dad. They're both regular listeners of Michael Savage, Sean Hannity, and Rush Limbaugh. They live on the outskirts of Washington, Missouri, a bustling town on the fringe of St. Louis. Theirs is one of the burgeoning exurban enclaves that are steadily dragging Missouri into the red column. Eighty percent of voters in downtown neighborhoods voted for John Kerry, but out in Allen and Daniel's small town the results were flipped — a 58 percent win for George Bush.

David talks class warfare, same-sex marriage, and creationism the way most boys talk baseball or Gameboy. He gets it from Allen, a big silver-haired guy in his mid-forties who still expresses deep regret about the vote he cast for Bill Clinton in 1992. In David's world an East Coast liberal uncle is more exotic (and in many ways, more fun) than a two-headed frog. "Maybe the deer [in Oklahoma] are all Hillary Clinton voters," he says with a grin. "Maybe that's why they like hunting out here so much."

"Give it a rest, Davey," Allen says. But his sentiments are pretty much the same. The very mention of Hillary Clinton makes his brow beetle. "Come *on*," he says, when I ask him about the idea of New York's senator running for president. "I think people out here would go crazy. I don't think she would survive."

If you're a secret service agent reaching for the red telephone, relax. My brother is one of the gentlest men I've ever met. But he knows his neighbors — not just the ones who live next door, but also the virtual homelander community that's scattered coast to coast. He surfs the right-wing-media scrum on a daily basis, the blog sites, the AM radio and Fox News blather-fests. He hears the hatred, the viciousness, and the unreason. "I hate that stuff," he admits. "All the mocking and the lack of civility. It's nutty how some conservatives talk. Just like it's nuts how liberals talk about George Bush. But that's how people feel."

It's late summer, and we've been driving for a week through southwestern Kansas, down across the interlocking panhandles of Oklahoma and Texas, dipping into New Mexico. For blue state types this is enemy territory, the undiluted heart of red America. For a hundred miles in any direction, the culture war is over. The Democratic Party has dried up and blown away.

A woman down in Texas told me, with a kind of superstitious awe of seeing a single Democratic sign in some poor fool's yard during the 2004 campaign, "It's like putting a bull's-eye on your property. If you ever told people you were a Democrat, like at a party or something, they'd think you were just plain crazy."

Most of the things that stick in the craw of conservatives are either nonexistent or invisible here. The nearest abortion clinic is half a day's drive north, in Wichita, Kansas. Gays and lesbians who live in this part of the country are tolerated, for the most part, so long as they keep their sexuality to themselves. "Of course we have gay people here, too," says David Scott, chairman of the Republican committee in Ochiltree County, Texas, "but it's sort of Don't ask,

Don't tell. They're treated well, but they're not marching down the streets either."

In some of these sprawling counties, nine out of ten voters chose George Bush to be their president, and they would do it again in a heartbeat. In summer 2005, as Allen, the boys, and I road-tripped through homelander America, Bush's approval rating was plummeting in much of the nation, battered by Iraq and endless scandals, but his rural base was unperturbed. One survey found that the president's popularity was actually growing in a half-dozen homelander states, up 25 percent in Utah, up 11 percent in Idaho, and up 5 percent in Oklahoma.

In this parallel America, the *New York Times* and CNN feel as remote and irrelevant as the *Village Voice* or *Le Figaro*. The radio dial offers a scratchy drone of conservative and evangelical chatter, delivered with complacent, easy-going certainty. These are the voices of men preaching to a vast, far-flung choir. With Rush and Dr. Dobson scripting the libretto, the music of rural America is scored by a parade of puff-chested country-and-western singers, thanking God for their families and the U.S.A.

"I'm just a singer of simple songs," croons Alan Jackson. "I'm not a real political man. I watch CNN, but I'm not sure I can tell you the difference between Iraq and Iran. But I know Jesus, and I talk to God . . ."

After six days of this stuff, even David is tired of it, or maybe he's just eager to dust off one of his corny jokes: "If you play country music backward," he says, "your wife comes back, your boat's fixed, and your truck'll start running." And maybe homelanders will start voting for Democrats again.

The occasional jangle of a Spanish-language *tejano* station begins to sound downright transgressive. It hints at far-off things, at impending change, like the rumbling of a thunderstorm on the horizon. And things are changing. This isn't a fair sample of modern America, not by a long shot. The Rockies rise out that way somewhere, and the Pacific slope stretches beyond with its vast suburban metroplexes. In the opposite direction, back East, there are cities so dense and byzantine that at this remove they resemble biological organisms.

Somewhere on this continent there are three hundred million people, a dizzying mix of different races and creeds and faiths, a crackling Internet, Starbucks, skyscrapers. But here there is only the humbling imperative of land and emptiness. It's so profound, so global in scope, that it reduces all the rest of creation to myth and figment.

Allen points ahead at a punctuation, a shape of light on the rim of the world. Grain silos anchor hundreds of these midwestern towns, rising bleached and massive like Mexican cathedrals. Their bulk suggests a hidden bounty, dispersed like manna over the emptiness. The two kids, David and my own son, Nicholas, stir with restless energy. "How long until we get there?" Nicholas asks. "Can we get hamburgers?"

His cousin is a political junkie, but at age ten my boy is baffled by this whole enterprise. Drive around asking people their opinions? Strike up conversations with complete strangers about politics? He thinks the whole thing is nuts. "You know what you think, Papa. And you know they don't agree with you."

"That's why I'm curious about their ideas," I tell him. "I want to know why they think the way they do."

"But you're not going to change your mind, are you?"

"No, probably not. Not much anyway."

"Are they?"

"I doubt it."

Nicholas is unconvinced. So is Allen, to be honest. He has gamely agreed to play the role of rural conservative, the red yin to my blue yang, but he's a little nervous. "You just can't make me look like a bumbling idiot," he says.

It's a reasonable enough concern. Metros have made a sport of denigrating rural Americans. Even as they lose battle after battle, urban pundits and politicians continue to dismiss homelanders as bumbling hicks, too stupid or misguided to look out for their own welfare. "People getting their fundamental interests wrong is what American political life is all about," Frank writes on the first page of *What's the Matter with Kansas?* "This species of derangement is the bedrock of our civic order; it is the foundation on which all else rests."

The day after the 2004 election, London's *Daily Mirror* published a front-page banner that was adopted as a talking point by millions of American metros: "How can 59,054,087 Americans be so dumb?"

There is practically a sub-genre of urban punditry that aims to diagnose GOP supporters like my brother. Depending on whom you ask, they are racists, neurotic failures, or morons. One scholarly paper widely circulated on the Internet (it served as the basis for an article in the on-line magazine *Slate*) attempted to identify the "specific variables that have been hypothesized to predict conservatism." The motivating factors included fear, aggression, "intolerance of ambiguity," and (my personal favorite) "anxiety arising from mortality salience."

Another analysis posted on-line claimed to prove that blue state voters were simply smarter than red state voters. The official-looking chart, later debunked, ranked Kerry voters at 100–115 IQ points, while slatternly Bush voters drooled along in the 85–100 point range. It received half a million hits in a single day and was fodder for articles in *The Economist* and Florida's *St. Petersburg Times*.

In March 2006 a University of California–Berkeley researcher published a paper in the *Journal of Research in Personality* claiming that whiny, insecure children grow up to be conservatives with right-wing traditional values. "The confident kids turned out liberal and were still hanging loose, turning into bright, non-conforming adults with wide interests," wrote Kurt Kleiner in a *Toronto Star* article that circulated widely on metro blog sites. "[The study] reasons that insecure kids look for the reassurance provided by tradition and authority, and find it in conservative politics."

"One of the biggest changes in politics in my lifetime," argued progressive journalist Bill Moyers, in a speech after the 2004 election, "is that the delusional is no longer marginal. It has come in from the fringe, to sit in the seat of power in the Oval Office and in Congress. When ideology and theology couple, their offspring are not always bad but they are always blind. And there is the danger: voters and politicians alike, oblivious to the facts."

This kind of fear and distrust is widespread in metro culture. When I began work on this project, a common objection voiced by friends and colleagues was that homelanders were simply too backward to warrant serious scrutiny. "I think you're taking this multiculturalism thing too far," a fellow writer told me. "Sometimes certain cultural values are just wrong. Maybe even evil."

I asked him for an example and after a pause, he said, "Genital mutilation. Or genocide."

"No, I mean give me an example of something evil that conservative rural Americans are doing."

He thought for a long time. I could see that he was determined to produce clear evidence that homelanders were as dangerous and threatening as a band of cannibals. "Supporting the war in Iraq," he said finally. "And pushing millions of Americans into poverty. And the deliberate erosion of civil liberties. And the separation of church and state."

All of which struck me as valid concerns, especially in an era when the Democratic Party offered only a token counterweight to the Republicans. But there's a sizable gulf between the Patriot Act and the Beer Hall Putsch, a lot of ideological bandwidth between picketing a Planned Parenthood clinic and genital mutilation.

"My idea," I said, testing it on another colleague, "is to look for the people and institutions that are disseminating these traditional ideas. I don't mean the screamers. I want to find intellectuals, writers and thinkers who are shaping the movement. I want to find communities where these principles are being applied. Let's see how well they work."

A skeptical silence followed. "Well, take creationism," I said. "It's inching its way into textbooks now. Tens of millions of Americans believe in it, including my own nephews. Nineteen states are talking about downgrading evolution in science classes, describing it as a theory on a par with intelligent design. So where does that stuff come from? How does it fit into in people's lives? There must be someone in the conservative community who's really thought deeply about this stuff."

"What if there's not?"

"What do you mean?"

"Do you really think you'll find someone who can defend that nonsense in a thoughtful way?"

"But conservatives have universities now. They have think tanks and journalists. They can't all just be lunatics and propagandists."

"What if they are? George Bush is their leader, and he's not exactly a thoughtful guy. It seems to me that the Right is made up of a few very bad and manipulative people and a lot of very stupid and gullible people."

This from a friend who is worldly and thoughtful and as open-minded as anyone I've ever met. He would never dream of talking dismissively about a traditional society in Africa, say, or Central America. The difference, of course, is that those rural tribesmen can't vote in our elections. They don't make decisions that affect our urban-centric lives. They can't tell us who we can marry. They can't tap our phones. They can't send our kids off to war.

This sort of fear and loathing has made it difficult for metros to understand what they're up against: not a group of crazy, Bible-thumping zealots but smart, aggressive political activists with a coherent agenda. Republican strategist Bill Greener often serves as a consultant on rural political campaigns. He shakes his head at urban America's sneering assessments of the homelander movement, delivered (as he describes it) "in the tone of 'What's wrong with these people?' I don't think that does the Democratic Party any favors," he says.

Certainly not with voters like Allen, who fumed for days after Howard Dean dismissed Republicans as "pretty much a white, Christian party" and complained that conservatives had "never made an honest living in their lives." Dean later said that he was talking about GOP leaders, not rank and file voters, and he complained that his words had been taken out of context. But for many homelanders, the flap was proof that top Democrats don't respect rural issues or cultural values. "That is the thing that sticks under my skin more than anything else: the level of condescension I often feel," Allen says, "when I'm talking to somebody and express a conservative viewpoint and they think that I must be a complete idiot for having those viewpoints. It's almost like a kick in the gut. You know that whatever you say the gulf between you and them is so vast that there's no way to even have the conversation. I want to feel like the positions of my people are respected."

The first signs of civilization on the outskirts of Guymon, Oklahoma, are a truck stop, a trailer park, and an empty cattle yard. Towns out here have the quality of settlements along some tenuous trade route. The houses are modest, the brick streets wide enough for a military parade. The sidewalks feel empty.

There are churches everywhere, some big and cocky looking but most of them modest and spare. God is ubiquitous in this country, on billboards, on the radio, even on the editorial pages of local newspapers, which often offer daily passages from Scripture. In my notebook there is a quote copied down from the top of a roadside picnic table: "The best drug of all is when Jesus calls." The words were carved with deliberate, calligraphic neatness into the pine planking, next to mustard stains and etchings of phalluses. "If you listen, you can hear. Jesus is with you everywhere."

For those of us from the other America, from the realm of cities and suburbs, rush hours and Google-enhanced globalization, homelander culture feels strange and arid. We suspect that there are pieces missing, as if the concept of a society had been sketched out quickly in rough draft, with the details and subtlety and nuance to be added later.

The people, too, seem improbably spare, their hearts filled with blunt notions of patriotism and kinship and the Holy Gospel. They believe that certain things are right and proper and certain other things just aren't.

This kind of thing offends the urban sensibility. Perhaps it's no surprise that city folk who encounter it so often respond with irony or flat-out scorn. "The tailgates groan with huge coolers, and groan even more when proud, gigantic rear ends are added," wrote Christopher Hitchens in *Vanity Fair*, after a reportorial dip into the rural culture of Virginia. "Should you desire to remove the right to bear arms from these people, you might well have to prize away a number of cold, dead, chubby fingers."

After buying the boys their lunch, I leave them with Allen and prowl around Guymon looking for people willing to talk. Folks on the street are curious about me. I stick out in a place like this. My hair's a little too long, my graying beard and accent a little too East Coast. Even without these telltales, people here would know. There aren't that many strange faces in the Oklahoma Panhandle. Again and again, people decline shyly to be interviewed. They say, "You should go and talk to Mr. Dixon."

Gerald Dixon is the type of guy I have come to think of as the rural grandee. Not that he's ostentatious or extravagant, far from it. He's not even all that powerful, in any easily definable way. But he knows everything and everyone, and over the years he has filled every imaginable role in the community's life, from politician to businessman to farmer to racehorse owner and historian. In semi-retirement, at the age of eighty-three, he remains a sort of figurehead, a symbol of continuity.

When I knock on his door and tell him I want to talk politics, he looks delighted. He clears a chair and insists that I sit. "Of course I'm a Republican," he says. "I was Republican when people here wouldn't admit they were Republican." His office is crammed with books and magazines and folders stuffed full of paper. "I love books," he says. "I love history." Dixon still serves as a notary public, meaning that his stamp of approval legitimizes much of the town's business. He has the tools of his office arranged on his desk. There's an old IBM computer in one corner but also a truly antique Royal typewriter that still gets a lot of use. "I bought it used in 1947," he says fondly. "I still type all my checks on it."

Guymon, he tells me, sits in a bone-dry chunk of Oklahoma. "There hasn't been any water in the river for twenty years," he says. Until the 1890s the Panhandle was known as No Man's Land — not a figure of speech, but a legal definition. Because of a dispute with the Cherokee, a territory the size of Connecticut remained for decades outside the jurisdiction of the United States. According to Dixon this place also had the dubious distinction of being the "geographic center of the 1930s Dust Bowl."

Dixon once penned a little monograph about the region. He presents me with a copy, salvaged from the bottom of a cluttered drawer. "Some farmers went seven years without harvesting a grain of wheat," it reads. "A portion of the movie *The Grapes of Wrath* was filmed north of Guymon." He himself started farming after the Second World War, renting land and buying some used equipment.

"Two years earlier we would have been complete failures," he says, but the climate was improving and so were irrigation techniques and commodity prices. "I stayed because I knew how to make a living here. I went into real estate, oil and gas."

I ask him about the Democratic Party, and he shrugs. "You know, they're sure not very active in this area. Not anymore. I voted for Harry Truman in 1948, and I was Republican county chairman at the time. I'm still proud of that vote. I couldn't see that things were so bad then under the Democrats. But they started fading gradually."

"A lot of people think it's mostly race that did it," I say. "Civil rights turned people out here against the Democrats. Do you think that had something to do with it?"

"Not in this area," Dixon says. He pauses to think and nods solemnly, as if agreeing with himself. "Probably in the South, sure, but in this part of the country there were no other races. There were no coloreds at all to speak of. I didn't see a colored man until I was a grown boy. Just us people who withstood the drought, the Depression, and the Dust Bowl. Race didn't have a thing to do with it."

"So what did it? Was it all these social questions? Family values, that kind of thing?"

"I don't use the *liberal* word a hell of a lot, if that's what you mean. I'm not in favor of same-sex couples."

"What's your opinion of George Bush?"

"I think he's doing a good job. He's got confidence in himself and his advisers. In the last election, that fellow Kerry started out okay, but his only platform was to run Bush down."

Dixon shows me pictures of his racehorses and his grandkids. ("I'm liberal with them," he says.) He talks about the hard work of living out here, a struggle against a horizon full of dust devils and sage. Natural gas is the big-dollar industry these days. The landscape is decorated with queerly shaped gas tanks, like an invasion of flying saucers. Deep wells provide water for the farms, draining the aquifer and giving a kind of borrowed lushness to vast irrigated fields.

It's a white man's world, ruled by fellows like Dixon who detest the idea of "big government" and regulations and bureaucratic meddling. Their faces have a kind of catcher's mitt roughness, sunworn and swollen with labor and fatigue. But change is creeping in even here, bit by bit and census by census. Drive down the main street of Guymon and you'll find Spanish *bodegas* and *panterias*. A new wave of Hispanic immigration has arrived in this part of rural America, drawn by the gas fields, the meatpacking houses, and fieldwork.

"What about all the Mexicans moving in?" I ask. "Do they make you uncomfortable? Are they changing things?"

"I bet we're fifty percent Mexican now in this town," he says, sounding a little perplexed. He crosses his arms. "But I guess they're about the only ones who will work hard."

"Are they involved in your politics? Are they getting elected?"

He makes a soft gesture with his hand, as if I've said something hasty or imprudent. "When they're a little bit more educated, their people will fit just fine into the political arena. And they'll probably take charge eventually, because they're multiplying faster than we are." He says it complacently, like a man does when he's discussing something that doesn't seem quite real, a thing that will happen long after he's gone.

"Some folks say the Republican Party is using people like you," I tell him. "They use your votes but don't do much for you, especially on pocketbook issues and the economy."

Dixon grimaces. "Anybody out here who wants a job can get a job. I don't see anybody going hungry."

There's something in Gerald Dixon's outlook that I encounter again and again in small towns. It's not simply that homelanders reject the Democratic Party's candidates or policies; the antipathy goes much deeper. For many rural Americans, the party as an institution has drifted outside the realm of the normal. To Dixon, the Democrats are as alien and remote as, say, the Greens or the Socialists.

Back in the van, I ask Allen to give me his gut impression of Democrats. After a puzzled moment, he says, "I guess I don't really know who they are. I mean, I know the personalities, John Kerry and Bill and Hillary and Al Sharpton. But there's nobody there that I can relate to. Democrats seem kind of stiff and fake. I think they lack common sense."

## 2

# My Brother's Keeper

Not so long ago, the opinions of people like Allen and Gerald Dixon didn't seem to matter much. Homelanders take umbrage at this neglect, but America is a democracy, after all, and urbanization is a fact of life. In the nineteenth century, small towns were vital hubs of American life. But by 2000 the Protestant farm culture that had defined our nation for nearly two centuries had been eclipsed by dense urban neighborhoods and sprawling suburbs.

Hispanics, African Americans, and Asians already outnumber rural whites by a sizable margin, and their numbers are growing fast. According to the U.S. Census, California's Hispanic population swells by roughly a thousand people every day. That's every single day, 365 days a year. Most of the immigrants pour into the state's massive cities. As of 2004, Los Angeles County alone was home to more than 4.6 million Hispanics. That's more people than live in six rural states combined.

It's hard to wrap your mind around. One city's minority group outnumbers every man, woman, and child in Alaska, Montana, North and South Dakota, Vermont, and Wyoming. Los Angeles County also has 1.4 million Asian Americans, which is more people than live in the entire state of Maine. And while California is on the cutting edge of America's multiethnic, urban transformation, other big metro states follow closely behind. Chicago's Cook County has 1.4 million African Americans, roughly the same population as the state of Idaho.

Signs of this demographic revolution are visible even in homelander country. In New Mexico, Hispanics already make up 43 percent of the population. In 2004, Texas joined the list of states where white people are in the minority. Arizona, Georgia, and Mississippi are expected to join their ranks in the next decade. Soon, nearly half of all Americans will live in states where gringos are just another slice of an increasingly jumbled pie.

America's rural-dominant states aren't just becoming more diverse; they're also becoming more urban. Between 1990 and 2000, the population of Texas's small towns stagnated but the metro population jumped by nearly three million people. That's like adding a new state the size of Alabama, all packed inside a few hundred square miles of suburbs and urban neighborhoods. Most observers assumed that this demographic shift would grind away census by census until small towns were buried, politically and culturally. Family farms would wither. The Rust Belt and the Bible Belt would merge into a vast depopulated wasteland.

As a natural extension of this shift, it seemed fair to assume that Democrats and moderate Republicans would set up permanent residence in the White House, dominate Congress, and push an ever more progressive, urban agenda. When *The New Republic* published a cover story in 1986 headlined *The Idiocy of Rural Life,* it reflected a growing conviction that small towns were already yesterday's news, hardly worth serious consideration.

In summer 2004, tens of millions of metros clung to this worldview. In our bright blue urban enclaves, we nurtured an increasingly bitter grudge toward George Bush. The brush pulling, the West Texas drawl, the bizarrely outmoded family values, and the stubborn anti-intellectualism triggered a kind of hatred not seen since the "fear and loathing" days of Richard Nixon.

We urbanites were convinced that we had the power to send Bush packing. He had crept into office while we weren't looking, the product of luck, silver spoon entitlement, and dirty tricks, but now we were riled up. We were volunteering, donating money, promising one another that we would get out and vote in droves. Metros knew that John Kerry wasn't the greatest candidate in the world, but he was sort of beside the point. Even many of my Republican friends were muttering darkly about Donald Rumsfeld's incompetent bluster, Karl Rove's cynical, poll-driven sloganeering, and John Ashcroft's in-your-bedroom social conservatism.

Meanwhile, my "Nader-Raider" pals on the Left were promising sheepishly that they would behave this time and vote ABB: *Anybody but Bush.*

Most years, I'm a dyed-in-the-wool moderate, cherrypicking candidates from both parties that strike me as centrist and levelheaded. I'm liable to vote Republican far more often than Democrat. I voted for George Pataki twice. I voted for Republican congressman John McHugh three times. But that summer, all my carefully calibrated centrism had come apart. I was furious. Heartsick. Terrified. One of my best friends, a pastor named Eric Olsen, was serving as a chaplain with a National Guard infantry battalion from New York that was stationed in the Sunni Triangle, north of Baghdad. His wife and two sons were counting the days until he could come home.

War is always tough, but a couple of things had me boiling. First, I felt betrayed. I had listened closely to Colin Powell's speech in front of the United Nations. I trusted Powell and after hearing him lay out the facts, I was convinced. A guy like Saddam Hussein couldn't be allowed to have weapons of mass destruction (WMDs), especially with all those "high-level contacts" between Iraqi agents and al Qaeda. President Bush had warned us unequivocally before the invasion that Saddam "could have a nuclear weapon in less than a year."

When the shooting began, I was sort of a small-time William Kristol, scolding my liberal friends for their indecisiveness, their dovishness, their "pre-9/11 mindset." By the summer of 2004, however, a majority of Americans knew the truth. Powell's hair-raising claims had been dead wrong. Bush's justifications for the invasion had been discredited before he sent the first soldier into battle. A poll taken by Fox News just two months after the invasion found that 41 percent of Americans believed that prewar intelligence was "intentionally misleading." Another 18 percent believed that "the truth about weapons intel lies somewhere between a mistake and an intentional deception."

But the administration's bungling of prewar intelligence (incompetence or deliberate lies, take your pick) wasn't the worst of it. The real outrage was the lack of diligence that went into preparing for the invasion. We pay billions of dollars in taxes to fuel the most powerful military-intelligence complex in the world, but the only Americans who seemed to have decent "intel" about the Iraqis were the peaceniks and protesters.

The ugly truth seemed unavoidable: Bush didn't just send our troops off on the wrong mission, he sent them in poorly equipped with a losing game plan. I was hearing from Eric about the shortage of translators, the lack of community-relations experts, the dearth of decent on-the-ground intelligence. American reservists were stealing equipment from their fellow soldiers, everything from body armor to Humvee doors, just to keep themselves alive. Boys who had been in high school vocational classes a few months before were frantically welding scraps of steel to the sides of their trucks.

Two kids with our local National Guard battalion had already been killed. One of them was a twenty-one-year-old reservist named Nathan Brown who was blown to ruin on Easter Sunday while riding in the back of an unarmored cargo truck. I had interviewed Nathan's mom, Kathy, a square-built bulldog of a woman, as blue-collar as one can get, from a tiny town north of Albany. Her scalding, sorrowful words were still ricocheting around in my head.

"Nathan was in a vehicle that was inadequate, there's no doubt," she said. "I just hope the rest of the soldiers over there get what they need to do their job and come home safe." But I could see she didn't believe it. Her faith in the president and his policy was gone. "Would I die for this cause?" she asked. "For this war? No, this war is unjust."

— — —

Kathy and my brother were exactly the sort of voters I expected to turn against Bush in droves. I felt as if I had one foot in their world, a decent sense of their political pulse. Then came a sobering day in August 2004 during a family reunion in Wichita, Kansas. My aunts own a big house on the bank of the Arkansas River, where our extended clan gathered for a week of happy bedlam, with middle-aged couples camped out on couches, toddler cribs tucked in corners, a nonstop buffet of baloney sandwiches and burgers grilled near the swimming pool.

Allen and I went for a walk, trying to work off another big meal, with our boys running in every direction like bottle rockets. It was melt-your-collar hot, the air so thick you could pour it in a glass. We lazed through the oaks and willows, and naturally we got to talking politics, mulling the future of the country. "I think maybe I could handle Bush's ideology," I said, "if the guy just had decent follow-through. But these chicken hawks didn't do their homework. So now our guys are stuck over there. And all Bush can say is 'bring it on.' And 'we'll stay the course.'"

You can guess where this is going. It turns out Allen was and is deeply devoted to Bush. Even after Abu Ghraib, the National Security Agency (NSA) spying scandal, the Valerie Plame affair, the Jack Abramoff eruption, and the national disgrace that followed Hurricane Katrina, Allen admires the man sincerely. He believes that Bush's policies and public demeanor steadied our country in those horrible months after 9/11. Even with the news from Iraq shading into the surreal, Allen felt that Bush was a guy he could trust.

"We have to give him the benefit of the doubt," he said. "He told us up front it wouldn't be easy, that there would be tough days. We have to be patient. I don't see this as a time for second-guessing."

The person who had Allen really steamed that summer wasn't Bush or Rumsfeld or Dick Cheney or Paul Wolfowitz. It was Michael Moore and the cabal of liberals who he felt were unfairly demonizing the war effort. He hadn't seen *Fahrenheit 9/11*, but he knew half a dozen scenes by heart, all refracted through the outraged punditry of right-wing talk radio. In Allen's world, the essayists and thinkers who frame the metro sensibility (from Moore to Nicholas Kristof to Maureen Dowd to Al Franken) are discredited before they open their mouths. They're too sneering, too sarcastic, and too urban.

Allen tells the story of listening to a local conservative radio show in his hometown who was interviewing a progressive about the Iraq war. The guest was arguing that the lives of average Iraqis hadn't been improved by the U.S.-led invasion. "Two different soldiers called in," Allen said, "feeling that some of the remarks were out of line. The liberal treated the one soldier as if he just wasn't smart enough to interpret things he had seen with his own two eyes. The other soldier didn't like the liberal's claim that the soldiers who died in Iraq and Afghanistan had died in vain and that President Bush, his commander in chief, was a moron."

Like a lot of folks in America, Allen and I were looking at one another across a painful and baffling divide. Bush and the war were metaphors, really, symbols of our very different takes on reality. In the days that followed we walked and talked, searching for points we shared in common without finding many. Everywhere we turned, there were land mines: tax cuts, public Christianity, choice and abortion.

We found ourselves living in completely different countries, getting our news from different sources, believing different people, even *liking* different people. Even when we agreed on hard facts, our interpretations were like night and day. Allen wanted to talk about Iraqi voters with purple fingertips. I wanted to talk about the growing body count and the president's lawyerly endorsement of torture.

In a sense, Allen and I are the perfect test case for the urban-rural standoff. We grew up in the same small towns. We both have solidly middle-class jobs and healthy families. We attend church regularly (Allen considerably more regularly), and we rely on taxpayers for at least a slice of our paychecks (Allen as a public school teacher, me as a public radio reporter). As kids we raised a fair amount of hell (Allen considerably more hell), and like a lot of baby boomers, we would be flat-out appalled if our sons tried half of the stunts we got away with.

In some ways we are still remarkably, reassuringly similar. We both like to read, and we love politics. We're both devoted to the idea of protecting the environment, though Allen comes at the problem as a hunter and a fisherman, while I'm more of a "take only pictures, leave only footprints" tree-hugger type. But over the last few decades, my sensibilities have been shaped by urban culture. Where Allen avoids the scrum and turmoil of cities, I make regular pilgrimages to New York and Montreal. He sees the rapid changes in American society over the last few decades as something akin to chaos; I'm fascinated and delighted by the constant negotiations of urban life. On most of the hot-button issues that divide metro from homelander, our views are as different as Gotham and Mayberry.

One of the most painful subjects that summer was same-sex marriage. I had just come from a wedding party in Canada (where gay and lesbian weddings are mostly legal) held to honor two dear friends, men who have shared their lives for decades. Their gathering had been almost indistinguishable from my family's reunion in Wichita, full of music, kids, softball, and catching up over bottles of beer. I couldn't think of one thing worth fearing or condemning in those good, middle-aged souls. But my brother's take on the subject was blunt and more or less non-negotiable.

"I don't hate gay people," Allen said. "They should live however they want. It's a free country. But marriage is a thing for men and women. It's tradition. The family is a cornerstone of American society."

By society, of course, Allen meant Judeo-Christian society. He meant a society built on the social structures that came out of agricultural Europe in the 1700 and 1800s. Allen is an educated man, not a flamer or a hater; you'll never find him shouting bitter words outside an abortion clinic. But he also lives in a place so truly rural —

not Berkshires rural, not southern Vermont rural — that it's easier to find a swimming hole than an espresso.

Allen goes out of his way to avoid the crowds and confusion of cities; even downtown St. Louis makes him grimace. "I'd rather live in a rural area almost anywhere than an urban area," he says. "It's a culture apart. I think it would be fair to say that I'm more comfortable with people from rural areas."

"What makes you uncomfortable with city people?"

"Living where I live, I don't have to be careful about what I say. About my enjoyment of hunting or owning firearms, for example. Those are things that are really important to me."

Allen's brand of homelander Christianity also bears little resemblance to the laissez-faire brand of Methodist worship that I've adopted. The Missouri Synod of the Lutheran Church drew attention in 2001 when senior officials chastised a pastor in Brooklyn twelve days after the 9/11 attacks. David Benke was suspended for eight months after joining hands with Hindus, Muslims, and non-Lutheran Christians during an ecumenical "Prayer for America" service at Yankee Stadium hosted by Oprah Winfrey.

According to *Christianity Today*, Benke was charged with "six sets of ecclesiastical violations, including syncretism (mixing religions), unionism (worshiping with non-LCMS Christian clergy), and violating the Bible's commandment against worship of other gods." The Benke case makes my brother uncomfortable, but he likes the fact that his denomination isn't wishy-washy. It makes sense to Allen that there are rules, lines you simply don't cross, and he accepts the notion that some of the boundaries won't necessarily make a lot of sense. You have to accept them on faith.

"That's how I feel about gay people," he says. "Homosexuality isn't something I have any interest in being involved with, or being around, but I don't actually see how it's sinful either, especially if two people are in a committed relationship. But you can't dispute that it's there in the Bible. It's forbidden. That's just the way it is."

— — —

This is where most metros tune out. The cultural divide feels too vast, too ugly. They tell themselves that white crackers in Alabama must have talked the same way in the 1950s: "Negros ain't bad, they just different." But Allen's not a bigot. He's not close-minded or blindly obedient. He is known in his church for challenging his pastor, for raising thorny questions about theology and faith and social justice.

Allen's cultural sources are also pretty nuanced. He tunes into AM talk radio and gets his nightly news from Fox, but he also listens regularly to public radio's *Morning Edition* and *All Things Considered*. He and David are both big fans of Jon Stewart's *The Daily Show*. The last political book he read was the autobiography of Illinois senator Barak Obama, an urban Democrat. "His life story is pretty inspiring," Allen says.

It turns out that in a very non-metro way, my brother's an idealist. He thinks there's a better, more decent America out there, a country that somehow got tangled up in niggling multiculturalism, derailed by political correctness, and deformed by tax-and-spend social engineering. He dreams of a future that's a little more honest, a little freer, and a little more prosperous than the one we've actually inherited. It's a nation where the politicians are humble and plainspoken, guided by clear moral values. Any blemishes in their past are redeemed by faith.

"And you think the Republicans will help you get there?" I asked. "Guys like Newt Gingrich and Tom DeLay?"

Allen shrugged a little wearily. He knows how I feel about those guys — that I find many of them to be ruthless, unsavory, and hypocritical. But a lot of the horror stories that metros swap about the Emperor Palpatines and Snidely Whiplashes of the Republican Right just don't have much currency in Allen's world. Often they don't get aired at all. The day that Tom DeLay was indicted, in September 2005, Rush Limbaugh's radio show was devoted to a snooze-enducing discussion of the nation's energy policy. By day two Limbaugh was back in full attack mode, accusing the Democratic prosecutor of trying to "criminalize the fact that people are Republicans."

The Abramoff scandal, involving the massive defrauding of Native American tribes by a top Republican operative, got remarkably little play on Fox News. Most of the coverage framed the scandal as a Big Government problem, not a Republican one. In the days following Abramoff's guilty plea, in January 2006, many conservative pundits maintained a deafening silence. The usually excitable crowd of right-wing bloggers mustered a collective shrug: "[O]ne almost gets the impression that campaign contributions and Congressional junkets are illegal," muttered *Power Line*'s John Hinderaker. "Time will tell how much of the Abramoff story is smoke, and how much is fire."

"You'd think, as the Jack Abramoff scandal burned its way through the Republican establishment faster than the space monster's blood dissolved the *Nostromo*'s bulkheads in *Alien,* that the [*Wall Street*] *Journal* editorialists would be exercising their own fangs," wrote Jack Shafer in the on-line journal *Slate*. "All the traditional themes that populate an outraged *Journal* editorial can be counted. An out-of-control majority party; dishonest lobbyists; a president who looks the other way; kickbacks and bribes. . . . Alas, no scathing 'Who Is Jack Abramoff?' editorial has appeared on the *Journal* page."

In part because they look through a very different window at our national politics, homelanders like Allen perceive a far more attractive version of the Republican Party. They also see the very worst features in the Democratic Party and its leaders. For millions of small-town folks, the portrait of John Kerry framed by the Right was a walking provocation, an incitement to get out and vote with vigor.

Even without the Swift Boat Veterans hysterics and the doctored photo of Kerry standing next to Jane Fonda, the Massachusetts Democrat's complicated soldier-who-joined-the-peace-movement backstory seemed to confirm rural America's worst fears about metro culture. Kerry reeked of the 1960s. He broke ranks with his fellow soldiers. He changed his mind too often, embraced too many -isms. He married a foreign wife. He played the wrong sports and seemed about as bicoastal as a politician could be, without being Hillary Clinton.

"John Kerry just doesn't work for me," Allen said. "He comes from another planet." But it wasn't just Kerry, it was the whole package. "When I think about Bill Clinton and all that stuff he did, I just get sick to my stomach. It's visceral. I know that's not the way we want our country to go."

The truth is I didn't much care about Allen's worldview. Not that summer. Monica Lewinsky and her soiled dress seemed downright quaint compared with missing WMDs and the growing body count in Iraq. Satisfied that my opinions were mainstream, I did my level metro best to set my brother straight. "Let's say I agree with you about the role of government," I said. "Maybe it is scary if the Feds get too intrusive. So how does that fit with the Patriot Act or with Congress telling people who can get married and who can't?"

"Legalizing gay marriage would mean that our society is endorsing it," Allen said. "Our government should tolerate the gay lifestyle. We shouldn't put them in jail or anything. But we shouldn't condone it either."

"It's fine with me if your church doesn't want to marry gays and lesbians. Don't let them in the door for all I care. But why should your convictions, or the federal bureaucracy, prevent another church — mine, for instance — from marrying two people who happen to be in love? How is that freedom of religion?"

"Your church can do whatever it wants," Allen said, "as long as the marriages aren't sanctioned by the government."

It went downhill from there. Not all the way downhill. Allen and I are still talking, still debating, still trying to find middle ground. But the conversation that summer drove home for me how thorny this mess has become. Positions that strike metros like me as basic common sense cause my brother to shake his head with dismay. And notions that homelanders see as bedrock American goodness make me want to give large amounts of money to MoveOn.org.

I left Wichita feeling sad and frustrated. I hated disagreeing so profoundly with a guy I love and respect, especially when the issues cut so deep. Here's the thing: We weren't just debating; it went to a much scarier place than that. We each held views that the other found troubling, ugly, and even morally wrong.

## 3

# Day of Reckoning

On Election Day 2004 I was assigned to a VFW banquet hall in Plattsburgh, New York. My job was to watch the returns come in with a group of local Democrats. It was a dreary night, damp and foggy along the shore of Lake Champlain. This northern industrial town is sort of a rust belt unto itself. The local air force base was decommissioned in the early 1990s. The population has stagnated, with so few young people sticking around to raise families that the local school districts have begun mothballing buildings. In 2005, Wyeth announced that it was shutting down its big pharmaceutical plant, axing thirteen hundred jobs.

Another institution that's struggling here is the Democratic Party. Plattsburgh hasn't elected a Democrat to the state senate or assembly since 1966. This congressional district has never sent a Democrat to Washington. Voters in northern New York used to elect Whigs, and now they elect Republicans. In most nearby counties, the Democratic Party is in shambles. In local races — judgeships, mayors, district attorneys — the whole "down ballot" menu that offers a snapshot of a party's depth, the Democratic column often remains empty.

The year 2004 felt different. The Democrats had a reasonably strong state assembly candidate, a genial, harmless-looking former high school principal named Bernie Bassett. He was a lackluster campaigner, but he hadn't done anything incompetent, and he was getting generous financial support from urban Democrats down-state. Local activists had managed to boost the Democratic Party's enrollment significantly. There was a sense among local politicos that George Bush had stumbled, alienating moderates. The Bush-Kerry debates had been a fiasco, with the usually folksy Bush managing to look both petty and imperious.

Through the afternoon, exit polls suggested that Kerry might just pull it off. Liberal blog sites churned with optimism, buoyed largely by leaked survey numbers. The stock market dipped a hundred points, a sign that Wall Street was bracing itself for a Democratic administration. The mood among Plattsburgh Dems turned jubilant as the networks reported that Kerry was holding a narrow national lead, sometimes as wide as 3 percentage points. In battleground states, the story seemed even better: Kerry was up by 9 points in Pennsylvania and neck-and-neck in Virginia. Florida, Ohio, and New Hampshire all looked winnable.

CNN showed footage of voting precincts in cities and suburbs, where long lines of people waited to cast their ballots. Many of the eager faces were black, Hispanic, or Asian. So many urbanites had turned out that polling places were clogged. Metros seemed to have shaken off their complacency. They were reasserting their dominant role, putting conservatives back in their place. But then actual returns began trickling in, and Bush's numbers looked stronger — and then, suddenly, very strong. One by one, states in the Midwest, the South, and the Rocky Mountain West popped up on the screen bright red.

Kerry won a few hard-fought victories: New Hampshire and Pennsylvania flashed blue. But Florida went for Bush by a safe margin, and the outcome in Ohio looked less promising by the hour. As Kerry's shadow victory evaporated, the Democratic crowd in Plattsburgh deflated. A glum silence replaced the laughter and back slapping. There was a feeling almost like shame, as people watched the tally board rack up more and more electoral votes for Bush and Cheney.

Metros across the country were understandably flummoxed. It didn't seem to make sense. The mood in their neighborhoods, on their morning commutes, around the office cooler, had been fervently anti-Bush. They had done everything right, giving money, mobilizing, firing up the blogosphere, working to turn out the African American vote. MTV worked with pop icons like Sean P. Diddy Combs and Eminem to mobilize the youth votes. Some would later claim that there had been vote tampering or fraud, but the illusion of Kerry's victory was really very simple: Reporters and pollsters had been gathering the bulk of their information in the nation's cities and sub-urbs. From Philadelphia to Miami to Cincinnati, they were hearing from people who rejected Bush's ruralist policies.

In homelander counties people were saying something very different. But as usual metros weren't listening, or they weren't listening hard enough.

For Democrats in Plattsburgh the night was doubly painful. After looking strong much of the day and winning comfortably in the district's most urban precincts, Bernie Bassett began to fade. In neighboring Franklin County, where you can drive twenty minutes on the main highway without seeing a house, the Democrat got creamed. By ten o'clock, folks in the VFW hall were shrugging into overcoats, hugging each other tearfully, and wandering out into the darkness.

I went back to my office and filed stories, business as usual. Another year, another election. But in fact I was baffled and dismayed. There were e-mails in my inbox from friends and colleagues baffled by the outcome. "I feel I don't know my own country anymore," was a common refrain. Folks were threatening only half-jokingly to head north to Canada. *Slate* even published an "explainer" that detailed the pros and cons of gaining Canadian citizenship. For the first time in weeks, I thought of my brother and something he told me in Wichita: "You think you're mainstream," Allen said. "But I think I'm mainstream. I honestly believe that my views are more normal for the average American than yours."

It turns out he was half-right. There are two versions of normal in America, two radically different takes on what our nation means, what we believe, and what our democracy should look like in the future. And in a head-to head matchup, Allen's side had won another round.

In the days and weeks after the election, metros scrambled to understand their humiliation. Who were these people who voted for Bush? How could they bring themselves to do it? For the first time, millions of metros confronted the notion that their predicament was more than an aberration. Perhaps the election in 2000 had been stolen, or could be blamed on Ralph Nader, or was a reaction to the drift and scandal of the Clinton years, but this time Bush had won a majority of the popular vote — the first candidate to accomplish that feat since 1988.

A 3 percent margin of victory isn't exactly a mandate, but metros were hoping for a full-scale public repudiation. Instead they got another dose of Bush's self-satisfied drawl as he declared victory. "I've earned capital in this election," he said, "and I'm going to spend it for what I told the people I'd spend it on."

I have friends who didn't read a newspaper for two months after the vote. They turned off the television and stopped listening to NPR. They simply couldn't tolerate the idea that "that man" was still their elected leader. *Salon*'s David Talbot published a column comparing the election to the nineteenth-century rift between the North and the Confederacy. "Secession is in the air again," he wrote. "And it's not just Southern conservatives who are openly discussing splitting the Union."

> It's increasingly resentful blue-state liberals, who complain they are shackled to reactionary Southern cousins. Nearly a century and a half after the South was defeated, it is the South's social agenda and the South's beloved president the rest of us are forced to live with.

— — —

In May 2005, *Salon* published another article describing embattled liberals as refugees from that other, more conservative America. "We've almost gone through a divorce with our own country," said Van Jones, with the Ella Baker Center for Human Rights.

This red-blue divide was widely adopted in the late 1990s as the standard shorthand for American politics. On brightly colored maps, recycled in newspapers and magazines and on network television, we saw progressive chunks of blue in the Northeast, along the West Coast, and clustered around the Great Lakes. Dividing and conquering blue America was a conservative red tide surging up from the South, flooding the vast Midwest, swamping the interior West.

Perched between these ideological hot zones are a handful of muddled battleground states. Florida, New Hampshire, New Mexico, Ohio, and Pennsylvania swing red or blue, depending on the year and the candidate. According to conventional wisdom, these wishy-washy souls can't quite decide where their loyalties lie, with Dixie or the New Deal. They're seen as sort of pathologically undecided. As a consequence, they're battered with obscene amounts of political advertising — inflating the revenues of local media companies and boosting TiVo sales.

This red-blue portrait of America's political culture is comforting for partisans on the Right and the Left. Ours may be a house divided, but both sides can look at the map and find big sharply defined territories filled with plenty of like-minded people. In the days after the election, an anonymous humorist circulated a new map via the Web, showing red America as *Jesus Land* and blue America as a frontier of *The United States of Canada*.

The red zone may be full of nutcase zealots and authority junkies, but our blue bastions are dependably progressive and even sort of European in their sensibility. You can find a decent loaf of bread, a good bookstore, a copy of the *New York Review of Books*.

The blue zone may be full of ecofreaks and feminazis and welfare moms and Al Sharpton liberals, but red America is still guided (thank God) by traditional values. People believe in something, and they stick to their convictions. They're not snooty, and they don't care what those damned Europeans think.

There's only one problem with this split-screen version of America's cultural landscape. It's utter fiction. It's not even good fiction, really. A good yarn can sometimes get at a larger and more compelling truth, but our imaginary red-blue divide hides far more than it reveals. Examine more accurate maps that break down the country's voting patterns by actual distribution and you find that those tidy ideological provinces dissolve. They simply vanish before your eyes.

Great swaths of homelander conservatism pop up in rural counties along the Great Lakes, in the Northeast, and in the West. Hundreds of small towns in blue California, Illinois, and New York are every bit as fervently Republican as those in the Deep South or the Midwest. Meanwhile, there are bright dots of metro liberalism deep in Republican territory. Right across Dixie and the Bible Belt, doughty pockets of urban progressives lean just as far left as their compatriots in California or Massachusetts.

Some observers, reacting to this messy reality, have described America as a "purple" nation, a murky broth of blue Democrats and red Republicans with no clear differentiation. "We are not defined just by religion or ethnic group, or region," wrote Robert Kuttner in *American Prospect*. "In the very close 2004 election, for instance, the contest was decided by 10 [percentage] points or less in twenty-one states. And a surprising number of states voted one way for president, the other for senator or governor."

But this model, too, disguises what has become a clear political and cultural divide in America, delineated not by state or region but by the boundary between our progressive cities and inner suburbs and the conservative rural culture that sprawls beyond the urban beltway.

Despite the historical tension between urban and rural culture, this sharp political segregation is a fairly recent phenomenon. As journalist Bill Bishop has noted in his groundbreaking reports for the *Austin American-Statesman,* small towns split their votes evenly between Republicans and Democrats as recently as 1980. Cities, too, were divided in their loyalties, often embracing GOP moderates.

All that has changed. In much of rural and exurban America, Democrats are pariahs. Motivated by issues that range from same-sex marriage and abortion to gun rights and affirmative action, small-town voters choose Republican candidates or they stay home. The average Republican-tilting county is now so rural that it has about one-third as many people as the average Democratic county. Counties that are markedly conservative — swinging for the GOP by 20-percent margins — tend to be even more distinctly rural, with only one-eighth the population of heavily Democratic counties. "The nation has gone through a big sort, a sifting of people and politics into what is become two Americas," Bishop wrote in the *American-Statesman.* "One is urban and Democratic, the other Republican, suburban and rural."

Obviously, there are people in small towns who vote for Democrats, just as there are Republicans in Manhattan and San Francisco. But the rural-urban divide is increasingly stark. One afternoon in Perryton, Texas — a tiny town near the Oklahoma border where 95 percent of voters cast ballots for George Bush — a woman named Micha Hardy told me flat out: "If I was to vote against the Republicans, it'd be like I was voting against America."

The fault line is so pronounced that "ruralness" has emerged as one of the best indicators of a state's political leanings. Twelve of America's fifteen most sparsely settled states are reliably Republican. Often, their bustling blue cities vote Democratic, but in states like Georgia, Nebraska, and Nevada, those metro islands are swamped in a sea of small towns. On the other hand, nine of the fifteen most densely populated states are dependably Democratic. In states like

Delaware and New Jersey, there simply aren't enough homelanders to offset the left-of-center cities and inner suburbs.

Most of the key battleground states are perched on the demographic divide, with metro Democrats and homelander Republicans competing on more or less even footing. Florida, Ohio, and Pennsylvania have population densities that average roughly 60 people per square mile. That's well above the comfort zone for Republicans, who perform best in states with about 30 people per square mile; but it's also well below the safety margin for Democrats, who fare best in states with around 120 people per square mile.

This tension wouldn't be so fascinating, and so dismaying for Democrats, if it weren't for the fact that small towns are winning the lion's share of battles, tipping big elections to Republican candidates. "The rule of thumb is that if the Democrat wins Cleveland by a hundred thousand votes, he wins [Ohio]," noted one political observer after the 2004 campaign. "John Kerry actually won Cleveland by two hundred thousand votes. He did almost everything right, turning out a huge urban vote. But Democrats still lost Ohio because the rural turnout was beyond anything we had ever seen before."

It's hard for metros to fathom how 20 percent of the American people, living in dusty small towns and far-flung business loop exurbs, can exert so much influence. A big part of the answer lies in the fact that homelanders are spread around unevenly. In California, Illinois, and New York, fewer than one in ten voters lives in rural communities. Republican presidential candidates haven't captured the electoral college votes of those states since 1988. But five American states have rural populations that top 50 percent — and four more states have homelander minorities that top 40 percent. In most of the key battleground states, small-town voters account for one-quarter to one-third of the electorate, making them a dominant power bloc. (Most of the states with a high quotient of homelanders also enjoy extra clout in the electoral college and in the U.S. Senate.)

A second big factor is that rural voters are zealous. They tend to be older and whiter than the population as a whole, which means they are far more likely to register and turn out to vote. Though they comprise only one-fifth of the American population, small-town voters cast one-quarter of the total ballots in 2004. Evangelical Christians like Allen, the hardest of the hard-core conservatives, make up just 7 percent of the population, but they cast roughly 11 percent of the votes. "If the Born Again public had shown up proportional to its population size," noted Christian pollster George Barna in a 2005 report, "Senator Kerry would have won the election by the same three-point margin of victory enjoyed by Mr. Bush."

But turnout alone isn't enough to swing elections, especially if you're a shrinking minority. Another big component of rural influence is solidarity. In the last two presidential elections, much of the nation split its vote evenly. We're like a bickering married couple out for a Sunday drive who can't decide whether to turn right or left. Exit polls conducted by CNN found that voters in the suburbs — where most Americans live — gave Bush and Kerry roughly 50 percent of their votes. They canceled each other out. (As we'll see in chapter five, even this "undecided" suburban vote breaks down on sharply urban-rural lines, with the inner suburbs trending Democratic while outer exurban neighborhoods vote solidly Republican.)

For rural whites that sort of fence sitting is ancient history. In battleground states, where voters were energized by lavish media campaigns, rural counties regularly offered up 75–85 percent support for Bush. The result was a David and Goliath mismatch, with dusty rural counties exerting more electoral influence than major cities. A textbook example was the bare-knuckled brawl over Florida's twenty-seven electoral college votes.

Miami-Dade County is one of the country's largest metropolitan areas, with 2.3 million residents. Those urban and suburban voters cast a lot of ballots, and Kerry won, but only by a fifty thousand vote margin. Orange County — which includes Orlando's nine hundred thousand urbanites, but also a swath of conservative exurban voters — was even more evenly divided. Voters there delivered to Kerry a razor-thin victory of just eight hundred votes.

Up in the rural Panhandle, meanwhile, you find sleepy Okaloosa and Santa Rosa counties, part of a stretch of scrub pine, resort towns, and turpentine mills that local tourism boosters call the "Forgotten Coast." You can bet Republican strategists didn't forget them. The two neighboring counties have fewer than 350,000 people between them, but they turned out in droves and voted lockstep for Bush. The result was an astounding Republican surplus of nearly 100,000 votes. With one-tenth of the population, this gaggle of small towns managed to deliver twice the political punch of Orlando and Miami combined.

That kind of political loyalty doesn't happen by accident. Republicans campaigned hard in Florida's rural communities, tailoring their message to energize as much of the homelander base as possible.

This development alone has changed the face of American politics. Historically, Democrats have lagged in the fund-raising matchup, but they have enjoyed a huge advantage over Republicans in the ground game. It's easier in dense urban areas to register and turn out large numbers of sympathetic voters. Volunteers go door-to-door; they can walk people to the polling place on the corner.

But in 2004, GOP strategists deployed new marketing and public relations strategies designed to target homelanders out in their lonely, rural-route subdivisions. Using consumer and lifestyle data, Republicans were able to identify conservative-leaning households, even if they were registered as Democrats. "Some people call themselves Democrats but in every behavioral indicator they're not," points out Democratic pollster Anna Greenberg. "Attitudinally they're really Republican."

"If you drive a Volvo and you do yoga, you're pretty much a Democrat," Republican national chairman Ken Mehlman told the

*Washington Post.* "And if you drive a Lincoln or a BMW and you own a gun, you're voting for George W. Bush."

Between 2000 and 2004, this GOP data mining turned up more than twenty million new potential voters nationwide, many of them outside the urban beltway. The likeliest prospects were hit with direct mail, one-on-one phone calls, and home visits conducted by local campaign volunteers. In the final crush of the campaign, key home-lander clusters received visits from top-level administration officials, including George Bush and Dick Cheney. "You felt like you were in the old Chicago organization that Richard Daley used to run," Mehlman told the *Post,* "because we ran for president in those places and among those people as if we were running for mayor."

Despite their small-town drubbing in 2000, Democrats were once again caught flat-footed. "A lot of Florida Democrats scoffed when President Bush flew into the little Democrat stronghold of Gainesville two days before Election Day," wrote *St. Petersburg Times* political editor Adam Smith. "And as Democrats chuckled dismis-sively, some seventeen thousand people from nearby rural counties drove in to cheer the first sitting president since Grover Cleveland to visit their area. Then those bucolic, often overlooked counties pro-duced some of the most dramatic Bush victory margins in the state."

In his column, Smith quoted figures provided by Florida Democratic pollster David Beattie. Beattie found that in 2000, Al Gore lost in exurban and rural counties by roughly 370,000 votes. But four years later, Bush's homelander margin surged dramatically to more than 684,000 votes.

"A lesson America learned from Vietnam," Beattie told the *Times,* "is you cannot win the cities and lose the countryside and expect to win the war."

"Democrats had assumed that you can't organize on the ground in rural areas," says Greenberg. "But the Republicans have shown that that's not true. At least in battleground states, I think you'll see more micro-targeting that will make rural areas even more important."

If Florida were unique, it would be possible to dismiss the home-lander phenomenon as a fluke, but a similar urban-rural border war played out in Ohio. Despite rumblings that black and Hispanic voters would stay away from the polls, the Democratic machine worked brilliantly. Five of the six most populous counties swung for John Kerry in record numbers, giving him a metro margin of more than three hundred thousand votes.

But rural counties swung with even greater fervor for George Bush. In much of southern and western Ohio, the Republicans swept 70 percent of the vote, enough to squeak out a 140,000-vote margin statewide. "As a political tale," wrote Paul Farhi and James Grimaldi in the *Washington Post,* "Ohio can be simplified into a story of city vs. country."

> Kerry's strategists had been hoping for months that urban voters, including such loyally Democratic blocs as organized labor and blacks, would push Kerry to an unbeatable margin, offsetting Bush's strength far beyond the cities. It almost worked [but] Bush had stormed to such an overwhelming advantage in rural and exurban counties that his victory was secure.

Naturally, Florida and Ohio drew the big headlines. That's where the national election was won and lost. But the homelander-metro rivalry was reprised again and again across the nation. In Nevada, Kerry dominated Las Vegas, winning the state's biggest city by a land-slide. He managed a tie in Washoe County, the state's second-most densely populated area. But with the help of Dick Cheney, who cam-paigned twice in the state's rural counties, Nevada's homelanders scraped up just enough votes to tilt the state's five electoral votes for George Bush. The margin was devastatingly close — not quite twenty thousand ballots. "Rural Nevada beat John Kerry," Democratic sen-ator Harry Reid told Gannett News Service. "I believe where the Kerry presidential bid failed was in not selling itself to rural America."

Bush's homelander victory in New Mexico was even closer. Rural counties managed to overwhelm urban Democrats in Albuquerque, Taos, and Santa Fe by a margin of fewer than six thousand ballots.

Some metro pundits have argued that this rural infatuation with George Bush is an isolated phenomenon, similar to the bond that Ronald Reagan established with blue-collar Democrats. But the homelander zeal in 2004 extended well beyond the presidential race. Voters in the Florida Panhandle swamped urbanites in Broward and Palm Beach counties, helping to elect Republican senator Mel Martinez. Erskine Bowles, Bill Clinton's former White House chief of staff, was unbeatable in North Carolina's cities, but the state's small towns managed to build a 160,000-vote victory for Republican Richard Burr.

Perhaps the most painful upset for Democrats was that of Senator Tom Daschle in South Dakota. As Democratic minority leader, Daschle was a key opponent of the administration's policies. He even dared to defy Bush on the eve of the Gulf War, declaring that he was "saddened that this president failed so miserably at diplomacy that we're now forced to war." But Daschle's metro sensibilities — he is firmly pro-life — left him vulnerable. In 2003, Sioux Falls bishop Robert Carlson took the extraordinary step of ordering Daschle publicly to stop identifying himself as a practicing Roman Catholic. Daschle fired back from the Senate floor, accusing Bishop Carlson of adopting an agenda "more identified with the radical right than with thoughtful religious leadership."

Despite the church's attack and a massive barrage of right-wing ads, Daschle eked out a narrow victory in Sioux Falls, South Dakota's biggest city. But voters in sparsely settled northwestern counties swung hard for Republican John Thune, helping the social conservative eke out a razor-thin margin of forty-five hundred votes. One of George Bush's most powerful enemies had been eliminated and homelanders had pulled the trigger.

# 4

# Going Rural

It's midafternoon on a weirdly mild August day in 2005, and I wander into a camera shop in Perryton, Texas. The spare, neat-as-a-pin town is the hub of Ochiltree County, a gorgeous expanse of scrub and hills, with thick stands of cottonwood trees and willows tucked down in winding arroyos. By some measures this is the most Republican place in America. More than nine out of every ten voters supported George W. Bush. Micha Hardy, a lean, crop-haired woman in her thirties, comes up, rests an elbow on the counter, and grins at me.

It turns out she's a German immigrant, her West Texas drawl laced with a strong twist of the old country. She's single, a business owner, with a sharp tongue and an acerbic sense of humor "This town is too pushy," she says, gesturing expansively. "How often do I get asked where I go to church? Way too many people run to church and then go to the bar and beat up their wife. They pretend to be religious."

Anyplace else in America you'd expect a woman like Micha to be a slam-dunk Democrat and a social liberal, but not in Ochiltree County. "I don't know anybody who would vote Democrat," she says, with a big laugh. "I can't imagine who that would be. No, I'm stumped. I can't imagine the person who would just come out and say, 'I'm a Democrat.' You'd just get bombarded with questions."

We talk for a long time, between customers, and Micha admits that she has a lot of reservations about the Republican agenda. She doesn't much like Bible-thumpers. She hates No Child Left Behind, because it's too meddlesome, too top-down. But in her mind these are quibbles, the sort of mild, inside-the-family complaints you might hear in Boston about Ted Kennedy or in San Francisco about

Nancy Pelosi. "In my case voting Republican is more of a personal like and dislike thing," she says.

One of Micha's employees, Christina Enriquez, comes up from the back of the shop. She's twenty-three years old, a white woman married to a Hispanic man who spent a year fighting in Iraq. She, too, has some beefs with the GOP. "The people who send soldiers over there don't know what it does to them," she says. "You don't see the senators' kids, the high-society kids, fighting over there."

When I ask her how she voted, she shrugs and says, "I went for Bush because he was better than Kerry, but not by much."

I tell her it doesn't make much sense to me, supporting a president who got us into a war she doesn't believe in, one that put her husband in harm's way. But like a lot of homelanders, Christina has a sort of love-hate relationship with Iraq and the president's leadership. She's skeptical and even angry, but also unwilling to hear criticism. Rural folks have a deep and personal investment in this war. "A local boy died over there," she says. "They shut down all the stores so that people could go to the funeral."

I ask Micha and Christina what they think of the Democratic Party, and of urban Americans in general. "The Democrats are too stuck up," Micha says. "I don't get along with city people. Towns like this are more laid-back."

Christina thinks for a moment and then says, "In cities you're more of an individual. You can do what you want, not what you're expected to do. Big cities have a better economy, but this out here is a way of life. A small town takes a long time to build up. It's time we got listened to by the big cities."

We talk for a while about abortion and Micha says bluntly, "I don't believe in killing babies. There's always room for one more baby in this world."

"I don't think it should be illegal," Christina says, "but there should be guidelines. I can't understand how anybody can go out and be a 'ho' every night and not use birth control. I was sixteen years old when I had my son. At the time, my mom was for an abortion, but I didn't think that was right."

In rural America, this range of attitudes represents the mainstream, the common-sense center of the debate. Both women are bright and open-minded. When I ask questions about the war, same-sex marriage, immigration, taxes, they think carefully before answering. Their answers are usually hedged with qualifications and shades of gray, not dogmatic or rigid. They also seem interested in my opinions. But in the everyday run of their lives, the metro point of view just doesn't get heard here. Or if it does get heard, it falls so far outside their sense of "normal" that it doesn't make sense.

Obviously, geography isn't the only thing that determines a person's political leanings. A black woman with a Ph.D. is far more likely to vote for a Democratic candidate even if she lives in Missouri's Boot Heel. A fair number of rural counties in the South and Southwest are predominately African American or Hispanic and regularly vote for Democrats. On the other hand, a white guy who served in the Marine Corps is likely to swing Republican, even if he lives in Boston. But there is a fair amount of evidence that even people in pigeon-holed categories of race, educational attainment, and economic class behave differently, depending on whether they live in urban or rural America.

Take the example of white men, generally considered a solid Republican voting bloc. In many states with high rural populations they've largely abandoned the Democratic Party. John Kerry's white-guy appeal in Alabama, Wyoming, and Arizona ranged from a dismal 18 percent to a tepid 36 percent. But in metro states like New York and Illinois, the percentage of white men voting Democratic was significantly higher, 46 and 48 percent, respectively. In highly urbanized Washington state, Massachusetts, and Rhode Island, Kerry actually polled higher than Bush among white men.

If Republican constituencies are vulnerable in urban areas, the

Democratic base can wobble in rural communities. Consider the African American vote. In urban bastions such as Illinois, New York, and Washington, D.C., black support for George Bush ranged from a sickly 10 percent down to a flat-line 3 percent. But in rural Georgia, Virginia, and Kentucky, George Bush attracted roughly 12 percent of the black vote. Not exactly a landslide, but a significant disparity. These numbers should give pause to metros who still think the Republican Party's southern appeal is solely the product of subtle bigotry.

So what makes rural America so unassailably conservative? How is it that people living a dozen miles outside the urban ring can see the world differently than their urban neighbors? For the moment, it's sufficient to say that in many small towns a dozen different factors converge at once. Homelanders tend to be whiter than the national average. They're also three times more likely to own guns. They have less education, on average, and they're more likely to attend church regularly. Most rural states have a lot of military veterans. In Montana, Nevada, and Wyoming, roughly 16 percent of the population has served in the military. In large urban states, such as California, Illinois, and New York, the number is closer to 10 percent.

These cultural differences are compounded by the fact that small towns have carved out an enormous degree of cultural autonomy. This alone is a remarkable homelander accomplishment, a major victory in the urban-rural culture war. When I was a kid, you drank from the spigot of urban culture or you went without. A rancher in Arizona turned to Dan Rather for his understanding of the world. A shop owner in South Dakota could choose from three television channels, all of them essentially urban and progressive in their content.

Growing up in Kansas, Oklahoma, and Alaska, we watched *All in the Family*, *M\*A\*S\*H*, and *Three's Company*, not because those shows reflected our values or experience, but because those were the only options. When MTV started flashing over cable television, the teens in my hometown started dressing and talking differently.

These days, rural Americans can get their news, books, art, movies, and music from sources that more closely reflect their traditional values. The break isn't clean or absolute; small-town folks still watch *Everybody Loves Raymond* and buy Stephen King novels and wonder about Jennifer and Brad's breakup. They try the latest fad diets, they get divorces, and they sneak peeks at porn sites on the Web. They still read *Time,* go to public school, and stand in line to see crummy blockbuster movies.

But now they can also get their news from Fox, Sinclair, or News Max.com. They can buy top-notch thrillers and romance novels written by evangelical Christians. Their kids watch *VeggieTales,* Christian cartoons on Saturday morning, and their teens hang out at youth groups, where they're encouraged to take "purity" oaths and wear "angel" jewelry that symbolizes their chastity. They listen to Christian rock bands that sound pretty much like mainstream pop acts, except that the guy they're crooning over happens to be Jesus.

When the time comes, young adults can go off to a rural-traditional college and then on to internships with a preselected list of conservative businesses or politicians. There are even dating and matchmaking services exclusively for social conservatives, where participants sign a loyalty oath guaranteeing that they aren't liberals.

"In good faith, I consider myself a conservative and typically represent myself as such when expressing my ideological views," reads the contract for ConservativeMatch.com. The company's logo is a hip-looking young woman, screaming in apparent frustration at all the sensitive left-leaning men who have driven her nuts. CM's slogan is "sweethearts not bleeding hearts," but the love net is cast wide enough to include "Republicans, Libertarians, Constitutionalists, 'Reagan Democrats' or similar parties from other countries."

Metro elites find all this baffling. They are used to dictating the national agenda, defining trends, setting political and cultural boundaries. Politicians trembled when Edward R. Murrow studied them over the tip of his smoldering cigarette. When Walter Cronkite expressed doubts about the Vietnam War, it was as if God himself had spoken. "Murrow taking on McCarthy and Cronkite going to Vietnam and coming back and saying, '*This isn't going to work*,' were two moments that are sort of the high points of broadcast journalism," director George Clooney told the *Daily Show*'s Jon Stewart.

But really it wasn't great journalism. Those were examples of political mentorship. Metro pundits were guiding America toward a moral and political conclusion. We saw a dim echo of this during Hurricane Katrina, when CNN's Anderson Cooper worked deliberately to summon the nation's outrage. But these days, such instances are rare and fleeting. The dialogue has fractured for good.

These days, for every Anderson Cooper, there is a Brit Hume ready with a rebuttal. For every Maureen Dowd, there is a Bill Kristol. For every Michael Moore, there is a Rush Limbaugh. "A political party is dying before our eyes," wrote Howard Fineman, a contributor to MSNBC. "I don't mean the Democrats. I'm talking about the mainstream media. At the height of its power, the American Mainstream Media Party helped validate the civil rights movement, end a war, and oust a power-mad president."

This media balkanization extends beyond politics and journalism. These days, for every Dr. Spock, there is a Dr. Dobson. For every Stephen King, there's a Tim LaHaye. For every Bill Moyers, there's a Bill Bennett.

The splintering of America's media culture dismays metros, but homelanders see the change as long overdue. It's fine if H. L. Mencken or Upton Sinclair (or their modern equivalents) want to talk trash about conservative culture, but why should rural folks be forced to tune in? Why shouldn't they have their own sources of information? Why shouldn't they have their own pundits, their own moral and political mentors?

The *Perryton Herald* is a tiny newspaper that comes out twice weekly and serves the scattered folk of Ochiltree County, Texas. The offices look like a stage set out of the 1970s, all fake wood paneling, threadbare carpet, big metal-topped desks that must be army surplus "Back when the three media networks controlled everything and AP and UPI were the only sources of news, that was our window on the world," says Jim Hudson, the *Herald*'s publisher. "Now I start my day with *Fox and Friends*. Then I do a computer check, reading *NewsMax.com*, a very conservative site. And I look at Matt Drudge's report. He finds stuff that you've never heard of before."

Hudson is a bluff sort of guy, by turns aggressive and gentlemanly, who sits in the back office filling a big ashtray. He writes the editorials and is famous for being somewhere to the right of just about everybody. Like most conservatives, he sees the downfall of the urban media monopoly as a something akin to the toppling of the Berlin Wall. "It's changed people's views of their world," he says. "They call me and say, 'Did you see on Fox News about so-and-so in rural South Carolina?' These days you can go on-line and read the *Washington Post* and also find the *Washington Times*."

When I ask Hudson about the urban-rural divide, he sits forward nodding and tapping his cigarette. "I lived in Houston for twelve years, and the people there forget where they came from. People in urban areas don't neighbor up. Here all the people know each other and they're friends. It builds a safety net, and you know you're not going to fall through."

"But I wonder if that would work in an urban area?" I say. "In city neighborhoods there are just so many people. Things are always changing so fast."

"You're right, it wouldn't work the same way. You have to rely a whole lot more on the government in cities. A rural area like us we depend on ourselves to get things done."

Like Allen, Hudson is convinced that city culture is fundamentally inferior, blighted by wrongheaded ideas that have led the country astray. "Urban America breeds things that will probably never be here [in Perryton], but it scares people." I ask what kinds of things he means and Hudson says, "Gay culture. HIV sure wasn't bred in rural America."

The statement is so ugly and raw that it takes me a moment to respond. "People in cities are scared, too," I say. "They're honestly afraid of the political ideas coming from folks like you. They think you'll take away their choices and try to impose your sense of morality."

"I would tell them that they have nothing to be afraid of," Hudson says. "I have liberal friends. They're afraid of the safety net being dismantled. But the changes aren't going to be radical or rapid. You can't change the government that fast."

Still, Hudson makes it clear that he thinks change will come — real, substantive change. He thinks his values make sense, that they're inherently better and will eventually win out. "The people who live here don't believe in killing babies," he says. "Every life is precious. In urban areas people have a throw-away-type society. If you don't want something, you just throw it away."

This sort of confidence is increasingly common in homelander circles. Hudson's side hasn't lost a lot of fights lately. When I ask about George W. Bush, Hudson sits back and grins: "He is hitting on all cylinders, as far as I'm concerned. He's a Texan, a rancher, a Christian, and a Republican. That covers all the bases."

Despite Hudson's reassurances, the militant rhetoric in homelander circles bears close watching. In May 2005, Pat Robertson described liberals and secular activists, led by an "out of control judiciary," as a threat more serious than Islamic terror: "If you look over the course of a hundred years," Robertson said on ABC's *This Week*, "I think the gradual erosion of the consensus that's held our country together is probably more serious than a few bearded terrorists who fly into buildings."

Much of the most venomous homelander rhetoric has been aimed at judges, who are blamed by rural Americans for "activist" decisions on abortion, school prayer, racial integration, and gay civil rights. In spring 2005, after judges refused to intervene in the Terry Schiavo case, then House majority leader Tom DeLay made a promise to supporters: "The time will come for the men responsible for this to answer for their behavior, but not today."

Texas Republican John Cornyn, a member of the Senate Judiciary Committee, was more explicit, suggesting that "raw political or ideological" decisions by the courts were to blame for a spate of violent attacks against judges. "I don't know if there's a cause-and-effect connection, but we have seen some recent episodes of courthouse violence in this country," Cornyn said in a Senate floor speech. "[J]udges are making political decisions yet are unaccountable to the public. . . . it builds up and builds up and builds up to the point where some people engage, engage in violence."

The culture-war jargon of Pat Buchanan and the treason talk of Ann Coulter resonate powerfully outside the urban beltway. Bitter words echo from pulpits, AM radios, and blog sites. In 2005 the pastor of a Baptist church in East Waynesville, North Carolina, made headlines after encouraging his congregation to banish Democrats from the church. Nine members were voted out. Slightly less than half of the church's members quit in protest — which means that more than half decided to stick around.

While driving with Allen in eastern Kansas, I stumbled across an issue of the *Daily Reporter*, a local newspaper published in Independence. Every Sunday the paper's editors turn over their lead editorial space to a Christian group called the Independence Ministerial Alliance.

"We are in a spiritual competition, not only for our spiritual lives, but others as well," wrote Pastor John Penrose of the Evangelical Friends Church, "and we are definitely out to win at all costs — even to martyrdom."

"What's up with this?" I said. "You can't tell me this isn't frightening."

After reading it through, Allen said, "I understand you being uncomfortable with that. Being scared even. Because it sounds like what he's saying is that everyone should *have* to be a Christian. That's not what he's saying. But an article like that, the language is so counterproductive. If he's trying to bring people to faith, that kind of article is the wrong way. It's so confrontational."

"A lot of metros think there is a growing intolerance," I said. "People in your world who think urban progressives aren't just different, they're bad or evil."

"In the mainstream Christian community — not just liberal churches, but churches like mine, really conservative churches — people would speak up with a lot of passion if that type of thing started to take hold. These big megachurches where everyone is going, they welcome everyone."

Seen in a historical context, the militancy of the homelander movement's language seems a little less ominous. In the 1960s and 1970s, anti–Vietnam War protesters regularly took over government buildings. Progressives armed with rifles and pistols occupied college campuses. They clashed with National Guard soldiers, blew up police stations, and robbed banks. African Americans angry about racial injustice set fire to whole neighborhoods.

Given that rural conservatives are just as fervent in their beliefs (one of which is the right to bear arms), it's remarkable that we've seen so little right-wing violence. You can count the number of Eric Rudolphs and Timothy McVeighs on one hand. Homelanders believe zealously in the moral rightness of their cause, but the vast majority also believe in the power of the ballot box.

Some progressives will dispute this. The Southern Poverty Law Center has identified sixty "terrorist plots" over the last decade allegedly organized by extreme right-wing activists, though they concede that most involved young skinheads or people with mental illness. A study by the National Abortion Federation found that between 2000 and 2005 there were a total of thirteen arson cases (and one attempted bombing) at clinics that provide abortions nationwide. There are also thousands of "hate crimes" reported every year, many motivated by racial or religious intolerance.

These facts not withstanding, it's clear that no national militant movement has arisen on the right in the mold of 1960s leftist groups, such as the Weathermen or the Black Panthers. Social conservatives haven't been occupying college administration buildings, blowing up statues, or planning confrontations with police. Their victories have come through aggressive grassroots organizing, lobbying, and peaceful political activism.

Still, words can be dangerous, and even many Republicans have begun to worry aloud that things have gone too far. "To assert that I am on God's side and you are not, that I know God's will and you do not, and that I will use the power of government to advance my understanding of God's kingdom is certain to produce hostility," wrote former Missouri senator John Danforth, an Episcopalian minister, in an essay published in the *New York Times*.

In March 2006 recently retired Supreme Court justice Sandra Day O'Connor, a Republican, gave a speech quoted by NPR's Nina Totenberg warning that politically motivated attacks "on the judiciary by some Republican leaders pose a direct threat to our constitutional freedoms." Connor's language was blunt and explicit: "It takes a lot of degeneration before a country falls into dictatorship, but we should avoid these ends by avoiding these beginnings."

Allen finds this sort of thing exasperating. He disapproves of the more poisonous rhetoric coming from hard-core conservatives — he describes Pat Robertson as "an idiot" and says a lot of Sean Hannity's opinions are "childish" — but he thinks all the hand-wringing about dictatorship and the loss of constitutional freedom is overblown. The way he sees it, America is in a struggle overseas against a dangerous enemy, an ideological conflict he likens to the Cold War. We're also deeply divided at home over what kind of society we should have. It's natural for tempers to flare, for angry words to be spoken on both sides. Allen believes that most of the complaints are politically motivated: "They just want to tear down the president, which in a time of war just isn't right," he says. "I think [Illinois senator] Dick

Durbin's comments about America running concentration camps were treasonous. If Durbin was right and there were concentration camps being run in Cuba, we would have a moral duty to put another government in place. Bush would have to go. But there aren't concentration camps down there."

"But what happened to all those conservatives who used to fret about black helicopters and big government sneaking around spying on us? You guys used to be the ones worried about this stuff. Now it's actually happening, and there's not a peep of protest."

"That's not true. Some Christians are pretty uncomfortable with the Patriot Act. A lot of Republicans think Bush is too big government. But I guess we trust him to do the right thing. I think his motives are pretty sound."

Like a lot of homelanders, Allen is convinced that Bush is a small-D democrat to his core. He accepts the argument that America is spreading freedom abroad and defending it here at home the best way we can. Conservatives point to the speeches Bush made after 9/11 encouraging tolerance. Will the administration make mistakes? Sure. But Allen points to Franklin Roosevelt's Japanese internment camps and John Kennedy's Bay of Pigs invasion as proof of a double standard.

"But why not take a stand against the torture at Abu Ghraib or the erosion of civil liberties under the Patriot Act? Your side has been silent on that stuff."

"I think it's horrible that people were mistreated, and I'm glad Abu Ghraib was brought to light," Allen says. "I support humane treatment of prisoners. I agree that we don't want to sink down to the level where the militant Muslims are. But I think in most cases these are just soldiers who got carried away."

"Really? There was no responsibility higher up?"

"I don't believe there was a program that went all the way to the president. And I guess I do support hardball tactics to get information out of people."

We had entered one of those fugue zones: Allen's sources of information were giving him one picture of the world and mine were giving me another. The newspapers and magazines that I read (the *Times*, the *New Yorker*, *Harpers*, and so forth) had documented conclusively a pattern of viciously brutal behavior, which had metastasized through the United States's shadowy penal system. It seemed clear that the Bush administration had approved the program and then gone to extraordinary lengths to prevent oversight by Congress or the judiciary.

But in Allen's world those media sources are largely discredited. "The *Newsweek* article [about the deliberate defamation of the Koran as a form of prisoner abuse] is an example of their overreaction," he said. "The Koran story was wrong; they didn't have the goods." Meanwhile, his own media sources regularly interpret Bush's policies as forward-leaning toughness. "I think we're being naive if we think we can prosecute this war without doing some of those things."

Not everybody in Perryton is comfortable with the homelander agenda. The *Herald*'s lead reporter is a spare, laconic guy named Gene Riley. He sits in the front office, serenely filling another ashtray. (Another of the small cultural divides that separate urban and rural America is the amount of tobacco use that still goes on beyond the suburban ring. People still light up at the dinner table. Square cigarette packs — or round chew tins — bulge in people's pockets.)

Riley has the slightly battered look common to newsroom veterans twenty years ago, when reporters never worried how they might look on television. "I like guns and I like shooting things," he says with an apologetic grin, after offering me a chair. "And I really dislike the welfare system, because I'm paying the bill."

But it turns out he's one of those old-fashioned conservative Democrats who used to be a regular fixture in small-town America. "I wouldn't let them stamp REPUBLICAN on my card," he says proudly. "I'm a Democrat and everybody knows it. Republicans say they're for the little guy, but basically they're for the big bosses. They always have been and always will be."

Riley's not an urban transplant. He's the real thing, born right here in Ochiltree County. He lives in the same house he grew up in. He's watched the growing rift between America's urban and rural tribes ("There's a serious divide between the two cultures," he agrees) and witnessed the steady erosion of the local Democratic Party. "The Democrats in this area all became Republicans. I'm not sure I can explain why that changed. When I was a kid, everybody running for office here was a Democrat. But the man who used to be head of the party moved away several years ago, and that just leaves me."

He's exaggerating, but not by much. Just 8 percent of the county's voters cast their ballots for John Kerry. That works out to roughly 250 people. Riley concedes that his views — he's pro-choice and thinks Republicans have sold out to big corporations — are unpopular in these parts. "I still swim upstream," he says with a weary shrug. "It's a slow-moving stream around here, but it's very wide and very deep. This is basically a one-party county."

"How does that work?" I ask. "I mean, how do people debate and talk about things that matter?"

Riley shrugs and says, "Republicans talk about how great democracy is, but everything they do makes me think they want *all* the politicians and judges to be Republicans. That's pretty dangerous, I think. That's what Saddam Hussein had, a one-party system. I tell folks, be careful what you wish for, you might just get it."

But the truth is that Riley's center-to-slightly-left views haven't made him a pariah. They earn him a lot of ribbing, but he still goes hunting with his childhood buddies. He's president of the local Kiwanis. When I ask him about the discomforts of being a political outsider, he laughs and says, "My boss, who is a hard-right-wing Republican, says he puts up with me because I'm an endangered species."

# 5

# Islands of Blue

The Republican Party has won the culture war in rural America. In the short term, this victory has paid enormous political dividends. But the GOP's embrace of homelander values has cost the party heavily in metro America, where the conservative movement's support is collapsing. "The South, small-town rural America, the exurbs are getting more and more Republican," Charlie Cook, editor of the *Cook Political Report*, told CBS News after the 2004 election. "[But] cities remain extremely Democratic, and closer-in suburbs are trending more and more Democratic."

John Kerry gets no respect as a national political leader, but he managed to win two-thirds of the nation's most populous urban and suburban counties. He didn't just win; he dominated by an average margin of 27 percent. In the city of Chicago, his margin over Bush was roughly eight hundred thousand votes. That's more people than live in the entire state of South Dakota. In Manhattan, where Republicans held their national convention, 82 percent of the voters swung Democratic.

Increasingly, our blue cities stand out on America's red landscape as an archipelago of Democratic progressivism. To the dismay of conservatives, this metro culture has extended its reach deep into the South and Midwest. Kerry won two of North Carolina's three most populous counties. He won five of the six most densely settled counties in Ohio. He won the two most urban counties in Tennessee and gobbled up two-thirds of the vote in Denver.

Social conservatives have worked hard to downplay their estrangement from metro America. Former senator Zell Miller, a homelander

Democrat from Georgia who endorsed Bush in 2004 and spoke at the Republican national convention in New York City, claimed famously that Democrats were "a national party no more." Miller cited his own disenchantment as evidence that Democratic appeal had withered to a few coastal provinces: "[Our party] is no longer a link to most Americans."

The media often echo this assertion with remarkable credulity, trotting out those red state–blue state maps to show that Middle America has turned its back on the Democratic Party. But the city of Atlanta in Miller's home state is a bastion of liberalism. El Paso, Texas, went solidly Democratic. Even Dallas, a city you would expect to be pretty happy with the Bush revolution, split its ticket evenly. "The real electoral division isn't between the coasts and the heart-land," wrote Sean Wilentz, a professor of history at Princeton University, in an essay published in the *Los Angeles Times*. "It's between cities all over the United States and the rest of the country."

> Alabama is supposed to be the buckle of the pro-GOP Bible Belt. But don't say that too loudly in Montgomery County, eponymous home to the state capital, which came in with a Kerry majority, as did Dallas County, home to the city of Selma, which voted for Kerry by a 60 to 40 percent margin. From Richmond, Va., to Jackson, Miss., from Salt Lake City, Utah, to Columbia, S.C., the Democratic ticket either won outright or ran well ahead of statewide totals.

Two of the ten most liberal cities in America, according to a 2005 study by the Bay Area Center for Voting Research, are found in the Midwest — Gary, Indiana, and Flint, Michigan. Eight of the top-fifty most Democratic cities are located in the South, places like Birmingham, Memphis, Jackson, and Richmond. Hardly the sort of thing you'd expect to find in Jesus Land.

Inner cities aren't the only areas that are swinging blue. A generation ago the suburbs around Chicago, New York City, and Washington, D.C., were solid Republican strongholds, part of the GOP's country-club fiefdom. Most are now rapidly trending Democratic. "If someone had said thirty years ago that the suburbs that ring Philadelphia wouldn't be codlock Republican, people would have told you that you were brain dead," says GOP strategist Bill Greener.

In his book *On Paradise Drive, New York Times* columnist David Brooks cited a 1998 study showing that America's inner suburbs had shifted to the Left in each of the previous five elections, a trend that shows no sign of abating.

> In 2000 the Democrats went over the top. A Democratic presidential candidate carried the area around the Main Line, outside of Philadelphia, for the first time in history. And the first Democrat ever won the area around the New Trier High School, north of Chicago. Once Republican strongholds, the inner-ring suburbs have become Democratic zones.

In 2004 the blue suburbs swung Pennsylvania to John Kerry. In the days after the election, Republican senator Rick Santorum chastised GOP leaders in Delaware County — the Philly suburbs — for failing to turn out a solid Bush vote. Local GOP chairman Charles Sexton fired back, demanding an apology from Santorum: "It doesn't take a rocket scientist to know what happened here," Sexton told the *Delaware County Daily Times*. "The parts of the county that have strong minority representation and the parts of the county with strong union representation turned out overwhelmingly for Kerry. Until the Republican Party wakes up at the national level and starts reaching out to labor, we are going to see these results continue."

The GOP's alienation from metro America extends well beyond unions and minorities. On a full range of issues — from moral values to tax policy — the burbs are becoming progressive: "In political terms and in lifestyle, the suburbs have changed dramatically in the past two decades," conceded conservative columnist Fred Barnes, writing in the *Weekly Standard*. "Cities have spilled into the suburbs, which are now densely populated and filled with singles, minorities, and people with an urban temperament."

The metro melting pot is overflowing. All those funky, modernist ideas about family and race and economics are oozing out into the cul-de-sacs and planned developments of Middle America. "I live in the socialist republic of Arlington, Virginia," Greener jokes. "In a state that went 55–45 percent for George Bush, Arlington's vote was upside down, 68–31 percent for John Kerry."

Like jilted suitors, some conservative pundits have begun to mutter that metro America — even those traitorous suburbs — might not be worth fighting over. If you want to find the real America, you have to look elsewhere, beyond the espresso-sipping yuppie metro enclaves of the urban-suburban core. "Sometimes people move to the exurbs to get away from the upscale snobs moving into the inner-ring neighborhoods," Brooks sniffs.

This sort of contempt is fine for the pundit class, but Republican politicians are justifiably nervous. Already, this metro alienation has swung key races to the Democrats. In Colorado's 2004 Senate race, Ken Salazar scored a powerful surge in urban Denver that accounted for his entire 100,000-vote margin over Republican beer magnate Pete Coors. In that year's gubernatorial scrum in Washington state, metro counties around Seattle prevailed over rural voters in eastern counties by a mere 261 ballots. In 2005 those left-leaning suburbs in northern Virginia muscled aside homelanders in southern parts of the state to elect Democratic governor Tim Kaine.

The metro hostility toward the Republican Party is deepening. In 2005 an African American woman ran for mayor in Albany, New York, on the Green Party ticket, outpolling the GOP's candidate five-fold. Normally that would be a bit of political trivia, but in the same election cycle Republican incumbents were swept aside in suburban Glens Falls and Saratoga Springs, as well as on Long Island, all traditional GOP strongholds.

Half a continent away, metro voters in St. Paul, Minnesota, were cheerfully ousting a popular first-term Democratic mayor. Randy Kelly wasn't guilty of corruption. There wasn't a sex scandal. His unpardonable sin was endorsing George Bush in the 2004 elections.

"Liberals, progressives, and Democrats do not live in a country that stretches from the Atlantic to the Pacific, from Canada to Mexico," wrote the editors of the Seattle alternative weekly *The Stranger*. "We live on a chain of islands. We are citizens of the Urban Archipelago, the United Cities of America."

> We live on islands of sanity, liberalism, and compassion — New York City, Chicago, Philadelphia, Seattle, St. Louis, Minneapolis, San Francisco, and on and on. And we live on islands in red states too — a fact obscured by that state-by-state map. Denver and Boulder are our islands in Colorado; Austin is our island in Texas; Las Vegas is our island in Nevada; Miami and Fort Lauderdale are our islands in Florida.
>
> Citizens of the Urban Archipelago reject heartland "values" like xenophobia, sexism, racism, and homophobia, as well as the more intolerant strains of Christianity that have taken root in this country. And we are the real Americans. They — rural, red-state voters, the denizens of the exurbs — are not real Americans. They are rubes, fools, and hate-mongers. Red Virginia prohibits any contract between same-sex couples. Compassionate? Texas allows the death penalty to be applied to teenaged criminals and has historically executed the mentally retarded.

In every region of the country, Republican politicians who compete in highly urbanized battlegrounds face a shaky future. Most are dancing to the Left, following their constituents further and further away from the GOP's national leadership. Much to the disgust of homelander Republicans, New York City mayor Michael Bloomberg and California governor Arnold Schwarzenegger are now all but indistinguishable from liberal Democrats on most of the social and economic issues that divide America.

Even Republican moderates look increasingly vulnerable on metro turf. Two powerful Republican governors, George Pataki of New York and Mitt Romney of Massachusetts, decided not to seek reelection in 2006 in large part because their urban and suburban poll numbers were crashing. In four other races where city voters will play a decisive role, Republican incumbents are struggling. Senator Rick Santorum of Pennsylvania, Senator Mike DeWine of Ohio, Senator Lincoln Chaffee of Rhode Island, and Governor Schwarzenegger are fighting to keep their noses above the rising blue tide.

Santorum's future is perhaps the most problematic because he made the mistake of broadcasting his homelander values openly. Once seen as a presidential contender, he published a book in 2005 called *It Takes a Family*. In it he questioned the role of women in the workplace and savaged the full range of metro institutions — "big news media, big entertainment, big universities and public schools, some big businesses and some big national labor unions, and of course, the biggest Big of all, the federal government."

The book reads confidently like a traditionalist manifesto, a no-holds-barred embrace of public Christianity and government-sanctioned morality. The very title is meant as a rebuke of Hillary Clinton, that bugbear of homelander culture, whose political book *It Takes a Village* was a national best seller. But Santorum clearly overestimated his message's appeal. His poll numbers plummeted in Pennsylvania's cities and inner suburbs. In 2006 he found himself in the awkward position of supporting spending increases for liberal social programs, a bid to mollify furious voters.

Despite his eleventh-hour scamper to the Left, Santorum may emerge as the next high-profile casualty in America's urban-rural culture war.

The loathing that mainstream metro culture feels for Republican policies and values has been clouded by a guileless media, which often equates the GOP's political wins with a wholesale shift in American values. "Ronald Reagan really moved us off to the Right," declared Leslie Stahl of *60 Minutes*, in an interview with the satirist Stephen Colbert in October 2005. "The center of the country has definitely shifted to the Right, and there we sit."

This claim is made fairly often, usually in the same matter-of-fact tone. Pundits speak casually of pendulum swings and backlashes, as if societies were as changeable as the weather, but really the notion is fairly radical. Hundreds of millions of people don't just shift direction, not without some major impetus.

In the 1930s and 1940s, Franklin Roosevelt used the New Deal and the Second World War to transform America into a fundamentally progressive nation. He built institutions and popularized ideas about the role of the federal government that have led to steady advances in civil rights, environmental protection, the reduction of poverty, and women's equality.

This basic model for American society proved remarkably durable, surviving the Cold War, national scandals, the assassination of a Democratic president, the ouster of a Republican president, the dismantling of Jim Crow, and a thousand other traumas. This cultural evolution also mirrored trends in other urbanized societies in Europe and Asia that were embracing more liberal values.

But observers like Stahl accept the notion that sometime after Reagan's election the United States suddenly reversed course. We became more conservative, more Christian, and more passionate about family values. Usually there's no reason given for why this supposedly happened. It's also difficult to find evidence to support the claim, which frames so much American journalism. In fact, there's an enormous amount of proof that nothing of the kind has occurred.

Consider as Exhibit A the Republican Party's track record in presidential races. In 1980, Ronald Reagan beat incumbent Jimmy Carter by 9 percentage points. Four years later, Reagan won reelection by a landslide. His understudy, the first George Bush, beat Michael Dukakis in 1988 by 8 points. By any measure, this three-election cycle represented a remarkable run of success.

But in the sixteen years since, support for Republican candidates has dwindled markedly. In 1992 the first President Bush lost badly to Bill Clinton, garnering only 37 percent of the popular vote. Four years later, in the wake of the so-called Republican Revolution, Clinton beat former Senate majority leader Bob Dole of Kansas by 9 percentage points. In 2000 the second George Bush campaigned as a centrist and a moderate, carefully downplaying his social conservatism. Rural conservatives supported him in droves and he still lost the popular vote to Al Gore, a clumsy campaigner who had penned a liberal treatise on environmentalism.

In 2004, Bush won reelection by just 3 percentage points, despite being an incumbent president in wartime who was blessed with a reasonably strong economy, a significant fund-raising advantage, and the astute guidance of Karl Rove. Republicans branded Kerry as an East Coast liberal and a flip-flopper, but the Democrat still won 48 percent of the popular vote. Nationwide that year, Republican congressional candidates received far fewer votes than did Democrats. In all, hardly a conservative mandate.

Indeed, surveys regularly show that broad aspects of the homelander agenda simply haven't caught on in urban America, where 80 percent of Americans live. Most metros aren't interested in more tax cuts. We're more worried about soaring budget deficits, health care, and education.

Pundits were shocked in 2005 when Bush's campaign to reform and privatize Social Security was rejected flatly, but a Harris Interactive poll released by the *Wall Street Journal* in October of that year found that three-quarters of the respondents actually favored universal health care. More than 90 percent backed full funding for Medicare and Medicaid programs to help the elderly and the poor.

The same survey found that 87 percent of adults wanted comprehensive sex education in their children's public high schools. Despite decades of bitter rhetoric, more than 60 percent of Americans still favor legal abortion. In 2006, when a Gallup poll asked Americans about Judge Samuel Alito's appointment to the Supreme Court, two-thirds of the respondents said he should be rejected by the Senate if he planned to overturn *Roe v. Wade*. One-third of Republicans shared that view.

The furor over same-sex marriage has energized social conservatives and shaped a general impression that Americans are increasingly hostile toward gays and lesbians, but in metro America, acceptance of homosexuality has taken root with remarkable speed. Many of my urban friends — including those who are churchgoing Christians — are far more creeped-out by conservative evangelicals than they are by the same-sex couples who are dropping kids off at day care.

Pollsters with the Pew Research Center found that opposition to same-sex marriage dropped by an astonishing 14 percent over the last decade, a period when conservative family values were supposedly on the rise. In 1996, two-thirds of Americans disapproved the idea; at present, the disapproval rate is just over 50 percent. The portion of respondents who — like my brother — "strongly oppose" gay weddings dropped from 42 percent to just 28 percent.

Young people are even more progressive, suggesting that the leftward trend is likely to continue. A Zogby International poll conducted in 2001 found that 85 percent of American high school seniors believed that "gays and lesbians should be accepted by society."

We've been led to believe that a new conservative religious awakening has swept the country, on a par with the great Christian revivals of the nineteenth century. Traditionalist pundits love to contrast our supposed fervor with the godless heathens of Western Europe. But surveys of religious activity in the United States tell a very different story.

The percentage of Americans who describe themselves as Protestant has plummeted below 50 percent for the first time in our nation's history. This is not just because there are more Roman Catholic immigrants pouring across the border from Latin America. As recently as 1990, according to a poll taken by the highly respected American Religious Identification Survey, 86 percent of respondents identified themselves as Christian. By 2001, the number had dropped to 77 percent — an astonishing decline in so short a period.

"The number of people who never go to church is rising quite dramatically," conceded conservative columnist David Brooks, in a 2006 interview with PBS's Charlie Rose.

"Now what is that a reflection of?" Rose asked.

"You go to some neighborhoods and the church is where people look to moral renewal and character building," Brooks said. "It's an essential institution. You go to other neighborhoods and the university is where people look. In some areas the university has displaced the church and is a growing part of society."

"There does not seem to be a revival taking place in America," concluded evangelical Christian pollster George Barna, in a report published on his Web site. "Whether that is measured by church attendance, born again status, or theological purity, the statistics simply do not reflect a surge of any noticeable proportions."

For tens of millions of Americans, Christianity is no longer the central moral influence in their lives. Even among metro churchgoers, the sort of fundamentalism favored by homelanders has gained almost no foothold. James Dobson and Pat Robertson dominate the headlines, but a Gallup survey in 2005 found that 72 percent of Americans believe "there are many true religions," while only 20 percent endorse the evangelical doctrine that "there is one and only one true religion." Only about one-third of Americans now believe that the Bible should be read as the literal word of God, another basic tenet of fundamentalism. This number, too, has declined sharply — down from 45 percent in 1990.

As recently as the 1990s, this urban sensibility defined our political culture. Activists like Dobson and Bill Bennett weren't powerless, but they were clearly outside the mainstream. Democrats had controlled Congress with dominant majorities for forty years. The first President Bush distanced himself deliberately from social conservatives and was infuriated by Pat Buchanan's culture war speech at the 1992 Republican National Convention. The national platform of both parties was broadly progressive and urban-centric, with poverty, race, and education at the top of the agenda. Liberalism was mainstream enough that many rural Democrats felt perfectly comfortable embracing their party's national platform.

Bill Clinton's election in 1992 seemed to confirm a permanent metro hegemony. Clinton won the White House thanks in part to Ross Perot's success in dividing the homelander vote, but the Democratic ticket also dominated inside the urban beltway. Metro voters saw in Clinton a reflection of their own thirty-something sensibility: He was smart, ironic, morally flexible, and culturally engaged. Despite his roots in southern white culture, pundits described Clinton as the "first black president" because of his popularity among African Americans. He was also the first boomer president. Hillary — his two-for-the-price-of-one First Lady — was the anti–Barbara Bush: "I've done the best I can to lead my life," she said. "I suppose I could have stayed home and baked cookies and had teas."

The statement outraged conservatives, creating a mini-scandal, but to millions of urbanites it sounded like real life, the America most of us experience. The Clintons were young, they were modern, and their values had incubated in the relativism of the 1960s. They seemed willing to take on some of the most revered institutions in America.

They supported gay and lesbian rights. With the Cold War over, they slashed defense spending in favor of domestic programs. They campaigned aggressively for the Brady gun-control bill, appointed a sort of rainbow coalition cabinet, slapped urban liberals onto the Supreme Court, and even dared to push for a national health-care system.

Enough ink has been spilled about Bill Clinton's travails. He lost a lot of battles. He allowed the Democratic Party's infrastructure to decay to a disastrous degree. In rural America he was an unmitigated disaster. But it's worth noting that even in the darkest hours of the impeachment crisis, when newspapers were calling for his resignation and Vice President Al Gore was edging toward the door, Clinton's popularity among metros never faltered. Six out of ten Americans thought he was doing a great job. After a decade of smears and personal attacks, he's still regularly named in polls as one of the greatest presidents of all time.

Given the weight of evidence to the contrary, why have so many metro pundits, journalists, and Democratic strategists accepted the notion that America has shifted to the right? Part of the answer lies in brilliant marketing. Barry Goldwater first claimed in the 1960s that America is a deeply conservative nation, held hostage by a cabal of urban elites. Goldwater lost to Lyndon Johnson in one of the biggest electoral drubbings in presidential history, but his assertion still echoes confidently in the right-wing media.

After the Republican Revolution in 1994, Republicans were able to justify their claim on the national zeitgeist, pointing proudly to the fact that they — and not the Democrats — were winning elections. George Bush, a man many urban Americans loathe to distraction, was reelected by a thin but undeniable majority of voters. Despite drifting further and further to the right, the GOP expanded its control over Congress and was able to confirm two ideological conservatives to the Supreme Court, where traditionalists now hold enormous sway.

Surely in the world's model democracy such a dramatic political shift must reflect a similar swing in the will of the people. If traditionalists like George Bush, Dick Cheney, Dennis Hastert, Bill Frist, Tom DeLay, and John Roberts have emerged as the most powerful men in America, their success must reflect a deeper truth about our society's values. But as the next two chapters will reveal, the abrupt rise of homelander politics doesn't reflect a radical change in national sentiment. It is instead the product of a massive imbalance in our political system, one that favors the social and political values of rural communities, while marginalizing the metro communities, where most Americans spend their lives.

# 6

# Red President

**M**ost people know that Al Gore won the popular vote in 2000 and still lost the election under the electoral college system, but few Americans understand that this outcome reflected a deliberate bias hard-wired into our political system.

In every election the electoral college redistributes power to so-called "lesser" states, such as Alaska, South Dakota, and Wyoming, which have small and disproportionately rural populations that tend to be whiter, more conservative, and more Christian than the nation as a whole. Meanwhile, the system sharply penalizes big urban states that tend to be progressive, diverse, and more secular in their leanings, like California, Illinois, and New York.

One often hears the phrase "One man, one vote," but in America it doesn't work that way. It never did. A significant amount of political power was shuffled around by the founding fathers, not to protect individual rights but to insure the continued independence of states. This arrangement is the legacy of an obscure and rather cynical debate held in summer 1787 at the Constitutional Convention in Philadelphia.

Delegates from sparsely settled states such as Delaware and New Jersey fought all summer long to preserve their autonomy and influence. "I suspect it to be of importance to the small states that their deputies should keep a strict watch on the movements and propositions from the larger states," cautioned Delaware's George Read. He and his allies fretted that powerhouse states like Massachusetts and Virginia "will probably combine to swallow up the smaller ones by addition, division or impoverishment."

Benjamin Franklin, George Washington, and James Madison thought this was nonsense. They were disgusted by the "demagoguery" of the small states, but in the end they capitulated. The deal struck by the framers made no provision for direct popular elections of the president. Instead, the new Constitution stipulated that each state would choose a certain number of presidential electors "equal to the whole number of Senators and Representatives to which the State may be entitled in the Congress."

In practical terms, this means that each state will receive a minimum of three electoral college votes. The trouble is that quite a few of our states have such tiny populations that they don't merit three votes. Based strictly on population, four states — North Dakota, Alaska, Vermont, and Wyoming — don't even merit one electoral college vote.

The impact of this deliberately imbalanced system wasn't obvious at first. At the time of the first U.S. Census, in 1790, there were only sixteen states, so the number of bonus electors gifted to smaller states was negligible. What's more, the disparity in population between large and small states was fairly modest. Virginia was just twelve times the size of tiny Delaware. (Currently, California is more than seventy times more populus than our smallest states — a ratio that's expected to grow to at least 90 to 1 by midcentury.) It's also significant that the voting population in that era was almost entirely homogonous, with political power restricted to white men. As a consequence, the political and cultural values of "greater" and "lesser" states were nearly identical.

Still, the more thoughtful framers of the Constitution worried that significant cultural and political gaps might develop as new states of varying size joined the Union. An influential delegate from Massachusetts named Elbridge Gerry warned that sharing power with these latecomers would eventually mean "putting ourselves into their hands." (Gerry is remembered these days primarily because he popularized the practice of gerrymandering political districts.) He suggested limiting the number of states so that any newcomers "should never be able to outnumber the Atlantic states."

Other delegates defeated the proposal, arguing (wrongly, as it happened) that "there was no probability that the number of future States would exceed that of the existing states." In the *Federalist Papers,* Alexander Hamilton and James Madison tried to soothe fears, predicting that any new states would "advance in population with peculiar rapidity," thus minimizing any demographic or cultural imbalances.

Through America's first century as a nation, this seemed to be the case. Former territories such as California, Florida, Ohio, and Texas matured quickly, developing into full-fledged mini-nations similar to the original colonies. They built diverse economies and thriving cities. But after the Civil War things changed. The nation's geographic expansion accelerated. We added fourteen new states at the heady rate of one every six years. The westward push doubled the nation's landmass, and most of the states incorporated between 1867 and 1950 were essentially empty.

With few exceptions, they remain thinly populated today, with settlement patterns that resemble the frontier of the eighteenth or early nineteenth century far more than the twenty-first-century urban reality that most Americans experience. Taken together, the states created after the Civil War still constitute only about 11 percent of the nation's population. In many cases their small towns and villages actually peaked half a century ago and are slowly dying away.

Yet because of the rural tilt built into the electoral college, these new states enjoy nearly 14 percent of the clout in presidential elections. That may not seem like a significant boost, but in effect the per capita clout of each homelander casting a presidential ballot in those states is automatically increased by about one-fifth.

It gets worse. In order to cede rural states more power, influence has to be drained away from somewhere else. That somewhere else happens to be the nine big metro states where most Americans live. Those states (five reliably Democratic, two battlegrounds, and two reliably

Republican) are home to nearly 55 percent of the population, but because of the system's artificial redistribution of power, they receive only about 44 percent of the voting clout in presidential elections.

Consider the example of New York. With nineteen million people, it's one of our most highly urbanized and progressive states. Social conservatives are a dying breed in statewide politics, and even the party's moderate Republican establishment is struggling. New Yorkers wield thirty-one electoral college votes, which sounds like a big chunk. But it takes the combined population of fifteen rural states just to equal New York's metro masses — and those fortunate homelanders receive a total of fifty-nine electoral college votes.

The same number of rural Americans are able to wield nearly twice the clout of their urban neighbors.

This homelander bias didn't matter so much when rural Americans were splitting their ballots, but as we've seen, small towns now vote by wide margins for Republican candidates. As a consequence, the system's tilt can skew a presidential election dramatically, electing a candidate that America's urban majority rejects, as in 2000.

Even when the results aren't quite as dramatic, the electoral college offers the GOP an enormous strategic advantage — what amounts to a running head start. Put bluntly, conservative candidates are guaranteed to win most of the rural states that receive a supersized allocation of electoral college votes. Democrats, meanwhile, receive most of their political support in the urban states that are most heavily penalized.

This imbalance was starkly visible in 2004. George Bush was able to reel in easy victories in twelve of those sparsely populated states that entered the union after the Civil War. (The two most highly urbanized states, Washington and Oregon, swung for John Kerry.) Taken together, the twenty-three million homelanders in this one rural-conservative cluster make up about 8 percent of the American population, but because of the system's bias they receive 10.9 percent of the total electoral votes. They were able to ante up a whopping fifty-nine electoral college votes, fully a quarter of Bush's entire tally.

Now consider John Kerry's easy win in California, a metro stronghold. All by itself that state boasts roughly thirty-six million citizens, about 13 percent of the American population. But because of the urban penalty, Californians receive only 10.2 percent of the total electoral college votes. The disparity is dramatic. With roughly twelve million more citizens, the Golden State contributed four fewer electoral college votes than their rural neighbors.

If only one state were affected, it wouldn't matter. But two-thirds of Kerry's wins came in the big urbanized states — California, Illinois, Michigan, New Jersey, New York, and Pennsylvania — that suffer the biggest systemic cuts in power. Before they raise their first campaign dollar or snag their first endorsement, Democratic candidates know that their political base will be sharply discounted. The urban African Americans and Hispanics, the Jewish community, the gays and lesbians, the professionals, the academics, the union members, all the tens of millions of metros who trend reliably progressive, will be stripped of 10–20 percent of their voting power.

In tight contests — and these days, most of America's national elections are tight — this kind of jury-rigging can make all the difference in the world.

To get an idea for how profoundly this homelander tilt has shaped America's political landscape, consider for a moment how our country would look if the founding fathers had seen things differently. What if they had decided that women deserved extra voting power, or African Americans, or Native Americans? Or what if they simply decided that every citizen, regardless of their race, their geography, or their class, deserved equal representation?

In a country with proportional voting, urban Americans would have the same sort of influence that one sees in France, England, or Canada. Metros would dominate elections for the simple reason that they represent the majority of citizens. It's likely that homelanders would still control many rural state governments, but their impact on the national dialogue would be no bigger (and no smaller) than warranted by their population.

This change would force Republicans to build urban constituencies, stumping in moderately conservative strongholds such as New York's Long Island and California's Orange County. The GOP would have to develop new campaign messages aimed at a wider cross section of minority and ethnic voters, a shift that would immediately empower the party's moderate Rockefeller wing. Candidates such as Rudy Giuliani, George Pataki, Colin Powell, and John McCain, all of whom have proven appeal with urban voters, would quickly supplant homelander icons like George Bush, Bill Frist, and Dennis Hastert.

Meanwhile, Democratic candidates like John Kerry would be free for the first time to pursue their natural constituency, wooing voters who are urban, multiethnic, and progressive. The party's platform would focus deliberately on the issues that metro constituents really care about: not the right to own guns or school prayer or banning same-sex marriage or even lowering taxes, but other civic values such as health care, the environment, public safety, education, and cutting the deficit.

A level playing field would also offer Democrats significant tactical advantages that would help to offset the Republican Party's traditional fund-raising superiority. Metro candidates would shuttle from city to city, focusing media dollars, personnel, and message on big pockets of urban and inner suburban voters. They wouldn't even have to do that much traveling. More than half of the American population now resides in just 147 big metro counties — many of which are clumped in vast megacities with more than five million people.

It's also safe to say that ditching the electoral college would end one of the more bizarre rituals in American political life: our rurally skewed primaries. Currently, presidential candidates spend years and tens of millions of dollars barnstorming through Iowa and New Hampshire. These states have come to serve as the gatekeepers in our national elections. They are a testing ground for politicians forced to compete in a homelander-biased political system.

"Iowa political leaders often say Iowans have the job of reducing the field of presidential candidates for the rest of the nation," boasted David Yepsen, political columnist for the *Des Moines Register*. "The people of Iowa pick corn, the people of New Hampshire pick presidents," quipped New Hampshire Governor John Sununu in 1988.

Politicians in these states insist that their primacy is a matter of tradition (the classic homelander argument), but the truth is that Iowa and New Hampshire no longer mirror mainstream America. The gatekeepers don't look like the people living behind the gate. According to the U.S. Census, their residents are more than 90 percent white — compared with 75 percent nationwide. Hispanics have emerged as our largest minority group, comprising one in eight Americans, but Iowa and New Hampshire have Hispanic populations so small (2–3 percent) as to be politically invisible.

On the other hand, both states boast homelander communities dramatically larger than the norm — 40 percent of the population in New Hampshire and 32 percent in Iowa, compared with just 21 percent nationwide. It's startling to realize that the rest of the country's population hasn't been that white or that rural since the 1930s.

Even without the electoral college's influence, holding a make-or-break primary in these two states might make sense for the Republican Party. Rural values have emerged as the cornerstone of the GOP's identity, and strong homelander appeal is required for national victory. But for Democrats, whose core voters are multi-ethnic and urban, relying on rural primaries to cull their field of candidates is simply bizarre. Frankly, it's hard to justify even within the context of our homelander-biased political system. It would be like the GOP holding make-or-break contests in New Jersey or and California.

In a system that relied on the principle of one-man, one-vote, Democrats would test their ideas and their campaigns in cities and inner suburbs, where the vast majority of their voters reside. (In the 2004 general election, John Kerry won only about a million votes in New Hampshire and Iowa combined, far fewer ballots than he received in just five metro counties around Philadelphia.) But as things stand, Democrats are forced to play on the other guy's turf and talk about the other guy's issues.

Once they've weathered the primaries, politicians like Kerry and Al Gore wind up slogging around on goose hunts, mumbling platitudes about NASCAR and family farms, desperately trying to scrape up enough homelander support to pick off a predominantly rural state like Arizona, Arkansas, New Hampshire, or Virginia.

Rural folks smell that kind of insincerity a mile away. Republican Bill Greener tells the story of joining a panel discussion with a Democratic strategist, who announced that his party needed to win back the "Wal-Mart vote." "God, do you know how patronizing that sounds?" Greener says. "Democrats sound like Republicans did ten years ago when we discussed going after votes from people of color. It's not that we like you, not that we have to listen to you. We just need a few more votes."

Urban voters, meanwhile, are outraged when their candidates do gutless, pandering things like proposing a constitutional ban on flag burning (Hillary Clinton) or refusing to talk openly about the environment (Al Gore). When Howard Dean suddenly starts quoting Scripture, metros shake their heads and think sincerely about voting for Ralph Nader.

But the hard truth is that Democrats don't have a choice. They know from painful experience that the system is stacked — you can't win the White House without winning small town votes. And for progressive politicians who reflect the political and cultural values of metro America, connecting with homelanders grows harder every election cycle.

Folks who think and write about rural issues, even liberal activists, often wax sentimental about our homelander-centric system for electing presidents. They insist that the process unifies the nation, forcing candidates to hear from and talk to a broader range of Americans. "I think it's fair to say that the U.S. Senate and the electoral college create a less monolithic approach to things," says Greener. By less monolithic, of course, he means less urban, less focused on the most populous states.

It's true that direct popular elections would de-emphasize rural America. There would be fewer photo ops in country diners and cornfields, fewer whistle stops at county fairs, and no more plaid shirts. But as things stand, presidential candidates already neglect huge swaths of the country. In 2004, four of the five most populous states — California, Illinois, New York, and Texas — were essentially ignored, except as reservoirs of campaign cash. (According to *New York* magazine, Democrats in New York City contributed a third of John Kerry's total war chest in 2004.) The two major parties neglected to visit twenty-five American states. Half the country never saw a single top-of-ticket candidate, Republican or Democrat.

The nonpartisan organization FairVote found that the two teams — Kerry-Edwards and Bush-Cheney — spent two-thirds of their campaign time in just six states, home to 13 percent of the nation's population. And the number of states where politicians spend time and advertising dollars dwindles every four years. John Kerry was lampooned for daring to commit resources in Virginia and quickly capitulated. George Bush's half-hearted bid for New Jersey was seen as bold initially and then as hopelessly quixotic.

After 2004, Florida and Missouri may be added permanently to the list of red states, while Pennsylvania begins to look unassailably blue. Far from unifying the country, the electoral college is narrowing presidential politics, squeezing the battleground, leaving most Americans — and the vast majority of metros — watching from the sidelines.

# 7

# The Homelander Senate

If the system we use to elect presidents were the only part of American politics rigged to benefit homelanders, it might not weigh so heavily on our culture. But the rural bias hard-wired into the U.S. Senate represents a far more profound redistribution of power. Our Constitution grants two seats to every state, regardless of population. As a consequence, a wildly disproportionate number of senators are chosen by voters in rural states where few Americans actually live. In half a dozen cases, homelander states are so sparsely settled that they barely qualify for a congressional district, yet they hold enough power in the Senate that they're able to control the national agenda.

The familiarity of this arrangement has caused most Americans to overlook the fact that it is spectacularly undemocratic. Consider again the woeful case of California. With nearly thirty-six million people, it's our most urbanized state, home to four of the nation's twenty biggest cities. The voters there tend to be socially progressive, electing a state legislature that approved same-sex marriage and legalized medical marijuana. Once a GOP stronghold and a testing ground for conservative ideas, the state hasn't backed a Republican presidential candidate since 1988.

Californians are ethnically diverse to a degree that rural Americans can scarcely comprehend. If the state's Asian community had its own, separate state, it would boast more residents than Oklahoma. If Hispanics had a separate state, it would rank in population somewhere between Michigan and Ohio. Liberals are often portrayed as tax-and-spend slackers, but California ranks as one of the most powerful economies in the world. It's a national engine for high-tech innovation and the arts. In 2004 the state's industries generated goods and services worth 1.5 trillion dollars. That's more economic output than eighteen rural states combined.

But because of our skewed system, the political values of California's citizens barely register in the Senate. They receive two votes, exactly the same number as the half-million people who live in Alaska. In fact, it takes the combined populations of twenty-one homelander states to equal the bustling crowds of California. The exact same number of people are represented by forty-two senators. Barbara Boxer and Dianne Feinstein can hardly hope to compete.

Given the rightward shift in rural politics, it should come as no surprise that homelander states elect far more Republican senators (twenty-six) than Democratic (sixteen). This homelander mandate accounts for most of the GOP's dominant eleven-seat majority in the Senate. Indeed, the urban-rural imbalance has grown so large that it creates a nearly insuperable hurdle for Democrats. Nationwide, Senate Republicans represent 4.5 million fewer Americans than their Democratic colleagues, yet they are able to control the nation's most powerful body.

This disparity is likely to expand as Democrats gain seats in such heavily populated metro states as Ohio and Pennsylvania and Republicans pick up wins in rural states like Nebraska and North Dakota. Within three or four election cycles, we could well find ourselves with a Senate dominated by a Republican Party that represents only one-third of the American people.

Defenders of the system will point out that the Senate's rural bias is tempered by proportional representation in the House of Representatives, but the fact that House seats are fairly and equitably distributed, based on population, doesn't balance out the Senate's spectacularly lopsided structure. For that to be true, a disproportionate number of congressional districts would have to be allocated to urban communities. In fact, the opposite has happened:

Republicans have used the redistricting process to diminish metro voting power in the House.

What's more, when it comes to much of our society's most important business, the ruralist Senate acts alone. The Senate reviews landmark treaties such as NAFTA (the North Atlantic Free Trade Agreement) and the Kyoto global-warming protocols. It alone oversees the appointments of key administration officials, such as Secretary of State Condoleeza Rice, former FEMA (Federal Emergency Management Agency) chief Michael Brown, and UN ambassador John Bolton. Senators also hold sole power to confirm or reject Supreme Court nominees.

The Senate's rural bias can shape these deliberations in profound ways. In 2005 senators took up the nomination of Judge John Roberts, who had been named by President Bush to serve as chief justice. Roberts is widely respected as a legal scholar, but his socially conservative views and public writings on abortion, women's rights, and voting rights place him well outside the American mainstream.

Activists on the Right and the Left saw the Roberts fight as a test of their influence. Ben Brandzel, with MoveOn.org, told the *Washington Post*, "There's going to be an opportunity for Democrats to show where they stand." But because of the Senate's structure, most of the individuals reviewing Roberts's nomination came from rural states where his traditionalist views are the norm.

Of the ten Republican Judiciary Committee members, six hailed from rural strongholds: Alabama, Iowa, Kansas, Oklahoma, South Carolina, and Utah. Most of the Democrats, by contrast, represented big urban states, such as California, Illinois, Massachusetts, and New York. The urban-rural disparity between the two parties was so stark that, even with two fewer seats on the panel, Democratic senators represented nine million more Americans than did their Republican colleagues.

It's interesting to note that within their own party, metro Democrats were stymied by rural opposition. Despite the fervent

efforts of progressive activist groups, several rural Democrats —
including Vermont senator Patrick Leahy — announced that they
would break ranks and vote in favor of Roberts.

In the final vote, twenty-two Democratic senators supported
Roberts, while twenty-two opposed his confirmation. Americans
were left with the impression that Democrats were evenly divided
and ideologically rudderless.

What wasn't generally reported was that the lion's share of
Democratic yes-votes came from homelander Democrats from states
such as Montana, Nebraska, New Mexico, North Dakota, South
Dakota, and Vermont. This urban-rural Democratic schism wasn't
perfect. There were Democratic yes-votes from Connecticut, Florida,
Michigan, Washington state, and Wisconsin. Harry Reid, the party's
minority leader from Nevada, broke with his rural colleagues to vote
against Roberts.

Still, most Democratic senators who opposed Roberts came from
big urbanized states, home to more than one hundred million
Americans. Meanwhile, the homelander Democrats who voted to
confirm Roberts tended to come from much smaller, rural states,
representing only about forty million people.

How did our democracy wind up with a Senate so jury-rigged that a
party elected by a dwindling minority of Americans can claim a
nearly filibuster-proof number of seats? Once again, the tale begins
with the founding fathers. Many of them were genteel farmers and
plantation owners. In 1787, the year of the Constitutional
Convention, Thomas Jefferson wrote a letter to George Washington,
insisting that "agriculture is our wisest pursuit, because it will in the
end contribute most to real wealth, good morals, and happiness."

Jefferson was utterly mistaken of course. Agriculture now employs
fewer than 2 percent of Americans and accounts for less than 1 percent of our gross domestic product. (There's also no evidence to support the notion that modern homelanders are happier or more

moral than their metro neighbors.) Other founders, including Benjamin Franklin, Alexander Hamilton, and James Madison were more prescient. They saw that power and wealth would eventually gravitate to cities and to industry, but they were decades ahead of their time, and they were also squarely over a barrel. The smaller colonies, such as Connecticut, Delaware, and New Jersey (the so-called "lesser" states of their day), quickly realized that they held remarkable veto power. They could scotch the new republic simply by refusing to join.

This is exactly what they threatened to do, unless their states were granted extraordinary influence in at least one chamber of Congress. Their motives weren't entirely cynical. They saw themselves not as Americans but as diplomats representing quasi-sovereign territories. They wanted to retain a significant amount of their independence. "The little states were fixed," declared John Rutledge, a delegate from South Carolina. "They repeatedly and solemnly declared themselves to be so. All that the large states then had to do was to decide whether they would yield or not."

The debate that summer in Philadelphia was bitter. A plan devised by Madison was introduced that would have distributed Senate seats proportionally, based entirely on population. The small states refused to budge, and the matter was tabled, with Madison fretting that a "chasm" had been left in the fabric of the new Constitution. The issue surfaced again a few weeks later when a lawyer from Connecticut named Roger Sherman proposed that "each State should have one vote and no more" in the Senate, regardless of population. "Otherwise," he declared, "a few large States will rule the rest."

The big states balked, and tempers flared. Benjamin Franklin issued a written statement urging calm, but he also came out firmly against the notion of giving extra power to small states: "I do not at present clearly see what advantage the greater states could propose to themselves by swallowing the smaller," he said, "and therefore do not apprehend they would attempt it."

The small states, led by New Jersey's William Patterson and Maryland's Luther Martin, fought back. Patterson insisted that proportional representation would strike "at the existence of lesser states." The struggle simmered on through the summer and appeared intractable. Hamilton declared that a "crisis marked our affairs." The mood deteriorated to such a degree that Franklin urged everyone to offer "prayers imploring the assistance of heaven."

At last, on July 2, 1787, the delegates did what all flummoxed politicians do: They formed a committee. The group was led by Elbridge Gerry, the businessman from Massachusetts, who promptly capitulated. Behind closed doors, he agreed that each small state should receive as many Senate seats as the big ones. His big-state colleagues were outraged, and Gerry later admitted that he himself had "very material objections" to the plan. "We were however in a peculiar situation," he complained. "If no compromise should take place, what will be the consequence?"

The committee's report was debated and fought over for two more weeks and finally approved on a less-than-enthusiastic vote of five to four. When they limped out of Philadelphia in mid-September, the delegates had agreed to permanently skew the playing field of American politics. The decision was far and away the most controversial bit of horse-trading to emerge from Philadelphia, much more divisive than slavery. In the *Federalist Papers,* written soon after the convention, Madison and Hamilton sound defeated and more than a little sheepish.

> The equality of representation in the Senate is another point, which, being evidently the result of compromise between the opposite pretensions of the large and the small States, does not call for much discussion.
>
> It is superfluous to try, by the standard of theory, [to justify] a part of the Constitution which is allowed on all hands to be the result, not of theory, but "of a spirit of amity, and that

mutual deference and concession which the peculiarity of our
political situation rendered indispensable."

As everyone well knew, the deference and concession were all on
one side and the peculiar political position was nothing more than
political blackmail. In the 1830s the French philosopher Alexis de
Tocqueville wrote at length about the American Senate's odd structure, observing that "the minority of a nation dominating the Senate
could entirely paralyze the will of the majority represented by the
other House, which would be contrary to the spirit of constitutional
governments."

If Democrats win control of the House in 2006, our country could
face just such a situation. Senate Republicans elected by a minority
of the American people would have ample opportunity to block the
agenda of metro politicians such as Representative Nancy Pelosi, the
presumptive Democratic House Speaker from San Francisco. In
theory, after 2008 this systemic split could become even more pronounced with Pelosi serving as Speaker, President Hillary Clinton in
the White House, and a conservative homelander from a tiny rural
state occupying the majority leader position in the Senate.

But let's return for a moment to de Tocqueville, whose observations
about the Senate's artificial distribution of power are worth quoting
at length:

> The moment the inhabitants of the United States were consid-
> ered a single nation, it would be natural for a simple majority
> of all the citizens of the union to make the law. [Yet] one
> appreciates that the small states could not consent to the
> application of this doctrine without a complete abdication of
> their existence in everything connected with federal sover-
> eignty; for they would pass from being a coequal authority to
> an insignificant fraction of a great nation. In this state of

affairs there occurred what usually occurs when interests are in opposition to arguments: the rules of logic were massaged.

Like other observers of his day, de Tocqueville was convinced that the U.S. Senate worked fairly well as a representative body, despite its obvious inequities. "All the states are young," he wrote. "They are close to one another; their customs, ideas, and needs are the same; differences stemming from their greater or smaller size are not significant enough to result in strongly opposed interests. As a result, the smaller states have never been seen joining forces in the Senate against the plans of the bigger states."

This was true enough in the 1830s. American society was sharply divided, but not on lines of urban and rural or "greater" and "lesser" states. Cultural loyalties in those pre–Civil War days were regional. Political divisions hinged on questions of slavery and territorial expansion in the West. But only a few decades after de Tocqueville published his essays, America began to change. The young republic began to grow up as rural folk quit their farmsteads and began crowding into cities. They were joined by swarms of immigrants from Europe and Asia.

In short order, the "customs, ideas, and needs" of urban life took on a character that was very different from the realities that shaped small-town life. Because of its brittle structure, this transformation wasn't reflected in the U.S. Senate. As far as that body was concerned, the swelling crowds in Chicago might not have existed at all. Illinois had received its two senators, and that was that. It didn't matter if California added another ten million people or another hundred million; their Senate delegation would remain identical. The same went for Massachusetts, New York, and Ohio.

In fact, over the course of America's great urban century, another trend developed that actually diminished the political power of our metro-dominant states. As previously mentioned, the end of the nineteenth century brought vast new territories into the union. In rapid succession Nebraska, Colorado, North and South Dakota, Montana, Washington, Idaho, Wyoming, and Utah all won statehood. The first half of the twentieth century brought in five more rural states: Alaska, Arizona, Hawaii, New Mexico, and Oklahoma.

On average, two additional members joined the Senate every six years between 1867 and 1950, increasing that body's ranks by nearly one-third. The new delegates didn't represent many people. These western states remain sparsely settled and intensely rural, with only one-tenth of the nation's population; yet they now hold 28 percent of the Senate's voting power. Meanwhile, the nine metro states that are home to most Americans have seen their portion of the Senate's voting clout dwindle dramatically, to just 18 percent.

As University of Texas historian Sanford Levinson has pointed out, this imbalance would have outraged the men who drafted the Constitution. "The framers, of course, could not have foreseen the country's population increase, migratory patterns, or huge disparity of state sizes," he wrote. And things are only getting worse. Over the next quarter century, half of America's population growth is expected to occur in just three states: California, Florida, and Texas. Between them, they'll add more than thirty million people.

Once again, this massive demographic tidal wave will not be reflected in the Senate. The fifty million people packed into California's barrios and megaburbs will have two votes. So will the half-million homelanders scattered across the wind-scoured plains of North Dakota.

The impact of the Senate's rural bias is starkly visible in the way the institution's power is distributed. From the 1920s, when the modern system of Senate leadership took form, politicians from big urban states have held the coveted majority leader position for a grand total of eight years. A Californian managed to secure the position for two years. A New Yorker has never had the honor. Instead, power has passed regularly between men from states such as Arkansas, Kansas, Maine, Mississippi, Montana, South Dakota, and Tennessee.

The main cause for this homelander hegemony is sheer numbers. Metro senators such as Barbara Boxer (California), Bill Nelson (Florida), Barak Obama (Illinois), and Chuck Schumer (New York) may reflect the values of most Americans, but the Senate's structure means they're certain to be outnumbered by politicians from homelander states such as Alaska and Wyoming.

The lack of proportionality also makes it difficult for urban politicians (in both parties) to compete for leadership roles. Put bluntly, it takes a lot less effort to be a senator from a small state than a big one. "Few are likely to deny that Senators from the more populous states, such as California, face a broader array of representational pressures than lawmakers from the smaller states, such as Wyoming," writes Levinson. "An indirect effect of Senate apportionment, some scholars contend, is that contemporary floor leaders of either party are likely to come from smaller rather than larger states because they can better accommodate the additional leadership workload."

Increasingly, metro and homelander senators compete on entirely different playing fields. Big, urban political campaigns tend to be massive affairs, involving complicated media markets, tens of millions of dollars, and finicky allegiances between donors and interest groups that often operate on a national scale. Once elected, metro politicians like California's Dianne Feinstein — who won 5.8 million votes in her 2000 reelection bid — struggle to satisfy complex and quarrelsome constituencies.

By contrast, homelander politicians invest a fraction of the money and fund-raising effort. After taking office, they have far fewer people to please. The Senate's most powerful Republican, Bill Frist from Tennessee, won his most recent campaign with just 1.2 million votes. The Senate's top Democrat, Harry Reid from Nevada, held his seat with fewer than five hundred thousand ballots. That's barely enough votes to elect the mayor of a top-tier American city.

Under a system that grants them greater leisure and flexibility, rural lawmakers are free to maneuver for committee chairmanships and party assignments, duties that translate into bigger staffs, more prestige, and greater fund-raising potential. By campaigning on behalf of other politicians and distributing surplus cash to political allies, homelanders rise quickly to national prominence.

In the end, voters in low-population states choose a disproportionate number of senators, and they also tend to be represented by politicians with far greater individual power than voters from the big urban states.

As in presidential races, the stark rural bias in the Senate went largely unnoticed through much of our history for the simple reason that homelanders used to split their votes between Republicans and Democrats. Rural folks elected some of the Senate's most progressive leaders. Democrat Mike Mansfield from Montana was the architect of Lyndon Johnson's civil rights legislation. He grew up in Great Falls and dropped out of high school to join the navy. Before heading to Washington, he worked in his state's copper mines.

In their day, these homelander Democrats were a centering and stabilizing force in American politics. They tended to be social moderates and often fought to slow or block the more aggressive elements of metro policymaking. At times this meant forging alliances with Republicans to temper the New Deal and the Great Society.

Still, rural Democrats helped lift America into the modern age. They backed rural electrification, universal telephone service, and the interstate highway system. They helped to dismantle Jim Crow and improved the safety and working conditions of American workers. Perhaps most significantly, their numbers helped to buttress the Democratic Party's Senate majority.

Fifteen years ago, Democratic leaders could still boast a sizable rural bloc in the Senate. Their candidates were winning handily in states like Alabama, Arkansas, Montana, Nebraska, and Oklahoma.

In 1990, Nebraska's James Exon dominated his GOP opponent by 18 percentage points. In Oklahoma, David Boren humiliated a conservative challenger, winning more than 80 percent of the vote. That year, Democrats held fifty-seven Senate seats.

It's been downhill ever since. In 1992, Democrats suffered troubling setbacks in Georgia and North Carolina. A year later Republicans won a special election in Texas. The big collapse came in 1994, when Republicans managed to strip away eight Senate seats. Pundits blamed the collapse on shifting loyalties in the South, but Republicans won in every part of the country where rural voters represented a significant bloc. Tennessee fell, but so did Maine and Oklahoma. Two more homelander Democrats, Richard Shelby of Alabama and Ben Nighthorse Campbell of Colorado, announced that they were switching parties.

When the dust settled, Republicans controlled the Senate by a margin of fifty-three to forty-seven and the Democratic Party's small-town base had been crippled. Over the twelve years since, the two parties have traded blows, gaining and losing seats, managing a brief tie, dealing with defections by disaffected members on both sides. The underlying trend has been a slow accumulation of Democratic seats in high-population metro states, including Illinois, Michigan, and New York. Republicans, meanwhile, have gained ground in homelander strongholds such as Nebraska, Nevada, and North and South Dakota.

The pattern isn't perfect. Moderate Republicans like Arlen Specter and Lincoln Chaffee still win races in urbanized states. Conservative Democrats eke out victories in Nebraska and Montana. But these crossover wins are increasingly rare, especially for Democrats. Tom Daschle's defeat in South Dakota showed that even well-financed incumbents are vulnerable, especially if they stake out liberal social positions.

For Democratic challengers hoping to unseat homelander incumbents, the future is even more bleak. In 2004, Democrats fielded strong, well-funded candidates in three rural states against Republicans who appeared vulnerable.

Alaska senator Lisa Murkowski had been appointed to her seat by the state's unpopular Republican governor, who also happened to be her father. The act of brazen nepotism alienated some of the state's most conservative voters.

Kentucky senator Jim Bunning behaved so erratically during the campaign (even accusing the Democratic candidate's staff of beating up his wife) that it was widely rumored he might be crazy or senile.

Oklahoma senator Tom Coburn, an obstetrician, endorsed the death penalty for doctors who perform legal abortions. He also condemned the network broadcast of *Schindler's List* because he thought it would encourage "irresponsible sexual behavior." (George Will, the conservative columnist, described Coburn as "someone simply uninterested in being popular.")

With firepower this good, Democrats hoped to prove that they could still bag a big trophy outside their urban strongholds. But all three incumbents were reelected by comfortable margins. Republicans also cruised to victory in supposedly competitive open races in North and South Carolina. The 2004 election suggested that unless Democratic leaders alter their national platform and moderate the party's core identity, even socially conservative Democrats will suffer in homelander-dominant Senate races.

This is grim news for metros. Because of the Senate's skewed structure, Democrats can't hope to regain their majority without winning back some of those homelander seats. The rural bias is so powerful that an urban-centric party can actually lose seats, even in election cycles when it wins more votes.

That's exactly what happened in 2004. In Senate contests nationwide, Democrats claimed a total of roughly 44.7 million votes, but because most of their support was clustered in big metro states, those ballots only leveraged wins in fifteen races. Republicans, meanwhile, were able to attract just 40 million votes nationwide; however, because their conservative base was distributed across those low-population homelander states, the GOP was able to claim wins in nineteen races.

In a year when Republican candidates took a beating at the polls, they were still able to expand their Senate majority by four seats and Majority Leader Bill Frist was able to boast once again of a national mandate.

If you're still not convinced that the Senate is a homelander institution, I've saved the best for last. The most conspicuous symbol of the Senate's rural bias is found right under our political noses in the nation's capital. Washington, D.C., is progressive, multiethnic, and staunchly Democratic. Despite recent population declines, the city is home to roughly 570,000 people. That's comparable to the population found in four rural states: Alaska, North Dakota, Vermont, and Wyoming.

Yet unlike the white conservative voters in those states, metros in Washington have no Senate representation at all. In the nation's most powerful legislative body, their voices are silent.

If you live in urban America, this probably has you feeling good and cheated. It's one thing to have George Bush sitting in the White House and Bill Frist running the Senate. It's quite another thing to discover that the system was rigged by farmers and plantation owners a couple of centuries ago to accomplish that very political result. You might even be thinking that it's time for us to scrap the electoral college and make the U.S. Senate more democratic.

Of course we should, but we can't. The founding fathers, in their wisdom, gave homelanders one last bit of extraordinary power: They granted rural states a de facto veto over any changes to our Constitution. Any amendment requires passage by a two-thirds majority in both houses of Congress. That means a lot of those rural senators would have to vote to eliminate a political arrangement that benefits their home states and insures their own employment. Were they foolish enough to do so, the change would then need ratification by three-fourths of the state legislatures.

Just thirteen homelander states, representing only 5 percent of the nation's population (not quite as many people as live in Los Angeles and New York City), could easily thwart any reform — even if it enjoyed the backing of two hundred million metros.

## 8

# Boomburg, U.S.A.

It's midmorning, and Allen and I are cruising downtown Washington, Missouri, an orderly, bustling place of thirteen thousand people or so. The redbrick buildings stand at neat intervals. The Missouri River flows by at the bottom of the steep hill. Looking upriver from the public park, we can see a tangle of forest and bluffs every bit as wild as the country that Lewis and Clark faced when they passed this way two hundred years ago.

"This is a pretty Republican area, but not exclusively," Allen says. "Up until very recently the Democrats were still strong, clinging to that Roosevelt loyalty." It turns out that several prominent politicians from this area, including Washington's mayor and the local state senator, are conservative, pro-life Democrats. "I vote for them regularly, but I can't for the life of me understand why they still call themselves Democrats. Because they're really not."

"Some Democrats are trying pretty hard to revive their party's rural support," I say. "They want to connect better in towns like this."

Allen shrugs. "I hear lip service given to that, but in this state the Democratic Party is controlled by urban politicians. The power players are never going to be rural Democrats who are pro-life and have more conservative values. On the social issues how are they going to bridge that divide?"

Washington is like a lot of small towns on America's swelling exurban fringe. On one flank sprawls a strip of brand new commercial ticky-tack: Wal-Mart, Steak 'n Shake, Ruby Tuesday, and Quik Lube. But just over the ridge you'll find acres and acres of rich corn and soybean fields made lush by the river's floods and by the humid sun.

The Amtrak station stands down by the river. The train and the highway are conduits that lead into urban St. Louis. The city is a distant but tangible presence, the source of local television news and wellspring of the big daily newspaper, the *Post-Dispatch*. That's where the Cardinals play baseball and the Rams play football. My sister-in-law Laura is just back from seeing *Jesus Christ Superstar* at one of the venues downtown. ("I wasn't shocked by it or anything," she says, "but it got so many things wrong.")

A lot of folks from Washington commute to jobs inside the urban beltway, but more and more of these exurban towns are turning their backs on the metro core. They are developing their own industries, their own government centers, and their own entertainment. Typically, these "boomburgs" retain the cultural characteristics of a small town. They look outward to homelander communities for their social and political orientation. They are often 80–95 percent white, predominantly Christian, and Republican.

"One symbol of the outer suburban life, particularly in the South and West, is the megachurch," wrote Gregory Giroux in *Congressional Quarterly*, "often a Christian fundamentalist congregation with thousands of members."

Gilbert, Arizona, is one dramatic example of this new homelander frontier. When Ronald Reagan was elected in 1980, five thousand people lived in this farm town on the outskirts of Phoenix. By the time George Bush scrapped his way into the White House in 2000, the population had exploded to more than one hundred thousand, and the pace of growth is actually accelerating. Over the past five years, this devoutly Republican sprawl added another sixty-five thousand people.

In 2003 the federal Office of Management and Budget (OMB) created a new "micropolitan" category to describe these communities. The OMB identified roughly six hundred exurban settlements scattered across America. "Some of the largest micros are more than just overgrown small towns — they appear to be exemplars of a new decentralized or even countrified city," wrote Robert Lang, director of the Metropolitan Institute at Virginia Tech.

In 2004 the swarm of micros and boomburgs and exurbs proved invaluable for George Bush, swinging several battleground states into the red column. Voters in Gilbert and surrounding Maricopa County, for example, delivered a margin of 175,000 votes to Bush, accounting for nearly his entire edge in Arizona. Washington, Missouri, doesn't wield anything like that kind of clout, but Allen's adopted hometown voted Republican by a 58 to 41 percent margin. Folks here helped to overcome Kerry's huge win in urban St. Louis, where the Democrat claimed 80 percent of the vote. Missouri's eleven electoral votes went to Bush.

As we drive, Allen tunes in Sean Hannity's program on the truck radio. The show is just switching over to a commercial break, and the announcer ends the hour with a smarmy invitation to stick around for more liberal bashing. "You *got* to admit it!" the voice croons. "What could be better than making fun of Hillary? She's *fascinating*! Sean Hannity is on the radio right now!"

"How often do you listen to this stuff?"

"Maybe three or four days a week. But I listen to NPR six or seven days a week."

"Do the two things balance out? I mean, how do you think Hannity fits in with other news programs?"

"They are doing two different things, I would agree. As much as I believe that there's liberal bias in the media, I don't think the *Washington Post* or NPR are biased in the same way that Hannity is. People should listen to him as much for entertainment value as anything else. He's kind of a cheerleader, and he provides kind of an emotional outlet for people who are frustrated. But I think it would be a huge mistake for anybody — and I know there are people who do this — to just listen to Hannity and feel like they'd received all the news they need."

"Is there anything about him you don't like?"

"All the mocking. I can't stand it, for example, when they do these Bill and Hillary impersonations."

The commercial break ends, and Hannity returns. He welcomes a female caller who sounds sort of giddy and breathless. She doesn't sound angry at all, but she says she's outraged by all the liberals in her office. "I'm surrounded with these vicious attacks every day. I need to know how to keep my sanity around it," she says.

"Women are the smart ones," Hannity says, in a voice so patronizing that it seems like self-parody, the sort of thing you'd hear on *The Colbert Report.* "What are the attacks? What are you getting?"

"For example, this Rove thing. They say he's a traitor. He's a criminal and he should go to jail and blah, blah, blah. I usually don't say anything because I don't want to start a fight. That's not what I'm there at work to do."

"Look at what the president goes through," Hannity says. "Look at the names *he* gets called. He gets called a Nazi, a liar, [they say] that he knew about 9/11. They don't like anybody he hires, anybody who works for him. And yet he believes so strongly in his cause that he's willing to accept the attacks that go along with the job."

This goes on for a remarkably long time. One of the outdated notions that conservatives still trot out is that their pundits are funnier and more entertaining than progressive mouthpieces. ("Those guys are bitter," Hannity says. "Al Franken hasn't been funny for twenty years, not that he ever was.")

But guys like Hannity, Savage, Limbaugh, and O'Reilly have become part of the Republican-homelander establishment, and that means they're boring. Even their venom has a tired aftertaste (Hillary Clinton's too shrill, Howard Dean's a howler, Bill Clinton's horny, and so on), as if they're rabble-rousing by the numbers. It doesn't help that their number one job is defending and lionizing George Bush, trying to make him seem less funny, less like a screwball. It's not exactly an easy task in the post-Katrina era.

Hannity gives the caller a final bit of fatherly advice, urging her to stay positive, just like the president. Above all, she shouldn't stoop to the nasty tactics of liberal Bush-haters, who are so blinded by their anger that they've abandoned civility. His spiel is so blatantly manipulative and dumb that I can't help groaning. "Come *on*, Allen. He just did that nasty routine about Hillary. It makes no sense."

My brother laughs sheepishly and says, "I totally agree. A lot of what Hannity does is on the childish side. But some of it's pretty entertaining. And it is informative. Sometimes he interviews Newt Gingrich and other leading Republicans."

"Does he challenge them in meaningful ways?"

"Never."

"Then what is he accomplishing?"

"I guess they come on to give their version of events."

"The mainstream media doesn't give them that opportunity?"

At this, he shakes his head firmly. "What I hear on the urban media are two versions of the liberal viewpoint, one that the left wing can absolutely salivate over and another that might challenge them a *little*. Rarely do I hear truly opposing viewpoints."

Hannity is deep into his routine now. He's been venting spleen and mockery for a full hour, but now he's suddenly appalled, shocked, and dismayed by the sour tone of public discourse. "When you look at Howard Dean, what do you see? An angry man. Look at Michael Moore, an angry man. Look at the Democratic Party in general. Who ever laughs, who ever smiles? Look at Nancy Pelosi. Look at Barbara Boxer. Are these people you'd ever want to hang out with? Then look at the president. The president's a nice guy, you know? You'd want to hang out with him."

It's too much for me: too obvious, too ugly and manipulative. Conservatives like this guy brand liberals with terms like *traitor*. They declare a culture war from the podium of the Republican National Convention. (Not a march, not a movement, but a war.) Homelanders embrace martyrdom on their editorial pages and call for the assassination of democratically elected foreign leaders on their syndicated television programs — but metros are the angry ones?

Allen turns off the radio. The air in the truck feels lighter. The pitch of tension drops. "I can't stand that you listen to that stuff," I say. "I'm sorry, but it's just that grim."

"You're taking it too seriously. I don't place any value in Hannity's opinions. They matter not the least to me. It all gets tossed in with my own thoughts. I have my own opinions."

It's one of those circles I can't quite square. I want to believe it. Allen's not vicious. He has a sense of right and wrong so firm and balanced that I've often used him as a guide. Inevitably, his advice urges me toward forgiveness, modesty. "Get over yourself" is the crux of his personal philosophy. On one level, he seems to shake off Michael Savage's vitriol and Rush Limbaugh's sneer, much the way a metro shakes off a hateful, misogynistic Eminem song. It's political hyperbole, that's all, the kind of cultural adrenaline that cuts through the media white noise and gives you a nice jolt of outrage.

But I can't help thinking that Allen believes this stuff. Maybe not all of it, but a lot. That's his anger coming over the tinny AM speaker, his frustration echoing through blog sites. A fair chunk of that spleen is directed at me. I'm one of those metro parents who would go ballistic if a public school teacher tried to mix Christianity in my son's science class. I don't want my tax money going to churches or church-operated schools. I understand all the ugly, complicated facets of abortion and I'm still firmly pro-choice. I don't want Supreme Court justices to make decisions by trying to channel the thoughts of eighteenth-century farmers and plantation owners.

Which means everything — and nothing. Two minutes later we're talking and laughing about some nonsense. Allen digs in the glove box and pulls out an old cassette tape of a comedian named Jeff Foxworthy. He's sort of the homelander version or Jerry Seinfeld or Chris Rock. "If your dad walks you to school because you're in the same grade, you might be a redneck," Foxworthy drawls. "If you've ever gone to a family reunion to meet women, you *might* be a red-neck. If you've been on television more than five times describing what the tornado was like, you might be a redneck."

The Republican Party's fascination with exurban culture makes per-fect sense — the people here vote reliably conservative. But it also smacks increasingly of desperation. In *On Paradise Drive*, David Brooks describes the outer-ring suburbs as a democratic nirvana, where the sins of class and race and shifting social norms are washed away:

> The exurbs are built to embody a modern version of the sub-urban ideal. Demographic studies show that they look like 1950s suburban America — intact two-parent families, 2.3 kids, low crime, and relatively low divorce rates. You some-times get the impression that these people have fled their crowded and stratified old suburbs because they really want to live in an updated Mayberry with Blackberries.

Brooks is sort of half right. Millions of white Americans do hunger for a modern version of Mayberry. But it's not the egalitarian vision he conjures up. To create a community that looks like a 1950s suburb, you have to begin with a hell of a lot of stratification and segregation. Many of the people flooding into these new ruralist communities hope to escape the muddle, the racial tension, and the sheer other-ness that come with urbanization.

From the homeland vantage point, urban America looks remote and discreditable. The vagaries of metro life are distilled to a reproachful mutter on Fox News, a disdainful *mot juste* in the *Weekly Standard*, or a sneering diatribe on Hannity's radio show. When writers like Brooks speak of America as a "segmented" country, they make it perfectly clear which segments are good and healthy, imbued with good old-fashioned, common-sense values, and which are bad and decadent and sort of silly.

"In rural America, churches are everywhere," Brooks writes.

> [I]n suburban America Thai restaurants are everywhere. In rural America it's unwise to schedule events on Wednesday night, because that is the night for prayer meetings. In the inner-ring suburbs, you can schedule events any night, but you probably don't want to go up against *Sex and the City*.

This is nonsense, of course. Anyone who actually lives in rural America can tell you that homelander culture isn't any healthier, wiser, or more salt-of-the-earth than urban communities. It's true that more small-town folk attend church, and they join the military with greater zeal. They tend to oppose abortion and generally espouse moral values that tilt to the right. But does all that produce better families or more decent neighbors or smarter schoolchildren?

Unfortunately, no. Crime rates are significantly lower in small towns, but in most other respects rural communities tend to be just about as dysfunctional as urban neighborhoods — sometimes considerably more so. The homelander economy is stuck in neutral and in many parts of the country is sliding rapidly into reverse. The result is a terrible rash of social ills, ranging from deepening poverty and hunger to domestic violence to a dire epidemic of crystal meth and heroine addiction.

As previously mentioned, the rural population is stagnant at a time when most metro communities are booming. Usually it's the best and the brightest kids who leave small towns first. One study found that better public schools in rural America actually accelerate the rate of brain drain, as smart, well-prepared kids go searching for better opportunities in urban or suburban America.

As a result, most rural communities don't innovate very well. The entrepreneurial culture is moribund. Academics who study rural

America have begun comparing the social and economic collapse in small towns to the implosion that hit urban black neighborhoods a generation ago.

After lunch we stop in at Allen's church. It's a handsome, no-nonsense 1950s type of building, no megachurch glitz here. The congregation runs a private elementary school that looks pretty much like any K–5 building in America (rows of lockers, scuffed tile floor, bathrooms with knee-high urinals) except that the walls are decorated with crosses, pictures of Jesus, and posters of the Ten Commandments. It's summertime, so school isn't in session, but the place is thrumming with well-ordered activity, more like a corporate headquarters or a government office than a place of worship.

My brother looks in and asks his pastor, Mark Bangert, if he has a few minutes to sit down with me. Bangert is a mild-looking sort of guy, with pale hair and a slightly weary smile. He seems a little nervous, but what conservative Christian pastor wouldn't be, confronted suddenly by a strange journalist from New York who wants to talk about America's urban-rural culture war?

He nods bravely and waves me inside his office, which looks like the study of a remarkably tidy college professor. We talk for a few minutes about his background (grew up in a conservative Lutheran family), his education (nearly a decade of university and seminary training), and his theology. "I don't believe that godly living or godly culture comes from within," he says. "I don't believe it's natural. I believe it's supernatural."

His manner is soothing after the experience in the truck. It's not that I agree with him, but it matters somehow that he's thoughtful and patient and occasionally uncertain. When I ask how his traditional worldview might work in modern society, he shrugs and says, "I have difficulty seeing past my own congregation and the families we can affect. But I guess it would be the same vision in a broader perspective."

I've encountered this before in my travels and in my own rural town, the Christian idealism that pervades the homelander movement. Social conservatives often play the role of scolds and puritans, especially when addressing metro audiences. There's nothing Wolf Blitzer or Joe Scarborough love more than interviewing Pat Robertson, host of *The 700 Club*, which is broadcast by Christian Broadcasting Network, not because Robertson is likely to say anything meaningful, but because his increasingly loony rhetoric makes for great theater.

But millions of conservative evangelicals have no interest in scoring cheap political points. They want Americans to share the joy and community of life within a Bible-centered congregation. The way they see it, their proselytizing isn't a demand or a threat; it's a gift offered freely. "I believe the gospel of God's love in Christ changes people," Pastor Bangert says.

"My sense is that there are a lot of Americans who don't want that kind of life," I say. "Either they're not Christian or they're not comfortable with this more conservative idea of what Christianity should be."

"People can live any way they want," he says. "They have that freedom in this country. I don't think Christians would ever be against freedom of religion. I don't think that's the intent at all. Some might fear that, I suppose, but I can't see that."

"What about some of these hot-button issues, though, like abortion? Isn't that an area where you want to decide for other people?"

"If human life doesn't begin when I'm a one-cell human being, when does it start? When does God somewhere along the line insert soul into the whole process? I believe it happens right from the very beginning. This is a human being we're talking about, and I can't get past that."

"So obviously, you support a ban on abortion?"

I expect a quick confirmation, a firm nod, but he pauses and sits back and suddenly looks wearier than ever. "We live in a pivotal time. I think we have gone beyond the founding principles of our country. This is speaking politically, not so much as a pastor. I don't see this right to privacy implied in any of the founding documents of our country."

The answer strikes me as oddly lawyerly, especially for a man whose understanding of public morality seems pretty straightforward. I prod him one more time, and he shrugs and says, "I don't know if a ban will ever happen."

"But if you had your way abortion would go, isn't that right? I mean, you seem a little unsure. I'm surprised that you even have to think about it."

He laughs and shakes his head. "It's just hard for me to imagine, I guess."

Away from the sound and fury of politics, this uncertainty is fairly common among homelanders. In recent years they've experienced a sort of political vertigo. It's one thing to crusade against the evils of modern society when you don't have the power to actually change anything. It's easy to condemn big government when you're not the one making the trains run on time or balancing the budget or responding to natural disasters like Hurricane Katrina.

But now that social conservatives are rewriting the laws and governing our institutions, they've been forced to confront the complexities and ambiguities of American life. From stem cell research to the fate of the Plan B contraceptive pill to the management of FEMA and Medicare, homelanders are struggling to match their vision of a more traditional society with the facts on the ground.

Abortion is a case in point. A lot of small-town folks see the procedure as an act of brutality perpetrated against an innocent child. They believe it weakens the moral fiber of our entire society. If you're willing to destroy a fetus, why not terminate the life of an elderly person, or a terminally ill patient, or a child with disabilities? They also see abortion as the by-product of licentious behavior, a barbaric form of contraception.

The reality is very different. There are roughly 1.3 million abortions every year in America, which means that it's one of the most common elective surgical procedures. "Abortion is a common experience," according to a report by the Guttmacher Institute. "At current rates, about one in three American women will have had an abortion by the time she reaches age 45." Despite homelander rhetoric, the vast majority of cases don't involve minors or late-term pregnancies or the "partial-birth" procedures. (To be fair, these cases also rarely involve rape, incest, or medical necessity, the usual arguments raised by metros.) Most women who end their pregnancies are doing so for the first time. They don't use abortion casually, as a contraception method. They're often young, poor, and desperate. Nearly 80 percent of women who terminate pregnancies report some religious affiliation, usually Protestant (43 percent) and Roman Catholic (27 percent).

Given that the procedure has become so commonplace — and the debate so fierce — it's startling to realize that after thirty years, the antiabortion movement hasn't offered a serious alternative. Homelanders rely instead on vague notions of encouraging abstinence and convincing Americans to live more virtuous lives. "When I was growing up here in the Wild West, if a young man got a woman pregnant out of wedlock they got married, and the whole darn neighborhood was involved in the wedding," South Dakota state senator Bill Napoli told PBS in 2006, after his bill banning abortion was passed by the state legislature.

But regardless of your moral framework, it's obvious that a ban (or even tight restrictions) would have enormous policy implications. Even if America were to cut the number of unwanted pregnancies in half (no serious medical professionals believe this is possible) we would still be faced with a deluge of seven hundred thousand babies every single year, most of them born to poor young women with little education and few prospects.

Asked if shotgun weddings were a workable solution, Napoli didn't blink: "[In the past] they wanted that child brought up in a home with two parents, and I believe that can happen again. I don't believe we're so far beyond that we can't get back to it."

This isn't policymaking; it's wishful thinking — a reflection of the idealism and romanticism that often shape the homelander movement. At times, it's hard to avoid the sense that rural folks know exactly what they want but have no earthly idea how to make it work. Pro-life advocates compare their crusade to the civil rights struggle of the 1960s, but progressives didn't just "ban" racism; they worked for two decades to build policies, institutions, and programs designed to combat it and make it less prevalent.

For their part, rural conservatives like Napoli have done none of the things that might make abortion less necessary. They haven't improved the availability or affordability of contraception. (In Missouri, Republicans took control of the state legislature in 2003 and eliminated funding for birth control at publicly operated clinics, arguing that the program encouraged promiscuity.) They haven't embraced the best and most comprehensive sex education for young people, even though the best independent research shows that abstinence-only programs are ineffective. In 2006, social conservatives convinced state and federal governments to spend more than $200 million on abstinence programs. But in a study published in the *American Journal of Public Health*, Harvard researcher Janet Rosenbaum reported that fully half of the kids who took "virginity pledges" later recanted, denying that they had ever made such a vow.

Homelander activists haven't proposed a new social safety net to catch unwanted children or help reluctant new mothers with limited means — just the opposite. They've helped the Republican Party weaken or dismantle the kind of health-care programs that might support expectant mothers and allow them to make better decisions. If abortion is banned in a significant chunk of the United States, this lack of foresight and preparedness will make Hurricane Katrina look like a minor flub.

Sitting in his office, Pastor Bangert concedes that not enough has been done. Despite his certainty that abortion is murder, he shakes his head and says, "You know, I don't know what it would be like if we do end abortion. Prohibition didn't work very well. How would this work? Would you give nine months' notice? I don't know how that would play out."

As Allen and I drive home, slipping through the outskirts of Washington, curving along dirt roads on the margins of soybean fields, he says, "You know, one thing I learned from Pastor Bangert is that God doesn't just impose his vision of the ideal society. I guess I have to resign myself to the idea that society is the way God intends for it to be. Hard as that is for me to understand, that has to be the way it is."

"You really do want abortion banned? You think that's a good idea?"

"The first thing I would do, I'd raise taxes to pay for social programs that would make it practical to end *Roe v. Wade*. Then, yes, I would outlaw abortion in this country. I'm passionate about that."

# 9

# Beating the House

We have seen how Republicans used this homelander base — small towns like Perryton, Texas, and exurban communities like Washington, Missouri — to win control of the White House and the U.S. Senate. The Constitution gives any political party with broad rural appeal a sizable advantage.

But in theory at least, there is no small-town bias in the House of Representatives. Congressional districts are allocated on the basis of population, with new boundaries drawn every ten years to reflect shifting populations as documented by the U.S. Census Bureau. After the 2000 census, most districts in the country were reshaped to include roughly 650,000 people, roughly a 10 percent increase.

Given the fact that 80 percent of Americans are metros, it stands to reason that urban and inner-suburban voters will elect the vast majority of representatives. All by itself, for example, New York City is represented by fifteen congresspeople. A 300-square-mile chunk of skyscrapers, brownstones, and tightly packed suburban neighborhoods wields more political clout in the House than do Alaska, Delaware, Idaho, Montana, North and South Dakota, Rhode Island, Vermont, and Wyoming combined.

Multiply that kind of voting power times all the cities in America and it stands to reason that urban politicians should control the House with an iron grip. Through most of the twentieth century that's exactly what happened. From 1932, when Franklin Delano Roosevelt swept to power, until the Republican Revolution of 1994, the GOP held the Speaker's gavel for only four years. For the better part of six decades, Democrats ruled the House as a private fiefdom, often with majorities so large that Republicans were completely marginalized.

Rural Democrats often held leadership posts, but they pursued an agenda that was increasingly urban and progressive. Men like Sam Rayburn from Texas and Tip O'Neil from Massachusetts collaborated on civil rights. They expanded the social safety net and pushed through populist economic policies. As recently as the early 1990s, it seemed a fair assumption that the Democratic Party's urban machine would chug along unchallenged for another sixty years. America's cities were continuing to swell. The Cold War had ended, weakening the position of conservatives, who had often campaigned on national defense and anti-communism. Domestic affairs were back on the front burner. "It's the economy, stupid," was Bill Clinton's battle cry.

How, then, to explain the fact that the homelander insurgency began in the House? How do we account for the astonishing rise of Newt Gingrich, a conservative history professor from rural Georgia who translated his "Contract with America" into an awesome electoral surge? How have all those metro congressmen managed to put themselves in the hands of rural traditionalists like Gingrich, Tom DeLay, and Dennis Hastert?

It's often forgotten these days, but when Gingrich rose to power, House Republicans were a fairly metro-centric bunch. There was little of the combative, ideological fervor that has colored the GOP's agenda over the past fifteen years. For most of the postwar era, moderates like Gerald Ford from Michigan, John Rhodes from Arizona, and Robert Michel from Illinois held a tight rein over their more conservative colleagues.

These Rockefeller-Eisenhower Republicans were generally pro-choice, progressive on civil rights, and comfortable with the idea of a sizable federal bureaucracy. As with Barry Goldwater a quarter century earlier, Gingrich's first big fight came with members of his own party. (He once described Senator Bob Dole as "the tax collector for the welfare state.") In 1989 he jumped into the race for the House minority whip post and after campaigning feverishly won by just two votes.

Almost from the beginning, Gingrich began characterizing himself as a "transitional" politician who would lead America away from the center-left, New Deal consensus that defined American politics. He took to giving self-indulgent speeches about culture and philosophy on late-night C-Span broadcasts. In the lead-up to the 1994 midterm elections, he convinced three hundred Republican candidates to sign his famous "Contract."

Gingrich later described the platform as a blunt repudiation of urban modernist society. "We have to say to the counterculture, 'Nice try, you failed, you're wrong,'" he declared. "And we have to simply, calmly, methodically reassert American civilization."

To tens of millions of metro Americans, Gingrich appeared absurd, even harmlessly nutty. It seemed that he was asking the country to turn back the clock on everything from the Pill to rock-and-roll. He was repudiating social programs and environmental protections fostered by both parties since the days of Truman and Eisenhower. Far from being alarmed, most Democrats paid little attention. They overlooked the fact that Gingrich's philosophy was backed by his skill as a tactician. He was a tireless organizer and a cutthroat campaigner who had little patience for his party's me-too centerism.

This is one of a hundred culture war skirmishes in which the metro side had plenty of warning but still managed to let themselves be blind-sided. In the 1980s Gingrich had proved his effectiveness by working almost single-handedly to disgrace and dethrone Democratic House Speaker Jim Wright, despite objections from members of his own party. "His evidence against Wright was slight, to put it mildly," wrote John Micklethwait and Adrian Wooldridge, conservative writers whose book *The Right Nation* is a mostly glowing account of the America's right-wing movement. "Wright's worst sin seemed to be getting a special deal on a contract to write a book."

In the early 1990s, Gingrich and the newly vigorous right-wing media were able to leverage several more substantive scandals. Illinois representative Dan Rostenkowski, one of the most powerful Democrats in Washington, was under indictment on corruption charges. (He eventually served a fifteen-month prison sentence.) Democratic leaders were embroiled in a check-kiting scandal, accused of overdrawing their House accounts by hundreds of thousands of dollars and trying to cover up the imbroglio. "It's unclear how much of [Democratic House Speaker Tom Foley's] reluctance to act was criminal and how much was sheer incompetence," wrote William McGurn in the *National Review*.

"You guys are our employees," fumed Rush Limbaugh, still a relatively new fixture in the political landscape, "and you treat people in the country like we are your employees and you're the boss."

It's no coincidence that Gingrich's revolution hit seven years after Congress repealed the Fairness Doctrine, which had forced broadcasters to offer audiences balanced political views. The change was a brilliant bit of Reagan-era deregulation that opened the airwaves to a cadre of influential right-wing commentators of a type not heard since the days of Father Coughlin's broadcasts on CBS radio in the 1930s. Limbaugh and his imitators gleefully adopted the Republican Party's talking points and offered conservatives a new pipeline to millions of listeners in rural America.

They quickly exploited (and inflated) the disarray of Bill Clinton's first term. Gays in the military, Hillary's bumbling effort to create a national health-care system, the Whitewater investigation, and Vince Foster's suicide were adrenalized into national outrages. To say that Democrats were unprepared for this constant barrage would be an understatement. But they weren't alone. In the months before Election Day 1994, few pundits understood the landslide that was about to hit.

In all, thirty-four Democratic incumbents would be thrown out of office, with between one-third and one-half of the losses coming in small-town-heavy districts. The most high-profile rural Democrat to topple was House Speaker Tom Foley from eastern Washington state. Republicans took out Judiciary Committee chairman Jack Brooks, a farmer from Beaumont, Texas. Democrats also lost twenty seats in open districts and for the first time in decades found themselves on the backbenches, down by a margin of 230 to 204 seats.

As mentioned previously, many pundits attributed Gingrich's coup to the conservative realignment in the South. This remains conventional wisdom among many metros. In fact, the GOP won its biggest gains north of the Mason-Dixon line, in districts across the Midwest and the Rocky Mountain states. The states that saw the heaviest Democratic losses were Washington (where Republicans picked up five seats), Ohio (three new GOP seats), and California (another three).

It was a historic victory, but winning control of the House wasn't enough for Gingrich. In the months after the election, he and his allies engineered two additional coups. First, they convinced other factions within the GOP that the new brand of homelander-style conservatism offered the only credible long-term challenge to Democratic control.

The old East Coast Republican establishment had played nice for half a century, and it had earned them nothing. They were paper tigers, country-club types. The future belonged to true conservatives who were willing to fight and scrap for every vote. This hearts-and-minds campaign was reenforced by a new form of party discipline. Gingrich and Majority Whip Tom DeLay restructured the House leadership, weakening the autonomy of committee chairs, centralizing power in a few positions, all of which were occupied by homelanders or their allies.

Here lies the first secret in the rural-conservative playbook. Through a brilliant combination of intimidation and reward, they were able to harness and control a group of thirty to forty moderate Republicans — most from urban and inner-suburban districts — who shared few of their homelander values. According to a survey by the *Christian Science Monitor*, roughly 8 percent of Republican congressional representatives are elected from metro districts that vote Democratic in presidential elections. These lawmakers represent a middle-of-the-road constituency, generally favoring small government and low taxes, but are liberal on social issues.

Visit the Web site of Congressman Vito Fossella, a Republican who represents Staten Island and a chunk of Brooklyn, and you'll find him trumpeting the virtues of the AFL-CIO and announcing, "Vito Restores Full Funding for PBS."

Without the collaboration of these metro Republicans, Gingrich's rural agenda would have faltered immediately. Every so often, there's a whiff of rebellion. In 2005, fifteen House Republicans voted to legalize medical marijuana. That same year, upstate New York representative Sherwood Boehlert, a twenty-four-year veteran, tangled publicly with Joe Barton, a conservative congressman from Texas. At issue was the GOP leadership's effort to discredit global warming research. In an open letter, Boehlert claimed that Barton was trying to "intimidate scientists rather than to learn from them, and to substitute Congressional political review for scientific peer review."

This kind of defection is rare, in large part because the metro wing of the GOP has remained disorganized and ideologically fractured. Unlike homelanders, they lack the support of strong allies in the Senate or the administration. They're allowed to vote their consciences on issues that aren't central to the Republican agenda (or when their votes won't influence the outcome), but on important items they know that any sign of disloyalty will be met with fierce retaliation.

In 2005, Boehlert fought against voting for President Bush's Medicare prescription drug plan for weeks. He clearly despised the legislation, which turned out to be a budget buster and one of the most confusing bits of Kafkaesque bureaucratic nonsense that older Americans had ever encountered. But they didn't call Tom DeLay "The Hammer" because of his ruthlessness against Democrats.

Under his regime, dissidents like Boehlert were threatened with the loss of their chairmanships. They faced challenges in Republican primaries. They lost financial support from key donors.

Boehlert capitulated and voted for Bush's bill. In 2006 he retired after a parting shot at the men who have shaped his party's direction for a generation. "I think most people reject the extremism of the far left and the far right," he told reporters. "They want us to find the common ground."

Cementing homelander control of the Republican Party was no small feat, but after 1994, rural conservatives managed an even greater coup: They convinced much of the nation that their triumph represented a major shift in American politics. The 1994 midterm election wasn't a one-time case of "throw the bums out" or a sign of dissatisfaction with Bill Clinton. It was a full-scale realignment of the national psyche, a rejection of New Deal–style federalism and a return to the glory days of the Reagan era.

"This lesson was really about some fairly big ideas," Gingrich wrote later. "Which direction do you want to go in? And those who argued for counterculture values, bigger government, redistributionist economics, and bureaucracies deciding how you should spend your money, were on the losing end in virtually every part of the country."

Homelanders swept into Washington claiming that they possessed a clear mandate to roll back policies that had enjoyed bipartisan support for half a century. "It's a different day," declared Kansas senator Bob Dole, the incoming Senate majority leader. "It's been forty years. Without any disrespect to my Democratic colleagues, I hope they'll relax and let us enjoy the day." Gingrich chartered a jet christened the *Speaker Express* and flew with supporters from Atlanta to Washington. "We're very excited," he declared. "It's going to be a historical occasion."

The right-wing media pitched in, trumpeting the conquest and relentlessly driving home the same theme: America's political landscape had changed. Voters weren't just cleaning house, they were building a new house. They wanted leadership that would question all the tired liberal wisdoms.

Polling, lifestyle surveys, and voting patterns contradict or raise serious doubts about all these claims. Americans remain deeply committed to safety-net programs — Medicare, Medicaid, and Social Security — that Gingrich hoped to dismantle. We're more comfortable every year with progressive social issues, so comfortable that we take our liberalism for granted. "Jim Dobson's [radio show] may be able to remind eight million Americans about the evils of homosexuality," wrote Michlethwait and Wooldridge, in *The Right Nation*, "but *Will & Grace*, a sitcom with several openly gay characters, is watched by twenty million people a week."

It's also fair to point out that in raw political terms, the Republican Revolution wasn't quite the earth-shattering event that Gingrich made it out to be. In modern times similar corrections have swept Congress at regular intervals. Roosevelt presided over a much larger defeat in 1938, when Republicans gained eighty-one seats. Four years later, he suffered through another drubbing, as forty-five Democrats lost their seats. During Harry Truman's first term, in 1946, the GOP picked up fifty-five seats and briefly won control of Congress. Over the decades that followed, big swings of twenty seats or more were common.

It's also worth noting that most of the Democratic incumbents who were defeated in 1994 captured at least 45 percent of the popular vote. Many of the races were much closer. (Owing to third-party challenges, six of the Republican insurgents squeaked into office despite winning fewer than half of the ballots.) In a campaign marked by low voter turnout, highly motivated conservatives were able to steal a march on moderates and liberals who were disorganized and apathetic.

Even so, the victory was narrow and hardly represented the sort of governing mandate that Democrats had enjoyed for half a century. "Everybody celebrated Republicans taking control of Congress for first time in 40 years, but nobody explained it was the smallest majority in 40 years," Kenneth Duberstein, a former White House chief of staff under Ronald Reagan, told the *Washington Post*.

Ironically, many of the Republican gains had come against moderate or conservative Democrats. Gingrich's foot soldiers picked off politicians who shared many of the GOP's social and economic ideas. Metro liberals were left largely untouched and have actually expanded their numbers in the past decade.

What makes the Republican Revolution of 1994 unique is its durability. Twelve years after their charge on Capitol Hill, the Republicans still clings to a twenty-nine-seat advantage in the House. But here again, homelanders and their media messengers often obscure an important fact: Following the initial gains, Gingrich's majority began to collapse immediately. In 1996, Republicans lost two seats.

In January 1997, having wrecked several other politicians' careers over ethical lapses, Gingrich himself stumbled into a morass of scandals. He was formally reprimanded and fined three hundred thousand dollars by fellow Republicans after entering into his own suspiciously lucrative book deal. The next year, after Republicans exasperated voters by shutting down the federal government, the GOP lost another five seats. Battered by political setbacks and weakened by rumors of an extramarital affair, Gingrich stepped aside. A few weeks later, his chosen successor, Bob Livingston of Louisiana, resigned after admitting to an extramarital affair of his own.

In 2000, the year that Republicans lost the popular presidential vote, House Republicans again saw two seats return to Democratic hands. Three election cycles in a row, their mandate had eroded, slipping to a razor-thin nine-vote margin.

This is hardly the track record of a confident and popular national movement. It's certainly not the sort of public affirmation Roosevelt received in the 1930s when he proposed to sketch out a new version of society. For all the rhetoric about paradigm shifts and visionary leadership, America's conservative realignment seemed to be nothing more than a footnote in the long history of metro dominance. The GOP's new brand of rural conservatism was playing brilliantly in small towns and on the new exurban frontier, but metros weren't buying it.

In 75 percent of the nation's urban and inner-suburban congressional districts, Republicans were taking a beating. "The Democrats, whose strongest congressional base remains in the nation's 90 urban districts, also do well in neighboring inner suburbia," wrote *Congressional Quarterly*'s Gregory Giroux, in a study of voting patterns published in 2005.

For House Republicans, this lack of metro support was potentially devastating for one simple reason: The urban population was rising, while the rural population was continuing to dwindle. The 2000 census found that America's cities and inner suburbs had surged yet again. Hispanics and African Americans (both Democratic-leaning groups) had grown dramatically in population. The leadership faced a rising demographic tide that would inevitably sweep the Republicans from power.

But if Gingrich was a skillful ideological salesman, DeLay was a bare-knuckle brawler. In 2000 he launched a new initiative to redraw the political boundaries for as many of America's 435 congressional seats as possible. The GOP controlled the legislature and the governor's office in thirteen states, giving its strategists remarkable power over the redistricting process in one-third of the country — including Florida, Ohio, and Pennsylvania. (At the time, Democrats held full sway in only seven states.)

In a typical move, DeLay and House Speaker Dennis Hastert dispatched a letter to Republican lawmakers in Pennsylvania, urging them to draft aggressively partisan districts. "We wish to encourage you in these efforts," they wrote, "as they play a crucial role in maintaining a Republican majority." The essence of their strategy was simple. By carefully tweaking the congressional map, Republicans would redistribute their loyal base of small-town and exurban voters. They would use those voters to leverage as many conservative-leaning districts as possible while also dividing and marginalizing urban and suburban voters.

This business of gerrymandering the political map to weaken one's opponent has been a favorite tool of Democrats and Republicans for generations. (Democrats in Georgia tried unsuccessfully to redistrict Newt Gingrich out of a job in the early 1990s.) But Delay's team took the strategy to a new level. They used sophisticated new polling and consumer data combined with state-of-the-art computer mapping systems to maximize the efficiency of their voter base. Pennsylvania's new districts were so weirdly shaped that they were given colorful names such as "supine seahorse" and the "upside-down Chinese dragon." Ohio's districts stretch and bulge like hungry amoebas.

It's important to note that these new districts didn't need a majority of homelanders in order to swing safely Republican. Rural and exurban voters tend to be extremely loyal and they vote at high rates. In many cases, a carefully deployed minority of small-town voters can tip the balance, out-competing their more numerous metro neighbors.

In 2002 the strategy worked brilliantly. Before redistricting, Pennsylvania's congressional delegation was evenly divided, with eleven Republicans and ten Democrats. Most observers agree that the split offered a fairly accurate representation of the state's political leanings. But in 2002 the new Republican district lines triggered an unprecedented triumph for the GOP. Voters elected twelve Republicans and only seven Democrats.

The same story played out in Michigan, an even more solidly Democratic state that voted for Al Gore in 2000 and John Kerry in 2004. The state's two U.S. Senators are Democrats, as is Governor Jennifer Granholm. But in 2002, using a district map developed by the Republican state legislature, Michigan's congressional delegation flipped from a nine-to-seven Democratic lead to a nine-to-six advantage for Republicans (one seat had been lost to redistricting).

Strategically distributed rural voters had helped to halt the GOP slide, and their zeal even helped Republicans reclaim eight seats. "There is no doubt, though, that on balance the 2000 redistricting cycle amounted to a major victory for Republicans," wrote Jeffrey Toobin in the *New Yorker*. "Even though Al Gore and George W. Bush split the combined vote in Florida, Pennsylvania, Ohio, and Michigan, Republican control of the process meant that, after redistricting, the G.O.P. now holds 51 of those states' 77 House seats."

This hardball strategy didn't draw widespread media attention until 2003, when Tom DeLay personally led the fight to redraw the political map in his home state of Texas. Typically, redistricting happens every ten years. But the GOP's House margins were still dangerously thin. A congressional map approved two years earlier by a bipartisan panel of Texas judges had done the unthinkable, allowing Democrats to compete on a more or less even playing field. In 2002, Texas voters elected seventeen Democrats and fifteen Republicans.

That year the GOP gained control of the Texas legislature for the first time. Under DeLay's tutelage, Republicans immediately launched an out-of-season mapmaking effort designed to eliminate Democratic seats. In 2003 the *Washington Post* acquired an analysis of the GOP plan produced by Joby Fortson, legislative counsel to Texas Republican representative Joe Barton. The document offered a fascinating insight into the Republican's homelander-based strategy.

"This is the most aggressive [redistricting] map I have ever seen," Fortson wrote gleefully. "This has a real national impact that should assure that Republicans keep the House no matter the national mood."

The plan specifically targeted moderate white Democrats such as Representative Chet Edwards. "Chet loses his Killeen–Fort Hood base in exchange for conservative Johnson County," Fortson continued. "They will not like the fact that he kills babies, prevents kids from praying and wants to take their guns."

According to the *Post*, Fortson's secret analysis "described how minority voters would be shifted into Republican-dominated suburban districts." Specifically, black and Hispanic voters in urban communities would be split up and swallowed. "Inner-city Ft. Worth will now be outnumbered in a Republican suburban district," Fortson gloated. If the plan worked, hundreds of thousands of Democratic-leaning metros would find themselves represented by homelander conservatives who shared few of their life experiences or their political values.

In drawing up the new boundaries, Republicans managed to eclipse the state's surging population of urban and Hispanic voters, which by some estimates had jumped by nearly a million people between 2000 and 2003. The plan was so cynical and so patently unfair to minority voters that civil rights attorneys at the U.S. Department of Justice opposed its implementation. Attorney General John Ashcroft, the homelander icon from Missouri, overruled their objections.

Democrats in the Texas legislature tried to filibuster the plan. Throwing dignity to the wind, they fled across the border into Oklahoma, hoping to postpone a vote. A furious Tom DeLay scrambled to locate the fugitives, going so far as to order the Federal Aviation Administration to track them down. (DeLay was later reprimanded for his involvement in the mayhem by a bipartisan House ethics committee.) In the end, Democrats were forced back to Austin and the redistricting scheme approved.

A lawsuit is still pending before the U.S. Supreme Court, but in 2004, Texas Democrats were forced to compete on a battleground designed by their opponents. The result was a predictable thrashing. Democrats lost a third of their seats, dropping from a seventeen-to-fifteen advantage down to a whopping twenty-one-to-eleven deficit. Four veteran Democrats, including Martin Frost, the third-highest-ranking Democrat in Congress, lost their seats. Another changed parties, running as a Republican in order to keep his job. Ironically, the only targeted

Democrat to survive was Chet Edwards, a top figure on DeLay's hit list. He held on by just nine thousand votes in the House district that includes President Bush's Crawford ranch.

The impact of the GOP's national campaign was examined in *Congressional Quarterly*'s 2005 report. The study identified sixty-four so-called mixed districts, where rural and exurban voters made up significant chunks of the population. "Most of these districts were drawn by state legislatures, many of them Republican, often with the aim of assembling territory that would reliably elect one party's candidate to Congress," wrote co-author Bob Benenson.

*Congressional Quarterly*'s study found that Republican candidates were able to win forty-two of the sixty-four specially made districts, a margin that accounts for their entire House majority. Indeed, the GOP's homelander redistricting campaign accounts for all of the party's gains in Congress since 2000. It wasn't ideology. It wasn't big ideas. It wasn't America's rightward cultural shift. It was a cunning use of the party's rural and exurban minority. Without the creation of dozens of new small-town-centered districts, Gingrich's revolution would have vanished completely in 2002.

One footnote about the Republican Party's rural strategy in the House: Redistricting has prolonged GOP control dramatically, but it has also reshaped both parties in ways that could have even more lasting consequences. As Fortson's memo makes clear, Tom DeLay and his underlings worked especially hard to squeeze out white moderates like Chet Edwards and Martin Frost who have long defined the Texas Democratic Party.

This is an important point, so let me repeat it: Conservative strategists weren't targeting liberals. They were hunting primarily for rural and suburban whites, hoping to eliminate Democrats with the kind of crossover appeal that might chip away at the Republican Party's homelander base. Before the 2004 election, ten of Texas's congressional Democrats were white men and seven were black or Hispanic.

But when the electoral ambush was over, the Democratic delegation was made up of five Hispanics, three African Americans, and only three white guys.

It's a brilliant bit of political manipulation. DeLay's plan doesn't just cut the number of Democrats. It also redefines the Democratic Party in a way calculated to make its leadership less appealing to white voters. Republicans get to map the political battlefield, and to an enormous extent they also get to choose their opposition. In the short term this strategy will likely make it even more difficult for progressives to win statewide elections in states like Florida, Georgia, and Texas.

But if anything, high-octane gerrymandering has had an even more profound impact on the Republican Party's identity. While homelanders worked hard after 1994 to anchor themselves at the top of the House hierarchy, new congressional boundaries offered another tool. The handcrafted districts were designed not only to elect more Republicans but also to expand the number of far-right social conservatives.

It works like this. Because the Republican candidate is certain to win the general election, the only real contest comes early in the process, when GOP leaders decide which politician should run. Because homelander activists dominate many local and state nominating committees, they're often able to choose the candidates who reflect their own traditionalist values. Even when primaries are contested, voter turnout is usually low, especially among Republican moderates. A tiny number of zealous conservatives can swing the outcome. As a consequence, many of the "movement conservatives" elected after 1994 hold views well to the right of rank-and-file Republican voters.

This ingenious redistricting formula has one more advantage for homelanders: It has made their communities indispensable to the Republican Party. Because small towns and conservative exurbs anchor a growing number of congressional districts, they're essentially hard-wired into the GOP's electoral strategy.

In 2004 Tom DeLay won reelection by a relatively narrow 55–45 margin, thanks to a massive turnout by loyal homelanders. His situation isn't unique. The Republican Party's rural constituency has been sliced dangerously thin to leverage as many new districts as possible. A minor defection or even a year of low turnout by small-town conservatives could have a ripple effect, devastating the GOP in ways not seen since the early 1930s.

As a consequence, white rural Americans enjoy enormous sway within the party. Far from being the patsies, homelander Americans are now the Republican Party's single most influential voting bloc. They've begun to throw that weight around with increasing abandon —against not only liberals and Democrats but also other factions within the Republican Party. Their indignation shredded any chance that Harriet Miers or Alberto Gonzales would sit on the Supreme Court. Their outrage scotched Dubai's 6.8 billion dollar bid to take over control of American shipping ports, a deal that was hugely popular among corporate leaders. In the 2006 midterm elections, the white rural vote will largely decide whether the Republican Revolution chugs forward or runs off the rails.

# 10

# The Great Schism

Describing rural Americans as a separate minority may sound like a stretch. After all, homelanders are mostly white, mostly Republican, and predominately Christian. That would seem to place them smack at the center of our cultural and political landscape. But the truth is that small-town folk are increasingly *different* from metros, a reality that has made the GOP's rural strategy possible.

Rural whites vote differently, as we've seen, and often hold markedly different social values. They also share life experiences — from education to employment to family life — that differ markedly from those of metros. A 2002 Kellogg Foundation survey found that rural voters prefer right-to-life candidates by significant margins, while in urban and suburban communities pro-choice candidates are widely favored. Forty-two percent of homelanders describe themselves as strong supporters of the National Rifle Association. That compares with just 25 percent nationwide. Rural voters are only half as likely to consider the environment to be a significant political issue.

Over the past quarter century, rural Americans and their leaders have embraced classic identity politics, which tends to exaggerate these attitudinal differences. It's one thing to be Christian and support gun ownership but quite another to think that being Christian or owning a gun is a defining political experience, on a par with being African American. But listen to Bill O'Reilly, Rush Limbaugh, or Pat Robertson and you will hear distinct echoes of Al Sharpton and Jessie Jackson.

Increasingly, rural Americans view themselves as an embattled group that exists outside the mainstream. They feel unfairly marginalized and economically victimized by urban elites. "Let me be very clear about something," declared Tony Perkins, president of the conservative Family Research Council, during a political rally in 2005. "We do not claim the right to speak for every American, but we do claim the right to speak."

In reality, of course, no one has the power to make Perkins shut up. The rally where he spoke, at a Baptist church in Nashville, Tennessee, was attended by Bill Frist and Tom DeLay; at the time, they were two of the most powerful men in America. The program was broadcast in all fifty states on cable channels that reach seventy-nine million households. Few progressive organizations can dream of matching that kind of reach or influence, but homelanders still feel like they've been pushed aside, ignored, and disrespected.

Metros scoff at this sort of thing. How can white male Christians feel besieged and marginalized when they run the country? It must be political posturing or cynical rabble-rousing, equivalent to O'Reilly's claim that there is a "war on Christmas," or the pamphlets distributed during the 2004 election that warned of John Kerry's plan to take away people's Bibles.

There's no doubt that conservative politicians and provocateurs regularly exploit homelander anxieties. "Simply put, we want to bring out the wackos to vote against something and make sure the rest of the public lets the whole thing slip past them," wrote Michael Scanlon, a former aide to Tom DeLay and at the time Jack Abramoff's lobbying partner, in an e-mail made public in 2005. "The wackos get their information [from] the Christian right, Christian radio, e-mail, the Internet and telephone trees."

It's worth pointing out, however, that even many small-town liberals share a growing resentment toward America's urban culture. At a conference in Washington, D.C., in 2005, I listened to the leader of one of the nation's top progressive rural think tanks speak eloquently about the estrangement and isolation experienced by homelanders. He ended by reading a passage from Kentucky essayist Wendell Berry:

I believe it is a fact, proven by their rapidly diminishing numbers and economic power, that the world's small farmers and other "provincial" people have about the same status now as enemy civilians in wartime. The small farmers and the people of small towns are understood as occupying the bottom step of the economic stairway and deservedly falling from it because they are rural, which is to say not metropolitan or cosmopolitan, which is to say socially, intellectually and culturally inferior to "us."

Berry is hardly a Fox News provocateur, yet he describes homelanders as victims of a slow-motion genocide, perpetuated by a callous and callow metro culture. Drive through the hollowed-out hamlets in rural Pennsylvania or the ghost towns of western Kansas and you'll see what he's talking about. You'll discover why so many rural folks believe that they've been abandoned and betrayed. In thousands of small towns, the poverty and malaise are as bad as anything you'll find in inner-city ghettos.

This rural indignation is heightened by the fact that small towns were once prosperous, powerful, and populous places. As recently as the 1950s, we were a nation of homelanders. Many of us lived on farms or were only a generation removed from the land. Farmers, ranchers, and plantation owners filled the ranks of our first political elites. "The American founders were provincials," writes historian Bernard Bailyn, in his essay *Politics and the Creative Imagination.* "[They were] living on the outer borderlands of an Atlantic civilization whose heartlands were the metropolitan centers of England, France, the Netherlands, and Spain."

The world they were born into was so deeply provincial, so derivative in its culture, that it is difficult for us now to imagine it as it really was — difficult for us to reorient our minds to that small, remote world. We cannot avoid reading back our powerful cosmopolitan present, the sense we have of our global authority and our expanded social consciences — reading back all of that into that small, unsure, preindustrial borderland world.

In his study of America's pre-metro society, Bailyn identified traits that still echo powerfully in homelander culture. Even the most powerful rural Americans see themselves as outsiders. They consider themselves uniquely connected to the true vein of national character. As such, they're uniquely qualified to judge and correct the broader society when it goes astray.

"They came to see that their remoteness from the metropolitan world gave them a moral advantage in politics," Bailyn writes. "Uncertain of their place in the established, metropolitan world, they did not think themselves bound by it; they were prepared to challenge it, and, as Thomas Paine put it, to 'begin the world anew.'"

In those days, of course, Europe's great capitals were an ocean away. America's fledgling cities hardly deserved the name. The first U.S. Census taken in 1790 found only half a dozen settlements with populations greater than five thousand people. Our three biggest cities — New York, Boston, and Philadelphia — had fewer than eighty thousand souls between them. They were little more than business centers, bustling port towns where men gathered to trade and conduct the business of government.

Over the next century, America's cities grew steadily, but as late as 1890 there were still only three metropolitan areas in the United States with more than a million people. The real hum of activity was to be found in the throng of dispersed villages and industrial towns, where mills, factories, and farms were fueling the nation's prosperity. Drive through the old hamlets of northern New York and you'll find proud brick facades, oversize churches, main streets laid out in grand style. Most are half-empty now, as derelict as the worst inner city, but it was a confident culture once, rich with experimentation and innovation.

During this long homelander epoch, America established many of the myths, institutions, and political mechanisms that still shape our society. We got used to the idea of politicians who grew up in log cabins rather than West End London townhouses. We grew to like the notion that our politicians came from simple rustic stock, not from an urban aristocracy. It fit our larger self-image of steepled churches, white picket fences, and neighborhoods and wholesome families that looked a certain way.

In those days, my brother's conviction that metro life was somehow unnatural and unwholesome was widely shared, even by the nation's intellectuals. "Cities force growth and make men talkative and entertaining," wrote Ralph Waldo Emerson, "but they make us artificial." As states entered the Union, their citizens were careful to build new capitals at a respectable distance from the crime, disease, and vice of big cities. Jefferson City, Missouri; Austin, Texas; Sacramento, California — these were small administrative hubs established by homelanders who wished to govern at arm's length from the urban mob.

Fortunately, it seemed that America was big enough to keep us sprawled out. We had a continent before us, a land of empty space and opportunity ripe for a people strong and virtuous enough to make it produce. In most small towns, churches were the center of civic life. The Bible and its teachings were standard intellectual equipment. Protestant Christianity was widely accepted as the foundation of public morality, even in our fledgling cities.

The urban-rural cultural divide that we experience today was all but nonexistent. A farmer traveling from the Virginia countryside into Richmond would find social and religious values that closely mirrored his own. He might encounter more vice and temptation than in his home village, but there would still be general agreement on what vice looked like and where such temptations fit in the moral order.

America's traditionalism was widely accepted even among the educated elites. In 1866 the great Harvard scientist and administrator Louis

Agassiz, discoverer of ice ages, returned from an expedition to Brazil claiming to have disproved the theory of evolution. "So there is an end of Darwinian theory," he said complacently, in an address before the National Academy of Sciences. In the 1870s the YMCA (Young Men's Christian Association) operated a Society for the Suppression of Vice, which convinced Congress to ban the trafficking of "obscene material," including information about birth control. In 1882 a district attorney in Boston threatened a publisher with prosecution, forcing him to suppress an edition of Walt Whitman's *Leaves of Grass.*

Many conservatives remember this homelander epoch with longing and regret, as a golden age. Ignoring all its sins of poverty, racism, and discrimination, they see it as a legitimate model for how our society might work in the future. What's more, they believe that traditional society was deliberately corrupted by urban liberals, eclipsed by big-government bureaucrats and academic secularists. Seen from the vantage point of rural Americans, the culture war didn't begin with Pat Buchanan's fiery speech in 1992. The first volleys were fired under Franklin Roosevelt's New Deal in the 1930s, when Democrats embraced a "big government" approach to solving national problems. The rift widened after World War II as small towns began to fall behind economically. The skirmish exploded into open battle during the social revolutions of the 1960s.

This homelander narrative is sort of half correct; the urban-rural culture war is much older than the 1960s. But the ruralist version doesn't go back far enough. The New Deal wasn't the opening salvo in the feud, only an escalation.

In fact, the long chapter of small-town supremacy began to close in the years after the Civil War. The frontier was shrinking rapidly, hemmed in by settlements and railroads. Modern industry was emerging, offering better jobs and higher wages. People began to abandon their farmsteads, crowding into urban neighborhoods in search of new opportunity. They were joined by growing waves of immigrants from overseas.

In the final decades of the nineteenth century, the nation began to sprout cities — not just big trading towns and industrial ports, but full-blown metropolises great enough to rival the capitals of Europe. It wasn't a gradual transformation; it was a revolution, an abrupt reinvention of what it meant to be American. New York City exploded in a single decade from 1.5 million to 3.4 million people. In 1890 there were twenty-eight cities with populations greater than one hundred thousand. By 1900 the number had jumped to thirty-eight. By 1910 it had jumped again to fifty, and for the first time in our history metros outnumbered homelanders. Ethnic ghettos were coming to life in San Francisco, New York, Boston, and New Orleans. Many of the newcomers had come straight from the cities of eastern Europe, South America, and Asia, bringing with them a new urban sensibility.

Homelanders weren't the only ones who felt threatened by the sudden swirl of change. Henry Adams — who was certainly no ruralist — wrote nostalgically about the "conservative Christian" civilization that was being displaced by "the dynamo" of urban modernism. In 1904, he traveled west by train to view the technological marvels of the St. Louis World's Fair and (in the words of historian Edmund Morris) "was struck by the raw power pulsating from landscapes once agricultural, now industrial — steam engines and smokestacks dirtying the air."

It was a violent era, marked by domestic terrorism, ethnic clashes, and street battles between religious groups. Many of the newcomers were Jews and Roman Catholics, groups viewed with suspicion or hatred by America's Protestant majority. The politics of racial and ethnic bigotry were mainstream. As late as the 1920s, Harvard president Lawrence Lowell felt comfortable stating openly that the admission of too many Jews would ruin his university: "The summer hotel that is ruined by admitting Jews meets its fate," he declared, "because they drive away the Gentiles, and then after the Gentiles have left, [the Jews] leave also."

Through it all America's cities kept growing. In every decade of the twentieth century, the nation became more urbanized. Three million new metros poured into cities and inner suburbs every year. Meanwhile, after 1930 small towns began losing population at the remarkable rate of two hundred thousand people every year, an exodus that continues to this day. This demographic upheaval echoed through American culture in a thousand ways. Men were leaving the farms, going to work in factories and shops and offices. Women, too, were leaving home, setting aside more traditional roles and making careers as secretaries, clerks, and factory hands. Between 1870 and 1900 the number of women working in offices grew from nineteen thousand to more than half a million.

These changes weren't the work of social theorists; they were the result of changes in technology that reshaped whole industries. A new urban middle class began to emerge, flush with unheard of luxuries like leisure time and disposable income. The automobile had arrived, and Americans were on the move, leaving their hometowns in search of opportunity. The first skyscrapers were going up, crowned not with crosses but with radio antennas, which crackled to life, spreading the influence of cities far beyond the horizon. It was fascinating, confusing, and terrifying.

D. W. Griffith's classic film *Birth of a Nation*, released in 1915, wasn't only a screed against African Americans; it was an indictment of the flood of change sweeping American society. President Woodrow Wilson praised the film. The same year, St. Louis native T. S. Eliot published "The Love Song of J. Alfred Prufrock," a poem that in Stephen Spender's description "provides metaphors for the squalor (and the mystery and the beauty) of a city unnamed, which nevertheless seems representative of other great cities. It is the universal temporal city of modern Western civilization."

> Let us go, through certain half-deserted streets,
> The muttering retreats
> Of restless nights in one-night cheap hotels.

But if some intellectuals were uncertain about the new urban modernism, others began to question the merits of rural life. A kind of metro backlash emerged as artists kicked against the restraints of traditional sensibilities. "The common characteristic of the remarkable group of [American] novelists who became famous in the 1920s," wrote the literary critic Alfred Kazin, "is that they were all from the Midwest, provincials seeking in the city a philosophy from which to attack the old values."

> The symbolic novel of the period, at least in America, was against the small town and embraced the excitement of the big city. The symbolic heroine was the "emancipated" woman; the symbolic crusade was against snoopers and vice-leaguers and book-censors.

Novelists weren't the only ones raising uncomfortable questions. Scientists, scholars, politicians, and artists began to poke at the facade of America's traditional culture. *American Gothic*, the famous painting by Grant Wood, appeared in 1930. It depicts a spartan house, with a stark and puritanical couple planted in the foreground. Their mulelike faces look rugged and bland. These days, the painting is seen as a classic bit of Americana, but to homelanders of the day, it felt like mockery. Outraged farmers in Iowa threatened the painter with physical injury. "*American Gothic* appeared to its first viewers as the visual equivalent of the revolt-against-the-provinces genre in 1910s and 1920s American literature," wrote Harvard historian Steven Biel, in his book about the painting.

If artists were edging away from rural culture, so were other institutions. Public schools were being established with a new philosophy of instruction shaped by secular academics, such as John Dewey at the University of Chicago. The big Ivy League universities, founded by Protestant congregations in the seventeenth, eighteenth, and nineteenth centuries, were feeling their way toward a more independent, secular identity. "Most were Bible-believing schools inspired by revivalists, precursors of today's evangelical Protestants," writes Richard Ostling, a religion correspondent for the Associated Press. "Yet in the 20th century [American universities] came to embrace thorough secularism, even hostility toward traditional belief."

The revolutionary concept of "cultural pluralism" emerged, holding that different civilizations might embrace different but equally legitimate values. This worldview offered a profoundly different framework for seeing the world, a framework that was decidedly at odds with the missionary ideals of Protestant Christianity. A half-century before, the nation's freethinkers had been harmless iconoclasts and entertainers, men like Whitman, Mark Twain, and the early secularist Robert Ingersoll.

But after 1900, academics, scientists, and artists trained in the urban tradition began to assume new confidence and influence. As Louis Menand describes it in *The Metaphysical Club*, his intellectual history of the United States, the new generation was devoted to "an unsentimental effort to reduce the explanation of phenomena to the physical laws of cause and effect, to restrict the scope of knowledge to things that can be measured."

> It meant doing without the hypothesis of a god — not only in the case of stars and rocks and fishes, but since Darwin, in the case of human beings as well. Squaring this enterprise with moral principles understood by most Americans to derive from divine revelation and to depend on the existence of a faculty of free will in human beings was a tricky business.

Tricky indeed. In 1925 the simmering tension between homelander society and the new metro upstarts boiled over in one of the most famous cultural confrontations in American history. John Scopes, a twenty-four-year-old teacher and football coach, was accused of violating Tennessee state law. His crime was telling high school students about Darwin's theory of biological evolution. But the trial wasn't a contest over natural selection (the judge refused to allow any substantial testimony about the theory's scientific merits). Rather, the case was widely seen as a fight over the soul of modern America. Who would set the parameters for popular culture? Would it be the traditionalists, who believed in the sacred origins of the Bible and the fixity of Christian dogma, or would it be the modernists and academics, thinkers who placed reason above faith?

Championing the homelander side was William Jennings Bryan from Nebraska. He was an old man in 1925, but for three decades Bryan had reigned over the Democratic Party. He was a daring progressive and a kind of folk hero, known as the "great commoner" and the "boy orator of the Platte." But he was also a devout ruralist and an evangelical Christian. In a speech before the trial, Bryan told an adoring crowd, "The contest between evolution and Christianity is a duel to the death. If evolution wins, Christianity goes."

The metro cause was taken up by a brilliant attorney named Clarence Darrow. The two men shared many of the same political convictions; in fact, Darrow supported Bryan in two of his failed campaigns for the White House. But their allegiance had ruptured over the issue of Darwinism and public Christianity. (Darrow was also disgusted with Bryan's refusal to disavow the Klan's resurgence in the South.) "I have always felt that doubt was the beginning of wisdom," he said, "and the fear of God was the end of wisdom."

In those days, Dayton, Tennessee, was a tiny southern town, population eleven hundred. The audience for the spectacle, however, was national. Correspondents from a dozen big-city newspapers and even a few radio stations crowded the village. H. L. Mencken covered the trial for *American Mercury* and the Baltimore *Sun*. He lost no time declaring his loyalties, dismissing Bryan as a "tinpot pope in the Coca-Cola belt and a brother to forlorn pastors who belabor halfwits in galvanized iron tabernacles behind the railroad yards."

Urban culture was in its adolescence, smart-mouthed and bare-
knuckled, and often insufferably callow. Throughout the trial, Bryan
and his supporters were regularly mocked and lampooned. Mencken's
dispatches portrayed the people of Dayton in bluntly prejudiced
terms, as "primates," "morons," and "yokels." He described their religious and cultural convictions (which had shaped American society
over the previousast fifteen decades) as "fundamentalist rubbish."

To no one's surprise, Bryan won the case; the jury was made up of
local farmers and shopkeepers. Scopes was duly convicted and
ordered to pay a fine, though the penalty was later dismissed on a
technicality. But in urban America the outcome was widely reinterpreted as a metro victory. Darrow had grilled Bryan about his belief
that the Scriptures were literally true, that biblical miracles had
occurred exactly as described in the pages of the New and Old
Testament. In the metro press, Bryan's views were made to look idi-
otic and out-of-date. It seemed that traditional Christian culture had
been exposed for its inherent contradictions and hypocrisy.

"Legislators might go on passing anti-evolutionary laws," wrote
*Harper's* editor and historian Frederick Allen Lewis, "and in the hinterlands the pious might still keep their religion locked up in a science-
proof compartment of their minds; but civilized opinion everywhere
had regarded the Dayton trial with amazement and amusement and
the slow drift away from Fundamentalist certainty continued."

In the glow of triumph, metro culture overlooked the fact that
homelanders saw the outcome very differently. After all, Scopes *was*
convicted. And if Bryan's opinions sounded primitive to urban audiences, they were still perfectly mainstream in small-town America.
Far from feeling defeated, Christian activists were delighted by the
proceedings in Dayton. "The Scopes trial actually energized religious
anti-evolutionists," writes historian Susan Jacoby in her book
*Freethinkers.* "The outcome and the publicity surrounding it led
many — arguably most — American secularists to underestimate
the vitality of fundamentalism."

The Scopes trial represents one of the first great schisms in America's self-awareness, when the two tribes of our culture began to see the same events through a radically different lens. Compounding the muddle was the fact that Bryan died only a week after the trial. His sudden and dramatic collapse "was frequently used as a metaphor for the death of the ideas he represented," according to Jacoby. "That was the way things looked from Harvard Square and Greenwich Village."

But in the rush to judge homelander culture, metros missed one other important reality. It emerges like bits of dusty light through the cracks in Mencken's ugly prose. Mencken's honesty as a journalist forced him to observe that the trial's audience in Dayton, Tennessee, was attentive and even open-minded. People argued and they prayed, but they also listened. The folks who should have played the role of rubes and yokels roared with approval when sound arguments were made on either side.

"The town, I confess, greatly surprised me," Mencken wrote. "I expected to find a squalid Southern village, with darkies snoozing on the horse blocks, pigs rooting under the houses and the inhabitants full of hookworm and malaria. What I found was a country town of charm and even beauty."

## 11

# The Curse of the Cities

If the first half of the twentieth century was a demographic earthquake, the decades after the Second World War brought a full-scale tectonic shift. In 1950 roughly half of the American population still lived in small towns. Thomas Jefferson could have traveled through much of his beloved nation and found people living by the rituals of field and barn and church that were common in his own day.

But by 2000, eight out of ten Americans were living in cities or suburbs. A third of the nation's population had settled in just ten supersized urban-suburban clusters. As if that weren't enough change for one society, the postwar period brought another fundamental break between the two cultures. Before the 1940s, America's rural communities were often more racially diverse than were the cities. Half the country's African Americans lived in small towns, mostly in the South. Between 1940 and 1970, however, five million blacks streamed north looking for a better life in urban neighborhoods. "The black migration was one of the largest and most rapid mass internal movements of people in history," wrote Nicholas Lemann, in his book *The Promised Land.*

Lemann describes the Illinois Central train station in Chicago as the Ellis Island of the black migration. When the wave crested, that one midwestern city was welcoming seven hundred new African American residents every single day. Blacks were also pouring into Detroit, New York City, Philadelphia, and Washington, D.C., searching for higher wages, better living conditions, and freedom. They were changing the geography of race in American life: "In 1970, when the migration ended," Lemann wrote, "*urban* had become a euphemism for *black.*"

This new racial dichotomy is striking. Homelander communities are often 90–95 percent white. But in cities like Newark, New Jersey, it's not uncommon for 80–90 percent of the citizens to be African American or Hispanic. As previously discussed, our Constitution favors one of these cultures (white, rural, conservative) over the other (ethnically diverse, urban, progressive). Alaska's senator Ted Stevens, a Republican, represents roughly the same number of people as Cory Booker, Newark's recently elected Democratic mayor. While Stevens is one of the most powerful and influential men in America (he wears Incredible Hulk ties on the floor of the U.S. Senate and is famous for his tantrums), Booker is largely unknown outside his home state.

But if homelanders enjoy enormous political advantages, metros have often dominated the culture wars. The tough street culture of Mencken's era has grown up into a full-blown consumer culture, a constantly whirring dynamo of fashion and experimentation, racial and cultural mingling, self-reinvention and industry. In the process, a thousand different rural institutions have come under siege.

Long before same-sex marriage made headlines, divorce was altering our traditional idea of marriage almost beyond recognition. Widely available contraception cleared the way for a revolution in the way we experience human sexuality, disrupting puritanical values that were the norm until a few decades ago. Driven by the realities of their multi-cultural lives, metros demanded that more Americans — minorities, women, gays and lesbians, people with mental and physical disabilities — be welcomed as equal members of the community.

"In the short space of fifty or so years, profound scientific, techno-logical, cultural, and social developments had so changed the condi-tions of life that one felt separated from the previous four hundred years by a wide gap," wrote Thomas Bokenkotter, in his history of the Roman Catholic Church.

The vast majority of Americans view these changes as progress. It's indisputable that people today are freer, healthier, better educated, and more prosperous than they were when the country's urban century began. But recent decades have brought social tumult and emotional confusion, as traditional roles change and old codes of behavior are discarded. "So many spiritual and religious landmarks were suddenly swept away that the average Catholic was left in a state of complete bewilderment," Bokenkotter writes. It's a description that could apply to traditionalists across America's rural landscape:

> No doubt this sense of uprootedness is simply one manifestation of a general feeling common to everyone today and so well described by Alvin Toffler in his *Future Shock* and attributed to the constant acceleration of change affecting every aspect of our lives — not only religion, Toffler says, but all the old roots, family, nation, community, and profession are "shaking under the hurricane impact of accelerative thrust."

One of the markers of this "constant acceleration" has been America's changing relationship to public Christianity. For most of our history, Protestant faith and prayer were widely accepted aspects of civic life. Occasionally, this led to trouble, as different Christian sects feuded over the kinds of religious doctrine that should be allowed in the village square. In the 1830s, Missouri churches waged pogroms against settlers from the Church of Jesus Christ of Latter-Day Saints, slaughtering seventeen people at a place called Haun's Mill. (A generation later, Mormons would return the bloody favor, slaughtering 120 mainline Protestant pioneers in Utah.) In 1844, Protestants and Catholics rioted for three days in Philadelphia following an argument over which version of the Bible should be read in public school classrooms. At least twenty people were killed, and two Roman Catholic churches were burned to the ground. In 1921, after consultations with Christian missionaries, the federal government issued an order describing Native American religious ceremonies as "Indian offenses" and established "corrective penalties" to discourage them.

In the 1950s, Congress added the phrase "one nation under God" to America's Pledge of Allegiance. Metros often describe the change as a bit of Cold War hysteria, but in those days government-sanctioned prayers were often spoken aloud by children in public schools. "Almighty God, we acknowledge our dependence upon Thee and beg Thy blessings upon us, our teachers, and our country," read the prayer penned by New York state's board of regents.

Most Americans saw nothing out of order in these small acts of civic worship, but in 1962 the tide began to turn. The Supreme Court ruled 7–1 that school prayer violated the establishment of religion clause of the First Amendment. "It is neither sacrilegious nor anti-religious to say that each separate government in this country should stay out of the business of writing or sanctioning official prayers," wrote Justice Hugo Black, "and leave that purely religious function to the people themselves and to those the people choose to look to for religious guidance."

Many Christians were outraged: "This is another step toward the secularization of the United States," declared evangelist Billy Graham. "The framers of our Constitution meant we were to have freedom of religion, not freedom *from* religion."

In the decades that followed, the federal courts systematically purged overt Christian influences from most of our public institutions. In 1980 the justices ruled that it was unconstitutional to post the Ten Commandments on school grounds. Five years later, they banned school-sanctioned moments of silence, if they were specifically intended to encourage prayer.

In 1989 nativity scenes were banished from school grounds. In 1992 the justices ruled 5–4 that it was unconstitutional for clergy to offer prayers at official public school graduation ceremonies. In 2000 the Supreme Court took the additional step of banning prayer at the beginning of school sporting events.

Metros often describe the strict separation of church and state as the product of a constitutional firewall designed to protect our civic institutions from overt sectarian influences. But homelanders claim quite rightly that American democracy survived without this interpretation for nearly two centuries without falling into theocracy. The notion that our founding fathers were secular thinkers in the modern sense is ridiculous; they were farmers and provincial gentlemen, living in a society where Protestant faith was a basic assumption of daily life.

Traditionalists like Supreme Court justice Antonin Scalia are convinced that no such legal separation exists and that democracy requires a Christian foundation. "The moral order is ordained by God," Scalia argued, in a January 2005 speech delivered to the Knights of Columbus in Baton Rouge, Louisiana. "To say that that's the basis for the Declaration of Independence and our institutions is entirely realistic.... [T]he minority has to be tolerant of the majority's ability to express its belief that government comes from God."

Scalia urged his audience to embrace traditional views, even when they fly in the face of modern thinking: "Have the courage to have your wisdom regarded as stupidity. Be fools for Christ. And have the courage to suffer the contempt of the sophisticated world."

This conviction about Christianity's role in public life is increasingly common in homelander circles. In March 2006, state lawmakers in Missouri introduced legislation that would recognize Christianity as the official state religion.

The trouble, of course, is that America has changed profoundly from the days of the nineteenth century, when a broad Christian consensus existed. Today as many as one-third of Americans no longer believe in Christianity in any form, with a rapidly growing slice of the population made up of Hindus, Muslims, atheists, and New Agers. (According to a survey by researchers at the City University of New York, the number of Wiccans in America jumped from 8,000 in 1990 to more than 134,000 in 2001.) An even bigger chunk of the population holds Christian views that would have seemed bizarre and heretical in the 1780s.

Metro thinkers and policymakers understand this reality. America is a messy stew of competing interests and values. In their clumsy way, urban intellectuals have dragged the nation into a modernist, multicultural interpretation of the Constitution. An essentially traditional document has been reinterpreted to reflect a dizzying diversity of races and religions.

In a 2000 decision that restricted Christian prayer at sporting events sponsored by public schools, Justice John Paul Stevens wrote that "sponsorship of a religious message is impermissible because it [tells] members of the audience who are non-adherents that they are outsiders." This argument might have seemed intrusive and heavy-handed in 1850 — or perhaps even in 1950 — but these days it's possible to find urban neighborhoods where the predominant faith is Judaism or Islam or Buddhism. It's even easier to find secular parents who have no interest in exposing their children to a government-sanctioned religious message in the classroom.

The truth is, a lot of us who are Christian don't necessarily like our neighbor's version of Christianity. There's a huge amount of disagreement, even among conservative Christians, over what their faith means. Many Protestant sects still aren't convinced that Mormons share a legitimate claim to salvation. Allen's Lutheran denomination refuses to share worship with other Christians, let alone other believers from other faiths. Many Roman Catholic churches refuse sacrament to Protestants.

This all looks very different in homelander America, where the Christian consensus remains largely intact in small towns. In rural communities like Saranac Lake, New York (or Dover, Pennsylvania), there's plenty of grumbling between Protestants and Catholics, but the landscape of faith still looks very much like it did a century ago. In Longton, Kansas, you don't go to baseball games and find sizable Jewish populations in the stands. There aren't clusters of proud mothers in Perryton, Texas, wearing saris at high school graduation ceremonies.

Stripped of the urban context, the secularization of America begins to feel like an unnecessary provocation. It's not a natural, pragmatic response to a changing society, or the logical evolution of an increasingly diverse culture, but a brazen attack on traditional sensibilities and time-honored customs. It's one more culture war outrage, perpetrated by a misguided, and probably malicious, urban society.

Conversely, urban Americans often view the homelander mingling of faith and politics as frightening — an evangelical Christian version of *sharia*, Islam-derived law. "Liberal columnist E. R. Shipp said conservatives wanted a 'Christian jihad,'" wrote Stephen Waldman, cofounder of a popular on-line faith discussion forum called Beliefnet, in a column for *Slate*. "The *Village Voice* declared Bush had a 'mandate for theocracy.' Others have compared the current administration to the Taliban."

> This is profoundly insulting to most conservative Republicans in the same way that it is insulting to liberals when they are called Communists or defenders of terrorism. Yes, religious conservatives want a greater role in public life — perhaps more than liberals want or the Constitution allows — but President Bush's faith-based initiative is highly pluralistic and he has spoken out for religious tolerance. Equating him or his supporters with regimes that execute dissidents or blow up buildings is heinous.

The vast majority of homelanders don't want a theocracy, but social conservatives do insist that we interpret our founding documents in a very different way than metros are accustomed to. This deep ideological difference is laid bare in the bitter dispute over the meaning of the U.S. Constitution.

What makes the Constitution so compelling to urban Americans is that it seems to offer a framework fluid enough to accommodate the changing needs of a modern society. It's not dogma or revealed truth but a set of guiding principles. This legal philosophy has shaped Supreme Court decisions from the mid-1930s, when Franklin Delano Roosevelt bullied justices into approving much of his New Deal legislation.

The classic articulation of this metro approach was written by Chief Justice Earl Warren in 1954 as part of the decision known as *Brown v. Board of Education.* The Supreme Court had been asked to review the constitutionality of segregated schools. Black children were being ghettoized in appalling, run-down buildings. They had few qualified teachers, few supplies. The central figure in the case was a black third grader in Topeka, Kansas, named Linda Brown, who was forced to walk a mile through a rail yard to reach her segregated elementary school.

Linda's father tried to enter her in a white elementary school just seven blocks from their home, but the principal turned the family away. The NAACP sued, demanding an end to segregation in Topeka's schools. The Topeka board of education argued initially that separate schools were the best way to prepare black kids for American life, claiming that racially divided schools made sense in a racially divided society. Later, local officials insisted that black schools were being brought up to code so that the two parallel institutions would be "separate but equal."

The Constitution and the Fourteenth Amendment (which guarantees "equal protection" to all Americans regardless of race) offered no guidance on public education. Strict constructionists argued that the courts and the federal government in general had no right to intervene. But Warren insisted that Americans should *build* upon the Constitution's legal framework, working in the light of modern-day values and circumstances.

"In approaching this problem, we cannot turn the clock back to 1868, when the Amendment was adopted," he wrote. "We must consider public education in the light of its full development and its present place in American life throughout the nation. Only in this way can it be determined if segregation in public schools deprives these plaintiffs of the equal protection of the laws."

It was the epitome of judicial activism. In one stroke a group of nine unelected justices — the "robed oligarchy" despised by modern-day conservatives — had begun the slow toppling of segregation. The decision was hugely unpopular in the South and still ranks with *Roe v. Wade* as one of the half-dozen most controversial decisions in U.S. history. "It may be just or wise or expedient for Negro children to attend the same schools as white children," wrote Barry Goldwater, in *The Conscience of a Conservative,* "but they do not have a civil right to do so which is protected by the federal constitution, or which is enforceable by the federal government."

The practical results of Warren's decision are beyond dispute. After three hundred years of isolation and vicious persecution, African Americans have moved over the course of a few decades into mainstream society. The nation has a thriving black middle class. Despite white flight and the continuing dilemma of segregation, our schools and other public institutions are multiracial to a degree that our grandfathers (let alone our founding fathers) would have found baffling.

Metros see this outcome as proof that a flexible interpretation of the Constitution is both legitimate and necessary. Writing in the *New Yorker,* Jeffrey Toobin summarized the legal philosophy of liberals like Justice Stephen Breyer who argue "that the framers never intended for future generations of jurists to resolve contemporary controversies by guessing how the framers themselves would have resolved them. Instead, their goal was to promote what Breyer, quoting the nineteenth-century French political writer Benjamin Constant, calls 'active and constant participation in collective power' — in other words, 'active liberty.'"

This essentially progressive idea offends traditionalists. It's not that they want a return to racial apartheid, but they are convinced that the *Brown* decision and others like it violated important principles, doing far more harm than good. "In effect," Goldwater wrote, "the Court said that what matters is not the ideas of the men who wrote the Constitution, but the Court's ideas. It was only by engrafting its own views onto the established law of the land that the Court was able to reach its decisions."

From the homelander perspective, decisions like *Brown* and *Roe* moved America away from an authentic reading of the Constitution, knocking us off our political foundation. We gained a measure of social justice but at the cost of a broken society, where established laws and traditional principles were vulnerable to all manner of radical tinkering. It's important to note that conservatives see this shift as fundamentally anti-democratic. Rather than achieving social progress through political activism, ballot box victories, and formal amendments to the Constitution, liberals were remaking American society on the cheap, through litigation and the decisions of a handful of "activist" judges.

From the perspective of traditionalists, the Constitution wasn't meant to serve as a progressive document. It wasn't crafted to inspire greater freedoms — in fact, just the opposite. According to home-landers, the founding fathers established clear boundaries and restrictions on the exercise of federal power, preventing the government from meddling with churches or guns or free speech or private property rights. Conservatives believe that America was *meant* to have a weak central government, incapable of overstepping its original role.

In recent years, this understanding of the Constitution has been colored by rural conservatives who want to go much further. They see America's founding documents — the Constitution, the Declaration of Independence and the Bill of Rights — not only as a limitation on government but also as a sort of political dogma, one that institutionalizes Christianity.

"Those who wrote the Constitution believed that morality was essential to the well-being of society and that encouragement of religion was the best way to foster morality," wrote Justice Scalia, in a June 2005 argument against the removal of a Ten Commandments monument from Kentucky courthouses. "The fact that the Founding Fathers believed devotedly that there was a God and that the unalienable rights of man were rooted in Him is clearly evidenced in their writings, from the Mayflower Compact to the Constitution itself."

To support his argument, Scalia quoted a letter written by President John Adams in 1798 to the Massachusetts Militia: "Our Constitution was made only for a moral and religious people. It is wholly inadequate to the government of any other." This claim, that America is a fundamentally Christian nation, surfaces again and again in homelander literature. Tour the Internet and you'll find Christian prophecy sites that intertwine American political history with biblical revelation. "[I] support the Constitution of the United States as the framework for establishing the kingdom of God on earth," writes one preacher.

Most Americans find this notion deeply unnerving, and with good reason. Some of the most powerful politicians in America believe that the Constitution should be used to codify a version of ruralist Christian values that few of us share. "Our entire system is built on the Judeo-Christian ethic, but it fell apart when we started denying God," Tom DeLay told the *Washington Post's* Peter Perl in 2001. The chief objective of the Republican Party, in DeLay's opinion, was "to bring us back to the Constitution and to Absolute Truth that has been manipulated and destroyed by a liberal worldview."

> I ask DeLay [Perl wrote] about the many citizens who would be quite uncomfortable with the idea that he would mold the government in the belief that his religion — fundamentalist Christianity — had the only answers to society's problems. DeLay looks me squarely in the eye and shakes his head sadly. "When faced with the truth, the truth hurts. It is human nature not to face that. . . . People hate the messenger. That's

why they killed Christ." And so Tom DeLay makes it perfectly clear that his personal mission is to reshape the moral fabric of the nation, to remake it more in his likeness.

This point of view is now held by at least four members of the U.S. Supreme Court. Samuel Alito, Antonin Scalia, John Roberts, and Clarence Thomas aren't "conservative" in the sense that they support governmental restraint — quite the opposite. They're convinced that the Constitution should serve the end of restoring virtue and Christian decency to America's civic life. "I believe very strongly," wrote Samuel Alito, "in . . . the legitimacy of a government role in protecting traditional values."

It's clear that this homelander activism falls well outside the American mainstream. Even many devout Christians prefer to approach their faith as a personal choice. They don't want their religion served up as a part of the nation's political establishment. They prefer to shop around for their churches, searching for the message that fits their individual sensibility. They also want plenty of room to live their lives outside the church without having its rules forced on them. We might be Roman Catholic, but we take birth control pills just like everybody else. We might be evangelical Christians, but we still get divorced and live together outside of marriage.

Indeed, one aspect of modern American life that troubles rural conservatives is the comfortable way that city folk have settled into their new urban identities. Only a few decades removed from the farm, our society has adapted to the constant churn and re-invention. We're not liberal exactly. One of the reasons I ginned up new labels for our two national tribes — metro and homelander — is that the old categories don't seem to fit very well.

These days, a lot of my urban friends are remarkably conservative on fiscal questions. I don't know anyone outside the hard-left fringe who thinks that massive Great Society poverty programs should be revived wholesale. At cocktail parties and conferences in Washington and Boston and New York City, I find academics and journalists talking comfortably about the eventual phasing out of affirmative action and the partial success of welfare-to-work initiatives. Their bitterness about George W. Bush and the Republican Congress has almost as much to do with soaring budget deficits as it does the Patriot Act and the Iraq War.

But these same urban-minded folks tend to be increasingly open-minded on social issues. They have gay and lesbian friends, many of them staid, middle-aged folk who've been "married" since Ronald Reagan was in the White House. Even churchgoing Christians in urban areas are living far more flexible lives outside the boundaries of traditional morality. They live together without getting married. They have children out of wedlock. They see tolerance, rather than judgment, as Christianity's chief virtue.

Metros are often deeply moral in their own way, but the well-springs of their values tend to be complicated and diverse. They might draw wisdom from the New Testament and also from a Philip Roth novel, from the Talmud and from a poem by Billy Collins. They are by nature experimental. They browse, they pick and choose, and (the worst sin of all, in the eyes of homelanders) they change.

"Unfortunately, familiarity with traditionally hallowed writings tends to breed, not indeed contempt," wrote the British writer Aldous Huxley, "but something which, for practical purposes, is almost as bad — namely a kind of reverential insensibility, a stupor of the spirit. . . ." This notion, which is antithetical to homelander culture, pervades the urban sensibility, where newness and innovation are cardinal virtues. Metros see everything as negotiable; change and motion are inevitable, while sameness and dogma are viewed as deeply suspect.

Information is a premium commodity in urban society, to be sure, but no one expects to discover "the truth." The great astronomer Raymond Lyttleton wrote lovingly and with precision about the construction of the universe. But when confronted with the question, "What is the meaning and object of it all?" he answered bluntly: "There is no indication whatsoever in the whole cosmos that there is any discernible purpose at all."

It's revealing that one of the most popular American books in 2005 was Joan Didion's memoir *The Year of Magical Thinking*. Didion describes the abrupt and devastating death of her husband and daughter. The essential architecture of her life, happiness, and self-meaning were reduced to rubble — a tale to rival the tribulations of Job. But in typical metro fashion, Didion's sources of understanding and comfort (if that's the right word) are remarkably diverse. There is a respectful nod to Christianity but also a reliance on poetry and science and an intensely personal reflection, which seems to have little in common with the homelander concept of prayer.

In the end, Didion's conclusion is profoundly modernist: "The craziness is receding but no clarity is taking its place," she writes. "I look for resolution and find none."

To rural Americans, who look to their cultural sources for certainty and firm assurance, this sounds like an admission of failure, a capitulation. But the willingness to leave a question unanswered — or to answer it with another question — is one of the revolutionary aspects of urban relativism. The hero of this society isn't someone who defends the old order or insists upon ultimate truth but, rather, the thinker who breaks the rules and looks honestly at a thing, even if the outcome is harsh or disquieting or ambiguous.

It's the domain of the scientist, the clown, the rebel and the intellectual. In this world, breaking down traditional barriers makes sense. Transgression is seen as a creative act, a form of experimentation and even play. Whether it's Abbie Hoffman yipping it up in front of the cameras at the Chicago Democratic National Convention in 1968, a crucifix dunked in a jug of urine, flamboyant drag queens at a gay pride parade in Atlanta, or a portrayal of Jesus' sexual awakening in

*The Last Temptation of Christ*, this is the way urban culture breaks new ground.

Obviously, most metros don't embrace this sort of thing intellectually or even consciously. A tiny percentage of New York City's population will ever drift through the twisting galleries of the Guggenheim, scrutinizing the experiments of Jackson Pollock. But a remarkable amount of this urban sensibility has been internalized, accepted as a matter of course as part of America's youth-corporate-urban culture. It's revealing that rapper Snoop Dog can turn up in a Chrysler advertisement with corporate icon Lee Iacocca and no one bats an eye. Dan Brown wrote a novel that played fast and loose with the basic tenets of Christian faith — and sold more than sixty million copies, according to his publisher. We're used to this irreverent, mix-and-match reality. New industries, religions, communities, and fads come and go. Our urban skylines are expected to rise and fall like the stock market. We change careers, looking for better opportunities. We change churches, picking the message and the vision of salvation that suits our taste. We even change families, divorcing and remarrying, having abortions, sharing kids between households.

This sort of thing appalls homelanders and their intellectual allies, who view ideas and behaviors that are increasingly common in metro life as symptomatic of a dangerous moral drift. "The nation we live in today is more violent and vulgar, coarse and cynical, rude and remorseless, deviant and depressed, than the one we once inhabited," wrote William Bennett.

The new pope, Benedict XVI, who grew up in a village in Bavaria, wrote that the greatest threat to Western civilization isn't racial hatred or militarism or genocide, but "a dictatorship of relativism . . . that recognizes nothing definite and leaves only one's ego and one's desire as the final measure."

When I talk about the metro sensibility with my brother, he can barely contain his unease. "It sounds like anarchy to me," Allen says. He's a loyal St. Louis Cardinals fan, and he subscribes to the *St. Louis*

*Post-Dispatch,* but his loyalties lie with the abstract idea of rural America — not with his own metropolitan hub. "I would rather live in any small town than in a city. *Any* small town. It doesn't matter where it is."

This kind of rejection leaves metros shaking their heads. It's true, of course, that big-city culture sometimes erupts into disorder and violence, from the urban riots and protests of 1968 to the crack epidemic of the 1980s to the gang violence that still plagues American cities. There is a constant (and sometimes exhausting) struggle for balance in urban life, a hunger for meaning and community that leaves many people deeply unsatisfied.

But for all the angst in Woody Allen's films, or the gun-crazy vice on the nightly news, the end product of urban modernism often feels remarkably *normal.* "The realization that Negroes are no better nor no worse, and at times just as boring as everybody else, will hardly kill off the population of the nation," wrote Zora Neale Hurston in the 1950s.

Urbanites today feel much the same way about most of the hobgoblins and bugbears that frighten their rural neighbors. We accept the idea that one generation's bra burners will be the next generation's corporate leaders (and grannies). Hip-hop artists talk like fierce "gangstas," but what they really want is their own apparel line. The guy marching in the gay pride parade will be in his cubicle tomorrow processing tax returns.

An acquaintance of mine used to moonlight in New York City producing phone sex recordings (this was before the Internet wiped out that particular cottage industry), and he summed up urban gay culture with a shrug: "Unlike heterosexuals, they pay their bills on time."

The fact is that metro America hasn't imploded or disintegrated into chaos. All the homelander prophecies of collapse, urban decay, and chaos simply haven't materialized, a fact that causes social conservatives

no end to discomfort. In 1999, William Bennett published an awkward
little book called *The Index of Leading Cultural Indicators*. I call it awkward because the book's rhetoric is almost pathologically dire (the
quote offered above — "rude and remorseless," "deviant and
depressed," and so on — comes from its pages) but the statistical snapshot of modern life is unavoidably upbeat.

After seven years with a Democratic president in the White House,
crime rates were plummeting, drug use was down, far fewer women
were having abortions, and the number of Americans on welfare had
been slashed. "Over the last few years, I have amended some of my
own prior views about the efficacy of politics and public policy,"
Bennett conceded, managing to sound both arrogant and sheepish.

> It turns out that some social pathologies are less resistant to
> legislative action and political leadership than I once thought.
> Consider two examples: the extraordinary transformation of
> New York City, which was once thought to be virtually
> ungovernable and the enormous drop in the welfare caseload
> following the passage of reform legislation. In short, problems
> that were once considered all but intractable have yielded to
> well-conceived and executed reforms.

By almost any measure, American society is more just, more equi-
table, more prosperous than ever before in our history. In the
decades since Jim Crow was abolished, the black middle class has
blossomed. Women have been welcomed into public and professional life, and can now claim an astounding degree of equality. Yet
despite these gains, Bennett can't help but look for the storm cloud
behind the silver lining.

> In two generations, America has undergone dramatic and
> traumatic social change — the kind that one would normally
> associate with cataclysmic natural events like famine, revolu-

tion, or war. Civilizations stand on precious few pillars, and during the last three and a half decades, many of ours have fractured. Although we have learned to live with the situation, much as one might learn to live with a thorn deeply embedded in the flesh, it is important to remind ourselves periodically just how much ground we have lost.

The simple fact that we have "learned to live with the situation" dismays traditionalists. James Dobson — founder of the Focus on the Family media empire, headquartered in exurban Colorado Springs, Colorado — tells the story of receiving thousands of letters from American teenage girls, more blasé every year about premarital sex. "[At first] they would write and say, 'Who says it's wrong?'" according to Dobson. "And they would argue. They don't do that now. They write and say, 'That's okay for you.' 'That's alright if it's your view.' 'It doesn't happen to be my view.' 'We all have to make up our own minds.'"

Many of the urban parents I know would count it a success if their girls were this smart, this well adjusted, and this empowered. We want our kids to make good choices, but from the homelander vantage point, those kids are flying blind, with no references, no sure compass. "Post-modernism says there is no God and there is no eternal standard, there are no rules," Dobson says. "That notion that there is no moral law to the universe has taken hold and taken root like cancer that's spread through this entire nation. It continues to spread. MTV works on it every single day."

Dobson is correct in one respect at least: The urban-modernist sensibility life *has* become the norm. We've become a culture of experimenters and individualists. The credo of "Life, liberty, and the pursuit of happiness" may have been invented by a bunch of white farmers, but it turns out to be a devilishly modernist concept, one we've taken to with gusto. Since the closing of the West in the late

1800s, cities have served as our new frontier. People still flood into places like Atlanta, Houston, New York City, and Portland, hoping to make their fortunes but also eager to try on new lifestyles, to experiment with new codes of behavior.

Despite our lingering cultural nostalgia, we are a nation that's more metro every year, far more *Friends, Seinfeld,* or *Everybody Hates Chris* than *Little House on the Prairie* or *The 700 Club.* While I was researching this book — driving endless miles of backcountry — one of the most popular songs on my truck radio was a ballad by *American Idol*'s Kelly Clarkson about escaping the "darkness" of rural America.

"Grew up in a small town and when the rain would fall down, I just stared out my window," Clarkson crooned. "Wanted to belong here, but something felt so wrong here. So I pray (I would pray) I could break away. . . ."

If most of America's cultural landscape is urban-centric, homelander activists tend to be more focused, more deliberate. *The Simpsons* and *Seinfeld* and MTV display an attitude that's distinctly metro. They have very high ratings. But *The 700 Club* and Focus on the Family's radio broadcasts come with a specific agenda. They're beating a smaller drum but banging out one very simple message over and over again: *We're normal. We're healthy. We offer a better way forward. Here's how to vote. Here's how to force change.*

This isn't just propaganda — or rather, it's the most powerful form of propaganda because for the most part rural folks believe it to be true. They see themselves and their values as the logical center of the nation's political life. They believe that their roots run deeper than those of metros, tapping into a truer vein of American culture. But social conservatives also understand that they have a lot of convincing to do. The Moral Majority didn't get its name by accident. Every time journalists used the phrase, they reenforced the idea that the organization's views were widely held and even mainstream. (In fact, evangelical Christians make up only about 7 percent of the population.)

At the same time, homelander activists frequently use terms such as "radical" or "extreme" to describe everyday values that the vast majority of metros share. This vocabulary and framing have been adopted to an extraordinary degree by pundits and journalists within the mainstream urban media. They feel perfectly comfortable welcoming Pat Robertson or Jerry Falwell onto their television programs, but fringe thinkers on the Left (Noam Chomsky, Howard Zinn, Michael Moore, and so forth) are regularly excluded.

Their pliancy reflects a latent bias in our political perceptions. Decades after our national culture became a solidly metro phenomenon, many of us still see small towns and their institutions as somehow more virtuous and normal than urban communities. We hear about black "welfare queens" in inner-city ghettos, but the media rarely bother to report that the average homelander receives more federal money, per capita, than the average metro. When the farm lobby demanded during the 1990s that their federal subsidies be doubled — at a time when welfare payments were being slashed — no one dreamed of suggesting that rural Americans were addicted to government handouts. But the truth is that taxpayers, most of them metros, now shell out 20 billion dollars a year to prop up two million farms and agribusinesses.

How many people know that small towns are being hit by a drug epidemic of crystal meth, heroin, and cocaine so devastating that drug experts compare it to the urban crack explosion of the late 1980s? Instead, news reports, television shows, and films are filled with portraits of urban vice and mayhem. In fact, big-city crime rates have been plummeting for forty years. In New York City, murders dropped 73 percent over the past decade. Robberies are down by 72 percent, and rapes have been cut by half.

The political impact of this cultural framing is enormous, especially in an age when reporters look for simple, boiled-down narratives to define political campaigns. Urban politicians such as Michael Dukakis, George H. W. Bush, Al Gore, and John Kerry are regularly described in news accounts as stiff, awkward, and coldly detached. They may be "policy wonks" or "intellectuals" or "micro-managers," but they are clearly divorced from the vein of hearty, down-home American culture. Their wives are often caricatured as bitchy and shrill. Their hobbies (wind-surfing, snowboarding, sailing) are held up as effete and elitist.

Homelander politicians, on the other hand, are invariably described as regular folks. Ronald Reagan was the first postwar president to self-consciously adopt a rural style. He used the rolled-up denim shirt and crooked aw-shucks grin to powerful effect. Reporters and pundits still regularly describe him as hugely popular, a man who bonded naturally with the American people, despite the fact that his poll numbers often hovered well below those of Jimmy Carter's. At one point during his second term, Reagan's personal approval rating plunged to just 37 percent.

Taking a page from the master, George W. Bush has made a point of being photographed frequently with his elbow hanging out the window of his pickup truck or pulling brush on his Texas ranch. "People sometimes have to correct my English," Bush boasted at the 2004 Republican National Convention. "Some folks look at me and see a certain swagger, which in Texas is called *walking*."

The homelander shtick paid off. Bush was portrayed during the 2004 campaign as more natural, a straight-talker, blunt and truthful — the sort of guy you'd like to have a cup of coffee with. Often even critical articles about his administration were framed by positive-sounding adjectives: Bush was stubborn. He was a black-and-white thinker. He was bold. He wasn't the sort of guy to second-guess a decision or turn his back on an ally.

For his part, John Kerry was hammered relentlessly for being patrician, pretentious, and a flip-flopper to boot, and not by just the right-wing media. *New York Times* columnist Maureen Dowd was so eager to drive home Kerry's snootiness that she *invented* a suitable Kerry quote: "Who among us does not love NASCAR?" circulated in the blogosphere for weeks. When Teresa Heinz scuffled with a reporter, the five-second encounter ricocheted through the electronic echo chamber. It was cited as a definitive moment, deeply revealing. It fit the pre-chewed portrait of the Heinz-Kerry marriage as weirdly oversophisticated.

But when President Bush's daughters giggled their way through a tasteless speech at the Republican National Convention — full of sexual innuendo at times aimed at their grandmother, Barbara Bush — reporters shrugged. It didn't match the pattern. It wasn't part of the accepted story line.

This kind of framing has buoyed Bush through the lowest points of his second term. When an AP-Ipsos poll asked in 2005 whether Bush was personally likable, 42 percent of the respondents said no. By May 2006, a *New York Times*–CBS News poll found that his job approval rating had dropped below 30 percent.

First Lady Laura Bush was deployed to shore up her husband's image. "I don't really believe those polls," she said. "I travel around the country. I see people; I see their responses to my husband. I see their response to me." Other administration officials argued that the president's sagging popularity reflected the bloody war in Iraq. "The American people like this president," Karl Rove claimed during an appearance at the American Enterprise Institute. "His personal approval ratings are in the sixties."

Rove's claim is simply fictional. In fact, Mr. Bush's personal "negatives" were running 20 points higher than Hillary Clinton's, with millions of Americans convinced that their president was incompetent and untrustworthy. Confidence in his domestic policies was grim, ranging from 22 percent approval for his economic program to 26 percent support for his immigration plan. Perhaps the worst blow for Republicans came in the revelation that Democrats now enjoy a 13-point lead on the GOP's banner issue — moral values.

There has been plenty of evidence over the years that Bush's private character doesn't match his carefully crafted folksy persona. Dozens of published articles quoted White House insiders describing Bush as cold, insular, standoffish, and petty. Journalists documented the fact that most of his encounters with the public were staged before friendly crowds. These "town hall meetings" were often tightly scripted, hardly the sort of thing you would expect from a natural politician who connects easily with average Americans.

It had also become abundantly clear that Bush was capable of a good healthy flip-flop when need arose. He was firmly against the Department of Homeland Security before he was for it. He opposed and then supported the 9/11 Commission. He assured voters unequivocally that all domestic federal wiretaps would be approved by a judge and validated with a warrant. When it became clear that he had secretly signed off on a campaign to spy on the American people without judicial oversight, his handlers retreated behind lawyerly equivocation.

Bush promised harsh, buck-stops-here treatment for any White House staff member embroiled in the exposure of undercover CIA analyst Valerie Plame, but refused to discipline Karl Rove or reprimand Lewis "Scooter" Libby, Vice President Dick Cheney's chief of staff, when they were implicated. Even on small bits of political hackery, Bush can swing with the best of them. He claims to be a hardline free trader — so much so that he was willing to allow a company owned by the United Arab Emirates to run American shipping ports — but when it seemed politically expedient, he supported a Democrat-style tariff on steel imports.

All of this is normal enough political behavior. George Bush is as malleable and poll-driven as any metro politician. What's not normal is the way he is perceived and portrayed. His homelander image is served up fresh every day, stripped of factual context. Why? Because the muddle of triangulation and political deal-making doesn't fit the story line or the comfortable narrative framework.

In autumn 2005, MSNBC chief White House correspondent Norah O'Donnell was still praising Bush as somehow more "real" and down-to-earth than John Kerry. "And that was Kerry's problem — was authenticity. As much as people may disagree with President Bush about the war, many other things, he does have, to some degree, authenticity."

"I like [Bush]," agreed MSNBC *Hardball* host Chris Matthews on a broadcast the next day. "Everybody sort of likes the president, except for real whack-jobs, maybe on the Left. I mean, like him personally."

Most Americans disagree with this assessment, but in home-lander country it's a given that George Bush is one of them, a neighbor-in-chief: "A majority of Democrats believe that the president's 'come to Jesus moment' was nothing but a political ploy," Allen says. "I don't believe that. Maybe he did have a string pulled for him at some point in his life. He probably did. But all those attacks that came out about his military service and drugs and everything else, it's just disrespectful."

# 12

# The Science of Faith

She's there again.

I'm drifting through a crowd on the top tier of the stadium at Liberty University, Jerry Falwell's thriving Bible college in southern Virginia. A radiant, fierce-eyed girl has been trailing after me the past two hours. She's eight or nine years old, with yellow hair down her back. She has bare feet, wears a sort of peasant dress, and has a stern, thoughtful way of smiling. "What are you doing?" she asks, pointing at my microphone and my tape recorder. "Why are you asking people questions?"

"I'm writing a story," I say, "about the way some Christians think about science and evolution."

"*I'm* bored," she confides. "I already know *all* this stuff. We go to these things all the time."

This thing is a gathering of creationists hosted by an international organization called Answers in Genesis. More than a thousand people have come from all over the world to sing folk songs, to pray, and to talk about the origins of the universe. It's one part high school science fair, one part tent revival, and one part Star Trek convention. There are vendors selling everything from religious tracts to DVDs to quasi-scientific textbooks about the technical design of Noah's ark.

The girl shadows me all day, and in the midst of all this absolute weirdness, I realize that *I'm* the oddity. Her sisters, who also look like hippie-chicks, come to gawk. "We drove a long way to get here," they tell me. "We slept in the van."

Most of the people at the conference look like the crowd in any shopping mall in America, but as I circulate, I find that the apparent sameness — slangy American speech, hip-hugger jeans, iPod wires dangling from ears — only exaggerates the differences. What looks like a Gap T-shirt is really a God T-shirt. A teenage kid is carrying a Bible bound in camouflage. I listen in on conversations and find people talking seriously about the biblical patriarchs making prehistoric pilgrimages to North America.

Small discussion groups form to swap theories about the interactions between human tribes and herds of dinosaurs. One fellow is holding forth on the discovery of Aztec gold in the Egyptian pyramids, proof positive that a pan-global civilization existed before the time of the Great Flood. Oddest of all are the dozen or so actual scientists handing out glossy brochures that purport to show the flaws in various biological and geological theories that appear to contradict biblical creationism.

"This is an intensive week!" promises Ken Ham, the Australian who founded Answers in Genesis. He speaks from the main stage, his ascetic face and long muttonchop whiskers projected on the rock concert-sized video screen. "Not many people would give up an entire week of their lives for creationism!"

To warm up the crowd, he introduces a portly country-and-western singer named Buddy Davis, a pop star in the fringe culture of young-world apologetics. Davis launches into a series of praise songs, thumped out with summer camp dutifulness.

> The Bible talks about a worldwide flood.
> If there really was a worldwide flood what would the evidence be?
> Billions of dead things buried the rock layers laid by the water
> All over the Earth!(God) made behemoth and t-rex
> He made the fish in the sea
> He created the bugs on my windshield
> He created me!

It's like a scene out of the movie *Bob Roberts*, complete with folk-kitsch and right-wing, fist-in the air defiance. The crowd roars, claps, and sings along, and I realize that they know all the words by heart. Davis wraps up after an obligatory encore, and video testimonials flash on the overhead screen. "If you cannot trust the Bible where it starts, where can you start trusting the Bible?" a woman asks, staring somberly into the camera.

These messages are streaming out worldwide over the Internet. "I want to remind you," cautions the announcer, "that we are being watched. We have received over nineteen thousand page views, and many of those are coming from sites that are not in favor of what's going on here. So praise the Lord and be on your best behavior."

This subculture of the homelander movement has pushed its way into the messy, turbulent heart of America's culture war. Noisy legal and political skirmishes over creationism and evolution have been fought in California, Kansas, and Pennsylvania.

In 2005 the National Center for Science Education logged twenty-one full-blown creationism controversies at schools in eighteen states. President Bush even weighed in, urging schools to include religion-based theories in their science classes and arguing that "part of education is to expose people to different schools of thought. You're asking me whether or not people ought to be exposed to different ideas; the answer is yes."

For millions of kids, creationist science is already the status quo. According to the Department of Education, roughly 9 percent of all American schoolchildren attend Christian schools, many of them run by "conservative Christian" congregations. Nearly a million more kids in grades five through twelve are being homeschooled, often using teaching materials provided by fundamentalist organizations. The federal government found that half of the parents cite "religious reasons" for keeping their kids out of public school or say they "object to what the school teaches."

My brother initially sent his boys to the creationist elementary school run by his Lutheran Church, though both are now in public school. "I'm as close to certain that Earth was created by God as I am about anything," Allen says.

"The strictest version of creationism holds that the earth was created in exactly seven days and is only seven or eight thousand years old. Is that what you believe?"

"I don't believe that. I'm of the old-earth viewpoint of creationism. I don't know if this is true or not, but according to people that I trust on this matter, the word for 'day' and for 'a long period of time' is the same in the biblical language. The interpretation chosen by the translators of the Bible was the single day idea."

"So you believe that each 'day' described in Genesis was in effect a mistranslation of a word that means something more like thousands of years or millions of years?"

"Yeah, something like that."

"How does it fit into your thinking that there are quite a few other major religions and all of them have their own creation stories?"

"If I believed those stories, then I suppose I'd be a Hindu or Buddhist or whatever. If I had faith in that story and that line of thinking, then that's what I'd be. But I don't. I don't ridicule them for what they think, but I have my own beliefs."

"But does it raise any suspicions in your mind that different traditional peoples before the advent of science came up with explanations for their universe that seem to have this same kind of myth cycle built into them?"

"I haven't really studied that idea."

"What I'm getting at is that I think many modernists believe there was a period of time in human development where tribal societies were looking out into the darkness and coming up with stories to explain things they didn't understand. We just happen to be descended from one particular tribe. Native Americans have their story; Hindus have their story. We have ours."

"Look, trying to prove to somebody scientifically that Christianity

is the proper explanation for what we observe in the world is utterly
ridiculous. The reason I believe the Creation story comes from a com
pletely different direction. It's not from scientific thought. It's faith."

"And it's an important part of your faith? A lot of evangelicals seem
to think that creationism is essential to Christianity."

"My own interest is primarily in what happened from the time that
Jesus was alive onward. And because I do completely believe *that*
story in every respect, to the point of Jesus being resurrected from
the dead and coming back and spending time with people, it's silly
not to think that there could be supernatural explanations for these
other events. I actually enjoy the faith that says, 'Where human
reason and Scripture part ways, then you have faith.' You accept what
God has to say on the matter."

Like much of the urban-rural culture war, this clash between secular
science and biblical creationism began quite recently. Within living
memory, it was common for most educated, sophisticated metros to
believe what Allen believes: that God created the earth in more or
less exactly the manner described in Scripture. Scientists believed
that the world was essentially a static place. They assumed that it had
been created fairly recently and in much the same form we see today.
Researchers often made references to biblical explanations of natural
events.

The trouble began with an English researcher named Charles
Darwin. In 1859 he unveiled an essentially modern theory of evolution. His idea, stated briefly, holds that the world is in fact so truly
ancient that it boggles the imagination. It also appears to be incredibly malleable. Constant change is the normal state of affairs, as
species emerge and shift and decline. Fossils buried deep in the earth
show that this process has been going on for a very long time.

In living organisms (including humans) the mechanism for this
change is mutation and natural selection. Creatures constantly
exhibit small variations that occasionally offer some advantage. If the

organism out-survives its fellows and creates more offspring, the mutation is perpetuated. Over long periods of time, these alterations may accumulate, forming a new creature that's substantially different from its distant ancestor.

Evolution was rejected at first as scandalous and absurd, even by many scientists. Louis Agassiz introduced modern scientific research at Harvard University. He was a cofounder of the National Academy of Sciences, but as late as the 1870s, Agassiz believed devoutly in the biblical Flood and argued that Darwin's theory was "a scientific mistake, untrue in its facts, unscientific in its methods and mischievous in its tendency."

Most scientists quickly came around. During the same troubling period in the late nineteenth century, when America was sprouting cities, we were also developing a new professional class of researchers and academics. They found that Darwin's theory was a remarkably useful tool. The principles of evolution found their way into a thousand different experiments. More and more facts emerged that supported the argument. By the time scientists celebrated the hundred-year anniversary of Darwin's theory, in 1959, it seemed to most academics and intellectuals that the Judeo-Christian cosmology was essentially dead. It was banished not just from public schools and universities but also from many churches and synagogues.

But millions of Americans, especially in rural communities, still accept the Christian creation story as, well, gospel. Surveys regularly find that as many as a third of Americans believe in a literal version of biblical cosmology, though this figure has declined sharply in recent years. Traditional believers live with one toe dipped in the hectic currents of a technological, information-driven society, but they keep their other foot firmly planted on the foundational teachings of their faith.

It's not that creationists are ignorant or stupid. Allen and his pastor, Mark Bangert, both have advanced university degrees. Many of the people attending the convention in Virginia are teachers and doctors and accountants — and a few are actual scientists. But homelanders maintain an intellectual relationship to the world that has far more in common with medieval scholasticism than with modern scientific inquiry.

According to creationists, the Bible isn't a collection of teachings; it's not even theology as most metros understand the word. Scripture is, rather, a collection of hard facts. Each passage offers irrefutable evidence about the structure of the universe. "The Bible is the true word of God," says Dr. Kevin Anderson, who holds a Ph.D. in microbiology and is head of the Creation Research Society. "Science supports; it doesn't deny. Science confirms; it doesn't contradict."

In order to understand how radical this statement is, let me spend another moment talking about mainstream science — what it is, and is not. Secular scientists develop theories based on observation. They then devise various ways of testing their theories. When those tests contradict or disprove the original notion, the process begins again. When various theories prove correct, scientists look for ways to fit them together. The resulting picture is again tested by experimentation.

Because science is self-correcting, bone-headed notions (such as phrenology, astrology, and racial eugenics) are modified over time or abandoned altogether. Social conservatives like to claim that scientists are themselves entangled in a secular-humanist religion, blinded by a dogma every bit as rigid as their own. Many homelanders believe this sincerely. "At least we admit our bias," Allen told me one afternoon. "I think we're more intellectually honest."

But scientists don't make their reputations by upholding established truths or defending tradition. They get ahead by questioning theories and replacing wobbly bits of information with better ideas. You don't get to be Einstein by proving that Newton had the universe neatly figured out. In order to get your name up in lights (or win a Nobel Prize), you have to find something new, you have to prove someone wrong. Science is a human business, which means that individuals cling to their biases and presuppositions. But those who come after are generally able to muddle forward, separating the wheat from the chaff.

These days, no modern scientist believes that Charles Darwin got everything right. Even Albert Einstein, who changed the way metros see the universe, got a few things incredibly wrong. In a sense, science is the purest form of modernism, the most powerful articulation of the urban culture that many homelanders despise. Inherent in the system is the notion that there are no fundamental truths, no ultimate authorities. There is no final equation that will serve as *the* answer (to borrow from Douglas Adams) to life, the universe, and everything.

Which isn't to say that we can't know quite a lot. In the past century, scientists have scattered like ants, each bringing back bits and pieces of information. Each team of ants (biologists, say, or physicists or astronomers) has managed to build coherent models about how stuff works. We know from the fossil record, for example, that a vast number of other creatures existed in the past but are now extinct. What's more, we can say with certainty that the organisms we see around us aren't "fixed" or "finished." Humans are experiencing a universe in a transient phase of its existence.

As creationists will point out, big gaps remain in each scientific discipline; there's still plenty that we don't know. But the jigsaw puzzle as a whole has formed a vast and consistent blueprint. The pattern has allowed us to begin predicting things with remarkable accuracy, from the existence and function of DNA to the presence of black holes. It's also significant that in the course of a relatively short span of time, scientists have disproved most of the major cosmological arguments formulated by traditional Christians. We know that our planet isn't flat; nor do the sun and the stars orbit around it. We know with utter and complete certainty that the universe is older than ten or twenty thousand years. (In order to disbelieve this, you have to discount not only evolution and biology but also most of what we know about geology, physics, and astronomy.)

What's more, scientists have answered a lot of questions that were, until very recently, considered by many religious thinkers to be unanswerable. Proponents of intelligent design and creationism insist that baffling levels of complexity in nature create veils of impenetrable mystery. They look at the intricacies of the tiny molecular "machines" within our cells and conclude that there must be some invisible clockmaker fitting them all together. "The human body is packed with marvels, eyes and lungs and cells, and evolutionary gradualism can't account for that," Phillip Johnson, the Presbyterian attorney who popularized intelligent design, told the *Washington Post*.

But the same divine providence that Johnson credits for the invention of complex biological structures was once used to explain the existence of plagues and the motion of the stars and the changing of the seasons and the conception of children. Thanks to the scientific method, those veils have been lifted one by one.

We know, for example, that AIDS wasn't a punishment sent by God, as some evangelical Christians claim. We know this not because the notion is morally and theologically revolting but because researchers learned that the disease is caused by a mundane and very nasty viral organism. Owing to the scientific method, we've already discovered how to subdue the invading creature. Sooner or later, we'll figure out how to kill it entirely.

One by one, scientists resolve muddles. Being the restless souls that they are, researchers then go on to investigate even more complex phenomena. It's noteworthy that in all this mucking about, we have yet to find a single fingerprint of God anywhere in the universe. We've looked deeply into subatomic particles. We've stared into the curved space around distant galaxies. Thanks to the doddering speed of light, we can even look back in time, catching glimpses of the early stages of the universe. So far, there has been no sign of any supernatural force, no phenomenon that hasn't succumbed to a naturalistic explanation.

But from the homelanders' perspective, that's not accurate. Homelanders would argue that evidence of the Creator exists and it can be found in the dresser drawer of any hotel room in America. I'm talking, of course, about the Holy Bible. Scriptural literalists believe that the texts of the Bible represent an indisputable collection of factual data. Each passage in Genesis, each mention of cosmology uttered by Jesus Christ in the Gospels, is seen as material evidence every bit as solid and irrefutable as carbon dating or the speed of light.

"If Scripture is true, which I consider it to be, then I would expect it to blend easily and adequately with my scientific investigations," says Dr. Anderson. "To move back and forth between two truths isn't really crossing any particular line. Moving back and forth between scientific and biblical truth is staying on the same plane."

One sometimes hears people debating whether the Bible is meant to be read as a historical document. (Most modern textual scholars believe that it wasn't. The concept of fact-based history was probably unknown to the Hebraic tribesmen who first copied out the passages of Genesis.) But according to many homelander Christians, the Bible is a scientific text, one that describes exactly how the universe came into being, how it functions now, and what will happen to it in the future.

"God meant what he said in the Scripture, that he's the creator and sustainer of all things," says Dr. David DeWitt, a biologist and head of the Center for Creation Studies at Liberty University, where the Answers in Genesis conference was held.

DeWitt's is one of the most prominent institutions to be exploring the factual and evidentiary basis for biblical Creation. To illustrate his point, DeWitt shows me the skeleton of a chimpanzee.

"The Bible tells me that God made all creatures, so I use that to inform how I look at things. From Scripture, I know that God made man separate, so I *should* find differences. And I *can* find that, and so I come at my study of science from that perspective."

In fact, biologists and primatologists have identified profound similarities between humans and chimpanzees, but DeWitt's reading of the Bible tells him *a priori* that humans will be radically different, so that's what he sees. Anything that doesn't reflect these differences is minimized or ignored — not because he is intellectually dishonest but because unlike most secular scientists he feels he knows the truth. It is already revealed in the factual evidence of Scripture. "It really all fits together," DeWitt says. "When you study geology from a creationist perspective, you have to take into account the flood that covered the whole earth. So how does that inform your interpretation of rocks?"

In creationist circles, the story of Noah and the ark and the global flood is a sort of litmus test. Hard-core believers insist that there was a historical calamity that occurred only a few thousand years ago, exactly as described in Genesis. The entire globe was covered in enough water to swallow every landmass including the Himalaya, which at present rise more than five miles above sea level. DeWitt believes that this single event explains a whole host of physical phenomena, ranging from stratified rock in the Grand Canyon to the disappearance of dinosaurs to the fossilized remains of extinct organisms scattered in layered deposits.

"That sounds like a fairy tale to me," I say. "To be honest, I can grasp the idea of a flood from a purely supernatural point of view. If you were telling me that God magically made a lot of water and took it away again, I could accept that as your religious conviction, like the miracle of Christ's resurrection, or walking on water. But you're saying this was a scientific event, obeying natural laws. You think a bunch of water somehow covered the world's surface?"

Nodding earnestly, DeWitt says, "People ask all the time, where did the water come from and where did it go? It's a legitimate question. But we have scientists these days excited about the idea of water on Mars, when there's no visible water on Mars right now."

"You think enough water to cover the whole earth to a depth of five miles somehow seeped underground?"

"My understanding is that it's likely that the ocean floors dropped after the flood, which would accommodate much of the water." He sees the look on my face, shrugs, and says, "I think there are a lot of processes that we haven't fully appreciated."

Creationists make this sort of leap often. They criticize small points of inconsistency or confusion in mainstream science, then comfortably argue incredibly far-fetched and thinly substantiated theories to support their own cosmology. When they come to a gap or a clumsy assumption in their own worldview, they shrug and move on. Again, this is not because they're being dishonest or deceptive (the usual accusation leveled by critics) but because they already feel they know the facts. The rest is just a question of illumination and glorification.

As a consequence, very few actual scientists believe any of this. A quarter century after it was founded, the Creation Research Society has found about six hundred people with scientific degrees of any stripe willing to associate themselves with biblical literalism. You can certainly find far more scientists who believe in UFOs. "Most of them don't look at our data and what we're saying," Dr. Anderson argues. "Ninety percent of your Ph.D. scientists know very little about evolution. They accept evolution because that's what they were taught. They don't feel motivated to step back and say, Is this really true? And you also lose your career by doing that. People say obviously you are mentally demented. You'll lose your tenure. They remain quiet to keep their positions."

There's no doubt that "coming out" as a creationist means tough sledding for academic researchers. And no wonder. Believers have built elaborate scale models of Noah's ark, designed to illustrate how all the world's creatures fit aboard one supertanker-sized ship. One notion currently in vogue holds that the thousands of pairs of animals tended by Noah's family were all immature — a cargo of pups and cubs, eggs, and pupa that fell into a state of hibernation. This sounds like mockery, but researchers like DeWitt and Anderson believe that every line of the Old Testament writing is as accurate as a peer-reviewed paper. Their job is to figure out how it happened. Of his own scientific work, Anderson says, "Isn't it amazing that it doesn't contradict Scriptural tradition? I myself have been stunned. I could have lived with it being less confirmational."

"If scientists were objective," agrees the Reverend Jerry Falwell, founder of Liberty University and a cosponsor of the conference, "they would reject ridiculous ideas such as the big bang and other unscientific ideas about how we got here. If they were objective, they would allow academic freedom. Instead they call us bad names. They will not and cannot debate us, because we have the facts."

If homelanders are eager to see some form of creationism included in the public school curriculum, this is another field where they have yet to offer a clear vision of how their society would work. For one thing, traditionalists can't agree on exactly what version of biblical cosmology should be taught.

Just as medieval scholars beat up one another over the angels dancing on the heads of pins, there are infinite branches of scriptural literalism, all completely at odds about what the Bible means. Some, like my brother, believe that the six days of God's labor described in Genesis represent vast epochs of time. Others argue that vast spans of time elapsed between each day of God's divine work. Intelligent design proponents are the most timid, claiming only that some kind of guiding force must exist to explain the universe's confusing complexity.

Even within this most "rational" of creationist circles, no one can agree on how the process works. Some believe that God created various animal species supernaturally at intervals spread over thousands of years. Others accept that a limited form of "micro-evolution" does now occur, but insist that a guiding force must have intervened at various points throughout history.

It's significant that these "liberal" creationists make hard-core believers sputter with indignation. John Whitcomb, the coauthor of

*The Genesis Flood*, one of the most influential books in the creationist canon, blames "progressive creationists for deceiving large numbers of Christians into abandoning Biblical creationism and catastrophism." Speaking from the main stage at Liberty University, Whitcomb dutifully fires a salvo at secular biologists and geologists. ("Our public schools need to be purged of evolutionary perversions paraded as science," he says.)

His real ire, however, is reserved for those like Johnson who don't accept that the entire account of creation as related in the Old Testament. "We humbly insist that it is essential to believe the Genesis record of origins, in order to please God," Whitcomb says. "Our Lord said, whoever is ashamed of me and my words, of him the Son of man will be ashamed. Careful, friends, this can lead to someone's eternal loss."

Biblical literalists tolerate intelligent design because it serves as the thin end of a creationist wedge. It's clear that intelligent design arguments have proven far more palatable to average Americans, who simply can't embrace the full Christian mythology as scientific truth. ("It's probably the biggest stumbling block for people outside the faith," concedes Allen's pastor.)

"We agree that discussions and debates concerning intelligent design can temporarily catch the attention of unbelieving minds," Whitcomb says. "But if we leave Christ himself out of the discussion, how can we help people who are walking in the darkness of materialistic evolutionism?"

"We [at Liberty University] affirm the Scriptures, the historic account that's given in Genesis," agrees DeWitt. "So we work with intelligent design proponents, but I don't think they go far enough. If you're talking about getting someone to understand the gospel of Jesus Christ, intelligent design doesn't get you there."

Despite the lack of a coherent, teachable theory, creationists insist their worldview deserves a place in public school. Teachers who hold fundamentalist views should be allowed to discuss their own beliefs

openly, sharing their convictions that Jesus Christ is a primary physical force shaping the universe. "At least we should teach the contro
versy," Allen tells me later. "That's just being intellectually honest, let-
ting people know that some of us don't accept [evolution] as fact."

But how far should a teacher be allowed to go? Is it enough to put a
sticker on textbooks stating that Darwin is "only a theory"? ("Give us
that much," Allen says, sounding exasperated. "What would that pos-
sibly hurt?") Most creationists don't think so. They want the liberty to
speak out, to offer their version of truth. The definition of an evangelical Christian, after all, is that he or she evangelizes. The point of
teaching biblical cosmology isn't to correct a student's scientific
understanding of the world. The purpose is to save that student's soul.

By almost any measure, early experiments in Bible-based science
education have been dismal failures. In 2006 the Odessa, Texas,
school district will join the growing number of public schools that
are adding a "Bible study" class to the curriculum. The teaching
materials supposedly represent a non-religious treatment of the
Bible, taught as a historical and literary text, but the curriculum was
provided by a Christian-activist group called the National Council
on Bible Curriculum in Public Schools, based in Greensboro, North
Carolina.

The National Council's materials claim that no scrap of modern
scientific or archaeological evidence "contradicts or denies one word,
phrase, clause, or sentence of the Bible, but always confirms and ver-
ifies the facts of the Biblical record." The taxpayer-funded program
cheerfully cites scientists who don't have legitimate science degrees.

*Then* it gets weird. The National Council informs students that federal researchers have confirmed two — not one, but two — biblical
accounts of the sun's standing still in the sky: "There is documented
evidence in NASA that two days were indeed unaccounted for in time."

"This curriculum is simply an attempt to use public schools to
interfere with the freedom of families to practice their own faiths

and pass on their own religious values to their children," argued Kathy Miller, in a critique of the National Council curriculum issued by the Texas Freedom Network in August 2005.

"It attempts to persuade students to adopt views that are held primarily within certain conservative Protestant circles," agreed Dr. Mark Chancey, a professor of biblical studies in the Department of Religious Studies at Southern Methodist University.

No one is sure how many public schools are teaching this stuff (the National Council is cagey on this point) but estimates range from three hundred to one thousand districts in thirty-seven states. There are more than fifty school districts in Texas alone. The *New York Times* estimated that as many as 175,000 high school students now receive this sort of biblical instruction every year.

The allure of creationism is obvious. Modern science offers questions, but the version of "biblical science" embraced by many homelanders offers concrete answers. One keeps changing and tossing off new conundrums; the other glorifies truth and tradition. One accepts a world that is vast and transitory and probably uncaring, while the other describes a cosmos that is intimate, personal, and nurturing. The one is moral because it is based on the idea of flawed humans collectively seeking truth; the other is moral because there exists a divine Father, who serves as a teacher and as a punisher of sin.

"If scientists recognized the existence of a creator," argues Reverend Falwell, "they would also have to acknowledge that he is the owner and the lord of the universe. And they don't want anyone to lord over them." Quoting from the very first line of the Bible, Falwell says, "'In the beginning, God created . . .' That is the one basic truth that the enemies of Christ must negate if they are going to take over the culture and destroy a nation."

# (13)
# Winning Red

The strangeness of homelander culture has led many urban Americans to believe that the ruralist vision is simply unachievable. The conventional metro wisdom holds that small-town voters are being manipulated by Republicans who want lower taxes and laissez-faire government regulations, but don't really care about the social issues that stir passions outside the urban beltway.

"In only one area have the Cons achieved a tangible, real world victory," argues Thomas Frank in *What's the Matter with Kansas?* "Their intractable hostility to taxes of all kinds has successfully brought disaster on the [Kansas] state government."

This formulation makes sense to metros. After all, you can't turn back the clock to the 1950s. How can you undo a couple of generations of rock 'n' roll, Martin Luther King, and *All in the Family* reruns? How do you erase all that pot we smoked? The Pill, the Vietnam War, Watergate, MTV, and a thousand other things seem to form a sort of critical mass, an unstoppable momentum.

There's no way you can squeeze a couple of generations of social change back into the bottle. Homelanders must be doomed to failure. Frank writes of a small-town culture that actually revels in its permanent victimization.

> Conservatism, they believe, can never be powerful or successful, and backlashers revel in fantasies of their own marginality and persecution. As culture war, the backlash was born to lose. Its goal is not to win cultural battles but to take offense, conspicuously, vocally, even flamboyantly.

This claim is simply and factually wrong. It's true, of course, that rural elites have made significant concessions. Some of their chief goals remain unrealized. But on a growing range of issues, the home-lander agenda is moving forward with remarkable speed. In 2004, voters approved ballot initiatives banning same-sex marriage in eleven states. Even in blue state bastions like Oregon and Michigan, rural traditionalists won by more than a 10-point margin, owing to a massive turnout in rural communities.

In the days after the 2004 election, Karl Rove acknowledged the importance of traditional values in reelecting George Bush. "Five thousand years of human history should not be overthrown by the acts of a few liberal judges or by the acts of a few local elected officials," he told Tim Russert on *Meet the Press*. "Marriage is and should be defined as being between one man and one woman."

Through the winter, rural-traditional leaders paraded in front of the cameras on CNN and Fox and MSNBC, declaring that their hour had come at last. Tony Perkins, head of the Family Research Council, told the *Washington Post* that opposing same-sex marriage was "the hood ornament on the family values wagon that carried the president to a second term."

Michael Crowley, senior editor at the *New Republic*, described Dr. James Dobson as the new "Republican kingmaker" whose grassroots influence had been especially significant in Ohio and Florida. Dobson "is already leveraging his new power," Crowley wrote in the on-line magazine *Slate*. "When a thank-you call came from the White House, Dobson issued the staffer a blunt warning that Bush 'needs to be more aggressive' about pressing the religious right's pro-life, anti-gay rights agenda, or it would 'pay a price in four years.'"

But the real measure of homelander clout comes when Republicans clash with one another. In the days after the 2004 election, Senator Arlen Specter, the pro-choice metro Republican from Pennsylvania, blundered into the rural buzz saw. He made the mistake of claiming that "*Roe v. Wade* was inviolate" and suggested that his Judiciary Committee would be unlikely to confirm a Supreme Court nominee willing to overturn the law. Specter was immediately targeted by a massive intimidation campaign, coordinated by pastor networks across rural America.

The deluge was so fierce and bitter that Specter nearly lost his chairmanship. At a press conference, he read a statement drawn up by the White House, promising abjectly to "support any individual President Bush finds worthy." The capitulation wasn't just symbolic. In the months that followed, Specter engineered the confirmations of Justices John Roberts and Sam Alito, men whose anti-abortion stances were clearly established.

Homelander activists have steadily pushed the abortion debate, and their wins are coming fast and furious now. At their behest, the Bush administration has kept a "morning-after" emergency contraceptive pill called Plan B bottled up at the Food and Drug Administration, ignoring scientists' recommendations that the drug be made available to women without a prescription. South Dakota lawmakers have made abortion illegal, triggering a likely Supreme Court challenge. In Kansas the Republican attorney general has harassed Planned Parenthood clinics with criminal investigations, even demanding the names of women who have sought to end their pregnancies.

"Some states attempt to pass complete bans on abortion," according to a report by the National Abortion Federation. "Other states have introduced bills banning abortions without adequate health exceptions or have tried to ban abortions in outpatient clinics."

Until recently, metro pundits were still downplaying the likelihood that *Roe v. Wade* might be dismantled. "I've long doubted that a shrewd Republican president would want to see *Roe* over-turned," wrote conservative blogger Andrew Sullivan. "It's too useful for voter turn-out and direct mail. So what we're seeing is an inevitable clash between the party's elite realists and its grass-roots true believers."

But rural activists have made it clear that on this point they will refuse to bend or give ground. Early in 2005 the Bush administration floated the possibility that Attorney General Alberto Gonzales, a moderate on abortion issues, might be nominated to the high court. The idea triggered a firestorm among homelanders. My brother dismissed the idea. "It'll never happen," Allen said. "We'd be done with Bush. That just won't work."

In a Web editorial titled "Christians warn Bush about his upcoming supreme court nomination" the influential Jerry Gaffney Ministries based in Centralia, Washington, offered a similar message:

> Conservative Christians around the country will once again unite behind President Bush only if he chooses a Supreme Court justice that meets their values, but warn him against choosing Alberto Gonzales. Conservative lobbyists . . . laid down the gauntlet to President George Bush at the weekend, warning they would oppose the nomination of his friend and confidant.

If the power relationship worked the way metros believe it did — with Karl Rove pulling the strings and homelanders dancing obediently — Team Bush could have quickly contained the small-town zealots. Most observers saw Gonzales as the perfect candidate for corporate America and its Republican allies. Gonzales is bullish on deregulation, he would have been a shoo-in for confirmation, and he was guaranteed to broaden the GOP's appeal among Hispanics, a top agenda item for the administration.

Bush sounded downright peevish about the homelander barrage, urging his base to "tone down" the heated rhetoric. "When a friend gets attacked, I don't like it," he complained. But then the White House did exactly what rural conservatives wanted him to do, abandoning Gonzales and appointing John Roberts. NPR White House correspondent David Greene summed up the political situation pretty neatly, pointing out that President Bush "absolutely needs to satisfy the conservative base, especially on this first pick."

John Roberts isn't a fire breather or a bomb thrower. He is an exceptionally bright, articulate jurist, one of the sharpest legal minds in America. Because these traits don't match the metro stereotype of social conservatives — no pomaded hair, no southern accent, no culture-war rhetoric — the urban media seized on the notion that Roberts might be a closet moderate. But Roberts is a conservative Roman Catholic who grew up in tiny Long Beach, Indiana. His writings on abortion, women's rights, civil rights, and the role of religion in public schools all display a traditional, pre–New Deal view of society shared by few Americans.

In the 1980s Roberts asked bluntly "whether encouraging home-makers to become lawyers contributes to the common good." He described the legal efforts aimed at bringing women's equality to the workplace as "highly objectionable" and "staggeringly pernicious." He penned legal arguments in opposition to *Roe* and described legal abortion as a "tragedy." Surveys consistently show that few Americans share these opinions. A Harris poll taken in 2005 found that 58 percent of Americans wanted the new Supreme Court justice to be either a moderate or a liberal, while only 23 percent wanted a conservative in the mold of Roberts.

But as one would expect, homelanders were delighted by the Roberts nomination. "I've just spent two days of intense meetings in Washington, D.C.," wrote the Reverend Rick Scarborough, one of the most powerful pastors in the United States, who is based in Lufkin, Texas. He continues, in his e-newsletter:

> I've met with some of the most respected conservative leaders in the land. To a man — and woman — they assure me that the president's first Supreme Court nominee is an authentic constitutionalist — not just a man of integrity and intellect, but one loyal to the real Constitution (rather than the fre-

quently distorted document it's become) and the Judeo-Christian values on which our Republic was founded.

Was Scarborough (with his network of five thousand conservative pastors) being tricked by the GOP's Wall Street minders? Had President Bush pulled a fast one on his rural-traditional base? Many metros would like very much to believe this is true, that Roberts will be a mainstream, tax-cutting corporate conservative who will pull a "Souter" and drift slowly to the left.

But in an interview with the *Washington Post*, Scarborough made it clear he sees the power relationship working the other way, with tradition-minded rural activists working to keep the GOP's elite in line: "We have a lot of gutless wonders who wear the tag conservative Republican. Anytime there's any amount of fire, they crater," he said.

As it happens, Roberts was confirmed with ease. A few months later, feeling that they had built a cushion of political capital, the White House tried again to nominate a centrist. Searching for someone to replace swing-vote justice Sandra Day O'Connor, Bush turned to Harriet Miers, a White House operative and another of his personal allies. Homelanders weren't satisfied, however, and they broke ranks again, this time with a collective howl, demanding the appointment of another movement conservative.

"It was a striking example of the grass roots having strong opinions that ran counter to the party leaders about what was attainable," Stephen G. Calabresi, a law professor at Northwestern University and a founding member of the Federalist Society, told a reporter. The firestorm intensified after evidence surfaced that Miers had supported feminist causes and the right of women to choose an abortion.

During the fight, James Dobson was often better informed about Bush's nominees than Republican members of the Senate Judiciary Committee, at one point even declaring, "Some of what I know I'm not at liberty to talk about." And once again, it was the GOP's "elite realists" who blinked. Bush is regularly portrayed as stubborn and deeply loyal, but after two weeks of fierce attacks from his supposedly servile small-town base, he backed down.

Miers was shelved and replaced with Samuel Alito, a man whose opinions are so far outside the mainstream that other Republican judges have written fierce critiques of his legal arguments. Justice O'Connor scolded Alito for concluding that in certain instances a woman should be forced to obtain her husband's permission before having an abortion.

It's understandable that metros would have a difficult time believing that homelanders could actually win their war. We see our kids zoning out with their Game Boys, listening to Eminem on their iPods, or e-mailing with pen pals in New Delhi, and the ruralist vision just seems too far-fetched.

Journalists who report on rural-traditional culture tend to come away convinced that it's all just a weird sort of charade — a conservative version of the Summer of Love that will rise and peak and then fade away. In June 2005, Hannah Rosin wrote a brilliant profile of Patrick Henry College for the *New Yorker* called "God and Country." The school, in exurban Virginia, trains young homeschooled conservatives for "careers of influence" and has been hugely successful in placing graduate interns inside the White House and Congress. Interviewed by Jon Stewart on *The Daily Show*, Rosin suggested that it was all a sort of pipe dream.

> **Stewart:** After spending time with them are you encouraged by their humanity or are you frightened by their cloistered nature?
>
> **Rossin:** They need a reality check, I would say. They live in this cloistered world and then they go out and work in politics, so things may change. It's hard to keep your pure, perfect world and live in the world. So it may not work.

Stewart: But when they go off-message, their worldview collapses and then they just weep slowly and . . .

Rossin: And crumble. And weep over the Jesus on the dashboard.

Stewart: See? So, there is hope.

Rossin: So, there is hope.

But homelanders are far more clever and organized than that. Schools like Patrick Henry, Liberty, and Bob Jones University aren't just winding up their kids and sending them off into the metro world to sink or swim. Graduates are deliberately trained to engage and confront American society. And they're not just educating politicians and political activists; the major Christian universities have developed programs aimed at creating a new generation of public school teachers, lawyers, scientists, and media professionals. These graduates are often highly qualified and ambitious, but they also see their own success as a means to an end. They're moles, not-so-secret agents, and cheerful subversives.

When you hear on the news that a schoolteacher has raised a protest over some alleged liberal wrong, or a scientist is protesting against a "bias" in a university department, or a student is raising concerns about an "improper book" that's available in a high school library, you often find that those activists are connected to a larger support network. They're chipping away deliberately at the metro hierarchy, at the urban-modernist mindset. They're opening more and more fronts in the culture war, bodychecking the national debate to a new center.

## 14

# The Republican Party's New Elite

Perhaps the single strongest piece of evidence that homelanders have the power to change America is found within the Republican Party itself. It's easy to forget that for much of the twentieth century, hard-line conservatives were pariahs within the GOP. In 1948, Senator Robert Taft, a Republican from Ohio, tried to block Harry Truman's progressive legislation. With Roosevelt gone and the Second World War won, Taft hoped to uproot the New Deal.

But his candidacy was rejected in the Republican primary in favor of a moderate metro, New Yorker Thomas Dewey. The party embraced a platform that called for the expansion of Social Security and more funding for public housing. Politicians across the political landscape were describing themselves openly as liberal. Dwight Eisenhower, the Republican Party's next standard-bearer, was a military man, but his convictions were so centrist that both parties courted him to be their candidate. "Should any political party attempt to abolish social security . . . and eliminate labor laws and farm government programs," Eisenhower wrote after his election, "you would not hear of that party again in our political history."

Ike created the department of Health, Education, and Welfare and rejected plans to cut federal school aid: "Every liberal — including me — will disapprove," he declared. A centrist brand of Republicanism had taken hold, with deep roots in the big urban states of the East and the Great Lakes. Center-left Republican leaders like Joseph Martin from Massachusetts and Everett Dirksen from Illinois had utterly eclipsed the GOP's homelander wing.

Small-town conservatism was at its lowest ebb. With the help of the rural bias in the political system, homelanders were still able to elect large numbers of politicians, but the leadership of both parties was moving steadily to the left, away from traditional social values and small-government ideals. When Goldwater published *The Conscience of a Conservative* in 1960, he wasn't railing against Democrats; he was howling against "liberals" and "apologists" within his own party, primarily Eisenhower and Richard Nixon.

"We were swindled," Goldwater wrote. "There are occasions when we have elevated men and political parties to power that promised to restore limited government and then proceeded, after their election, to expand the activities of government."

> I find that America is fundamentally a Conservative nation. And it is all too clear that in spite of a Conservative revival among the people[,] the radical ideas that were promoted by the New and Fair Deals under the guise of Liberalism still dominate the councils of our national government.

Goldwater believed that the nation's entire history after 1932 was an aberration, a betrayal of social and political principles established by the founding fathers. He spoke openly of his Christian faith and promised a return to limited, Jeffersonian-style republicanism, with a shackled federal government. He voted against the Civil Rights Act, arguing that it was a principled stand for states' rights. He proposed making Social Security voluntary and called for the sale of the Tennessee Valley Authority.

"The good Lord raised this mighty Republic to be a home for the brave and to flourish as the land of the free," he declared, "not to stagnate in the swampland of collectivism."

Observing the mob of Goldwater delegates at the 1964 Republican National Convention, party icon Henry Cabot Lodge famously demanded, "What in God's name has happened to the Republican Party? I hardly know any of these people."

New York governor Nelson Rockefeller, a center-left moderate, was the most popular Republican in the nation. He was pro-choice in an era before legal abortion rights existed. But Rockefeller discovered that Goldwater had already captured the nomination, locking up so many delegates that the convention's outcome was a foregone conclusion.

In a tirade that anticipated Hillary Clinton's "vast right-wing conspiracy" speech by four decades, Rockefeller spluttered impotently about "subversion by a radical, well-financed and highly disciplined minority wholly alien to the broad middle course that accommodates the mainstream of Republican principle."

Goldwater's victory wasn't a coup. The truth is that rural conservatives had rolled up their sleeves and gotten busy, seizing control of local and state committees, filling key staff positions with their activists, taking on one grunt assignment after another until they dominated the Republican Party's apparatus. Their nineteenth-century ideology was widely discredited, even with the GOP, but their grassroots tactics were ingenious and would serve as a model for the homelander insurgency over the next three decades.

In the years before Goldwater's death, in 1998, his reputation was largely rehabilitated. Conservatives remembered him fondly as the founder of the modern conservative movement. But the Arizona Republican also helped usher Richard Nixon from office, and in later years he followed the rest of the nation in its leftward drift, becoming an advocate for gay and lesbian rights and defending a woman's right to choose an abortion.

"A lot of so-called conservatives today don't know what the word means," he told the *Los Angeles Times* in 1994, just as the Republican Revolution was surging to power. "They think I've turned liberal because I believe a woman has a right to an abortion. That's a decision that's up to the pregnant woman, not up to the pope or some do-gooders or the religious Right."

In his day, however, Goldwater was seen even by many mainstream Republicans as a dangerous radical. During the presidential campaign in 1964, Pennsylvania governor William Scranton wrote

Goldwater a public letter accusing him of "casually" prescribing nuclear war "as a solution to a troubled world." Democrat Lyndon Johnson was more explicit, describing his opponent as "a raving, ranting demagogue" who wanted "to tear down society."

Confronted with the starkest of choices, Americans went to the polls and chose a distinctly metro future. They voted for Johnson by unprecedented margins, giving him more than 61 percent of the popular vote and a landslide in the electoral college.

The 1964 election is widely remembered as the moment when the South peeled away from the Democratic Party. But Goldwater's hard-core homelander rhetoric ("Sometimes I think this country would be better off if we could just saw off the Eastern Seaboard and let it float out to sea," he told reporters in 1961) resonated with tradition-minded voters across the United States.

In the five southern states that Goldwater carried, he won a total of 2.5 million votes, only about 10 percent of his national tally. He received far more support in the single state of California (roughly 2.8 million ballots) and even claimed a respectable number of ballots in New York state (2.2 million). In Idaho, Nebraska, Kansas, South Dakota, and Oklahoma, the Republican ticket won between 44 and 49 percent of the popular vote.

Despite a disastrously managed campaign, Goldwater had outlined broad themes that resonated with rural voters. What's more, he had revealed a geographic base that was primed for a conservative revival — not just southerners but a national rural bloc that was increasingly disenchanted with urban progressivism. At first, Republican leaders hardly noticed. After Goldwater's humiliation, Rockefeller resumed control of the GOP and veered once again to the left, showing little interest in courting an ever-smaller homelander base.

"[Rockefeller] was a social liberal with notable support among black voters," wrote social historian Mark Kurlansky, in his book *1968*. "He called for the Republican Party to become the voice of the poor and oppressed." But once again, Rockefeller's overconfidence was crippling. In a stunning misstep, he withdrew from the 1968 presidential race, apparently expecting Republicans to summon him back by popular acclaim.

This coyness on the part of a national candidate was once an accepted tradition in American politics, but by the 1960s it was dangerously anachronistic. A *New York Times* editorial begged Rockefeller to reconsider, arguing that his refusal to run meant "the nomination of Richard M. Nixon by default" and would leave "moderate Republicans leaderless and impotent."

Rockefeller eventually reentered the fray, but once again he was too late. "His mishandling of the 1968 campaign when he had everything in his favor meant the undoing of Rockefeller's career," Kurlansky wrote, "which in turn meant the orphaning of the liberal wing of the Republican Party. 1968 was the year in which the Republican Party became a far more ideological party — a conservative party in which promising moderates have been marginalized."

For thirty years the center-left consensus created by Franklin Roosevelt had endured, but now the grand metro vision began rattling apart. A new generation of Republican politicians was emerging, inspired by Goldwater's nostalgia for a pre–New Deal America and willing to link their political fortunes to small-town culture. When Ronald Reagan declared that government "is not a solution to our problem, government is the problem," he was breaking formally with the postwar urban values of his own party.

As governor of California, Reagan had signed a liberal abortion bill, but as he stepped onto the national stage, the former Democrat embraced the homelander notion that Christianity was a necessary element of American society and democracy: "Freedom prospers when religion is vibrant and the rule of law under God is acknowledged," he proclaimed.

Naturally, the Republican Party's transition wasn't immediate. For decades, House Republicans remained a fairly metro bunch, with none of the homelander fervor that now colors the party's political image. The only Republican House Speaker in the postwar era (before Newt Gingrich) was a man named Joseph William Martin, a former newspaper reporter from Massachusetts. Minority leader posts were held by GOP moderates like Gerald Ford from Michigan, John Rhodes from Arizona, and Robert Michel from Illinois.

The shift in the Republican Party's center of gravity accelerated during the 1980s. Reagan's administration nurtured a new cadre of public officials (including Dick Cheney, Donald Rumsfeld, John Roberts, and Samuel Alito) who embraced social conservatism. The power of the new rural base was reflected in the insurgent candidacy of Pat Robertson, who fared well in 1988 against the first George Bush in rural primaries and again during Pat Buchanan's right-wing rebellion in 1992. Groups like the Christian Coalition, the Moral Majority, and the National Rifle Association continued to expand their influence within the GOP.

In those days my parents were stalwart Republicans, the sort of no-nonsense businesspeople that the chamber of commerce loves to put on the cover of their glossy magazines. My stepfather sold insurance and ran a small tourist shop, and he was elected on the GOP slate to the town council. My mom ran a small community college campus and actively opposed the environmental groups that wanted to shut down the local pulp mill.

When Moral Majority types took over the local Republican chapter in the late 1980s, my parents were indignant. Mom tells the story of sitting in a local caucus meeting when the chairman called for a voice vote to ratify the group's opposition to abortion rights. "They were going around the room," she says. "Yes, yes, yes, every-body saying yes. What could I do? I got up and walked out. I couldn't say yes, but I wasn't going to be the only one in the room saying no."

Like establishment Republicans all over America, my folks grumbled and wrung their hands — and then they stayed quiet. After my stepfather lost a mayoral primary race by a healthy margin, they stopped going to meetings. "Those people" — social conservative activists —

were "mean." They held grudges. They wouldn't come to your store if you crossed them. It wasn't worth the ugliness and the hassle.

It's fair to point out that moderates like my folks didn't have much leadership. Few centrist Republicans on the national stage were willing to stand up and say, "Wait a minute. That's not what our party is about." In a symbolic sense a whole generation of Rockefeller-establishment leaders fled the room. They stayed silent while their party was changed forever.

Really, it wasn't even a fair fight. Social conservatives came at the GOP's old guard from every angle. Newt Gingrich sent out thousands of cassettes and videotapes, urging rank-and-file congressmen to adopt his ideology. Tom DeLay passed out cash and elevated rural allies like Dennis Hastert and Roy Blunt. One of his biographers described the former majority whip as "a political infighter who thrived at being taken lightly — it coaxed opponents to lower their guards while it bolstered his will and heightened his intensity."

Jim VandeHei, the political reporter with the *Washington Post*, tells the story of Dennis Hastert's abrupt rise to power in 1998. "When the House speaker's job opened up," VandeHei wrote, "Rep. Christopher Cox (R-Calif.) — a telegenic policy intellectual from the nation's most populous state — seemed like a logical candidate."

> Cox certainly thought so. He brooded over his options and mused about a possible run on CNN. But while Cox was in the studio, J. Dennis Hastert was winning the cloakroom. With powerful backing from Rep. Tom DeLay, Hastert — a decidedly untelegenic, nuts-and-bolts pol from small-town Illinois — was working the phones, cutting deals and forming alliances. Within hours, he locked down the most powerful job in Congress.

Homelander leaders are often described as rubes and hayseeds. But men like Gingrich, Hastert, and Delay always seem to be one step ahead of the moderates. They drew their intensity from a vibrant grassroots community. In Thomas Frank's description of Kansas politics, he writes of small-town insurgents rallying from "a place of peeling paint and cheap plywood construction and knee-high crabgrass and shrubbery dying in the intense heat and expired cars rotting by the curb."

> The Cons were organizing at their fundamentalist churches on the edges of town; they were turning out for primaries in numbers that casual Republicans could never hope to match; they were trouncing [moderate Republicans] in races for everything from precinct committeeman to sheriff.

It sounds sort of ominous, like a scene from *Children of the Corn,* but the fact is that homelanders won the GOP's intraparty culture war fair and square. From the first salvos in 1964 to the final assault in 1994, they got organized and they got passionate. They built their membership lists and recruited candidates who represented their points of view. For better or worse, that's democracy. That's populism. That's how people rise up and demand change.

Far from being pawns of the Republican Party, homelanders now control much of the party's internal workings. It can be argued that the GOP was the first and most successful target of the rural revival. Social conservative Republicans dominate many state legislatures, the training ground that develops future national politicians. Rural elites wield a remarkable amount of influence at a national level, shaping presidential primaries and setting the legislative agenda.

In 2000, social conservatives in South Carolina crushed the candidacy of Arizona senator John McCain with a nasty whispering campaign about his sanity. For all his bluster, McCain accepted his humiliation and went back to playing the good soldier. Despite this remarkable loyalty, rural social conservatives have made it plain that they will do anything necessary to derail a McCain candidacy in

2008. This may sound arrogant or presumptuous, but it's actually nothing more than a clear statement of power.

It is now de rigeur for Republican presidential hopefuls to audition before Dr. James Dobson, making the pilgrimage to Colorado Springs. A group of evangelical leaders has announced that they will hold joint interviews with presidential hopefuls before the 2008 primaries. Gary Bauer, president of American Values, told *USA Today* that the coalition would be "a very effective way to nail down where people are on cultural issues."

It goes without saying that pro-choice Republicans and non-ideological centrists need not apply. Indeed, even the most popular members of the GOP's metro wing find themselves blocked from real power. At the Southern Republican Leadership Conference in March 2006, John McCain finished fifth in a straw poll. He tried to conceal his unpopularity by urging delegates to vote for George Bush as an act of solidarity, prompting Matt Drudge to report that "the move seemed to expose the McCain team's insincerity about its position with the base."

If nominated by his party, McCain could practically guarantee Republicans another eight years in the White House, but homelander activists don't even rank him in the top three most popular GOP candidates. McCain's not the only odd man out; in an otherwise glowing profile of former New York City mayor Rudy Giuliani, Associated Press political writer Beth Fouhy acknowledged that his metro views make him a long shot in 2008.

> Analysts agree that Giuliani's long record of support for gay rights, gun control, and legal abortion could very well disqualify him as a candidate among the conservatives who dominate GOP presidential primaries.

# ⑮

# The Big Homelander Payoff

U rban Americans cling to the myth that homelanders are naively working against their own economic interests when they vote for conservative Republicans. "If you earn over $300,000 a year, you owe a great deal to this derangement," writes Frank. "Raise a glass sometime to these indigent High Plains Republicans, as you contemplate your good fortune."

Progressives take it for granted that working-class people in small towns should give their loyalty, almost by default, to the Democratic Party. They assume that rural voters can be wooed back into the fold if we can only convince them to "vote their pocketbooks" instead of their moral values.

"Democrats should start by talking about economics," insists pollster and strategist Anna Greenberg. "I believe there has been a startling absence of economic narrative. We didn't challenge Bush on tax cuts in 2002. There's a political price to pay." But Greenberg acknowledges that changing the channel won't be easy: "Kerry tried to bring economics in. Some of that's not in [the Democratic Party's] control."

That's putting it mildly. In order to convince rural Americans to rearrange their political priorities, Democrats will have to displace some of the homelander community's most deeply held moral and cultural values. Folks like my brother see their crusade against same-sex marriage and abortion in much the same way that progressives viewed the civil rights and antiwar movements of the 1960s.

"Liberals tend to think that right-to-life activists are motivated by a desire to control women's bodies or sex lives, and to impose a religious doctrine," Steven Waldman wrote in *Slate*. "[But] the heart of the pro-life position is the belief that life begins at conception and therefore abortion is murder. Liberals should ask themselves, if they honestly believed that life began at conception, wouldn't they do exactly what the pro-life forces do?"

Even if a progressive marched into the 2008 campaign armed with a New Deal–style plan to revive rural America, most small-town voters simply wouldn't buy it. Few of the people I interviewed over the past year trust metro Democrats. They certainly don't believe that the MoveOn.org crowd will solve their problems — and with good reason.

During the roaring 1990s, Bill Clinton shoved NAFTA down the throats of small towns, a move that helped dislodge hundreds of rural factories and manufacturing plants. Clinton helped the Republican Congress slash social spending. According to U.S. Census data, the urban-rural economic divide grew dramatically during his eight years in office. In my own corner of northern New York, the Clinton years were punctuated by the loss of a shoe factory, a couple of cheese plants, and two paper mills, all drained away by a global economy that was fostered by metro Democrats like Robert Reich and Robert Rubin.

During Kerry's campaign in 2004, Democrats continued to shift to the center on economic policy, blurring distinctions between the two parties. A poll by Democracy Corps before the 2004 election found that 53 percent of rural voters perceived either "small" or "no" difference between the two candidates' economic policies. Almost by default that left social policy as the deciding factor. In small towns, Republicans will win that matchup every time.

The embrace of traditional values — and the rejection of "pocketbook" voting by homelanders — will be a hard nut to crack for another reason. The psychological shift reflects a growing economic malaise in small towns, on which Republicans have capitalized brilliantly.

From the mines of West Virginia to the grain belts of the Midwest to the logging towns of Idaho, rural industries were once the bedrock of American prosperity. By the 1950s, however, private-sector capitalism was tanking in small towns. The Great Depression was an anomaly in metro society, a painful hiccup, but in hundreds of rural counties, it was a dark sign of things to come.

The Second World War offered a brief respite as factories churned overtime and the government paid top dollar for the sort of commodities that small towns produce. But postwar globalization stripped away tens of thousands of jobs, decimating whole regions. Farms failed, consolidated, or were bought out. Industries that managed to hang on often relied on government subsidies or massive giveaways of public land, water, or minerals.

"The mass lay-offs in rural America are going to be a structural issue that will stay with us," says Mark Drabenstott, director of the Federal Reserve Bank's Center for the Study of Rural America. "We thought in the past that the driver of growth in rural America would be cheap labor, cheap land, and cheap taxes. But with globalization, there are plenty of places in the world that have those things. Why would a factory move from Chicago to western Iowa, when it could move from Chicago to China?"

Homelander communities contribute an ever-shrinking portion of the nation's gross domestic product. Small towns that continue to thrive are generally close to urban centers. They serve as bedroom communities, or vacation home destinations, limpets on the rock of the vast metro economy.

"In rural America we have very low innovation capacity," Drabenstott says. "It really starts on the suburban edge of Chicago and goes all the way to Dallas and back up to Glacier National Park. Within that area you have a huge swath of small-town America that's asking, 'How do we reinvent ourselves?'"

Anyone baffled by the resentment and anger festering in small towns should look at the economic numbers. Although 21 percent of Americans live in small towns, a study conducted in 2003 found that rural counties are home to only 17 percent of the country's private businesses. Even worse, homelander industries attract less than 1 percent of the nation's venture capital funding, which means they're less able to innovate, often incapable of taking the sort of risks that create new jobs.

For all the up-by-the-bootstraps rhetoric and talk of a proud ownership society, the churn and risk of modern metro American capitalism make a lot of homelanders nervous. "I think people are troubled today by the pace of change," Iowa's Democratic governor Tom Vilsack told *Salon* magazine. "I think they're insecure; I think they're nervous, and with some justification, because things are constantly changing."

Here lies one of the most profound differences between the two tribes. Metros often organize their lives around capitalist striving, professional advancement, and greed-is-good careerism. It's not just white yuppies; take the subway up to Spanish Harlem and you'll see more hustle in one square block than you'll find in all of Elk County, Kansas. Urban culture can be caustic and even brutal at times, but it's still largely a meritocracy. People who work hard expect to get ahead.

Often those options just aren't open to homelanders. Rural folks who want to join the entrepreneurial race generally leave town; they head to the city or the suburbs. Those who stay behind tend to build their value systems, their identities, and their political sensibilities around other things, such as family, church, and community. "People have personal standing in a discussion about what a good marriage is and what a bad marriage is," says Republican strategist Bill Greener. "They feel comfortable in that dialogue. It's about something they understand, a lot more than a discussion of trade policy."

"While many young people move away [from small towns], those who remain decide that money is not their god," writes columnist David Brooks, in *On Paradise Drive.* "There is intense social pressure not to put on airs. In many rural precincts, if you had some money and tried to drive a Mercedes, you'd be asking for trouble. If you hired a cook for a dinner party, people would wonder who died and made you queen."

This sort of thing reflects a kind of ideological schizophrenia among conservatives, who regularly lambast urban loafers (especially African Americans) who display a lack of capitalist zeal. But among rural conservatives, it is seen as proof of humility and earthiness — a virtue rather than a vice. "The error of liberals is that they concern themselves over much with material things," wrote Barry Goldwater in the 1960s.

> Liberals regard the satisfaction of economic want as the dominant mission of society. They are, moreover, in a hurry. So that their characteristic approach is to harness the society's political and economic forces into a collective effort to compel "progress." In this approach, I believe they fight against Nature. Conservatism looks upon the enhancement of man's spiritual nature as the primary concern of political philosophy.

One of the great ironies of modern politics is that homelander communities are the last place in the United States where the welfare state remains wholly intact. Thanks in great measure to Republican largesse, New Deal–style jobs programs are ubiquitous outside the urban beltway. Rural industries still enjoy massive taxpayer subsidies, protectionist trade restrictions, and government price supports.

This slacker reality is often ignored or disguised by the national media, where small-town folk are portrayed either as disenfranchised victims or as rugged, self-sufficient individualists — or both. We're used to seeing homelanders who work harder than metro, who get by on their own sweat and doggedness.

At a conference for rural journalists held in Washington, D.C., a newspaper editor from Nebraska complained that rural communities just "aren't on the radar screen" for government agencies. "The governor has a small part of his budget devoted to ethanol," he complained, shaking his head with real disgust. "That's his whole plan. Even our [rural activists] are out there saying, 'You have to pull yourself up by your bootstraps.'"

"It all comes down to people having to fix themselves," agreed the Kellogg Foundation's Ali Webb. "We hear that that's how [small-town folks] want it. There's no role for government."

But the notion that rural towns are stoically going it alone simply doesn't wash. A report prepared in 2005 by the National Rural Network found that homelanders receive roughly $6,020 per person in total federal spending each year. On the face of it, that's identical to the per capita spending enjoyed by metros, but rural folks usually live in towns where the cost of living is significantly lower, which means that the government checks go further.

What's more, according to the study, rural communities also spend far more of their federal funds on direct "transfer payments to individual citizens, such as Medicare, Social Security, and Farm Commodity Program payments." Metro communities, by contrast, tend to invest public capital in infrastructure programs and long-term economic development.

When one looks at direct cash payments to individuals, homelanders generally receive about 20 percent more per person from the federal government than do their urban neighbors. In Arkansas, according to a study by the National Committee to Preserve Social Security, rural folks are one-third more likely to rely on Social Security than are their urban neighbors. The same is true in Montana. In Michigan small towns are nearly twice as dependent on those government checks as Detroit and its suburbs.

This reality is a nervous subject for homelanders, rarely discussed in public. When I mentioned the issue to Allen, he bristled. It was the first time in our long series of conversations that he became truly angry. "I don't believe it," he said bluntly. "No way. I know so many people in my town who refuse to take government money. They'd rather go hungry. They'd rather see their kids go hungry."

I promised to check my facts and make sure my argument was sound, but Allen urged me to drop the issue: "You'll just alienate people," he said. "You'll make rural people so mad that they won't listen to anything else you have to say."

Small-town folks don't only wait for government checks to arrive in the mail; they also look increasingly to the public sector for jobs. Because welfare carries such negative connotations in small towns, Republican politicians prefer to spend dollars putting people to work. Indeed, homelanders look increasingly to the public sector for their jobs and in many rural counties government has emerged as the single largest employer.

Take Grant County, Nebraska, in the Sandhill cattle country north of Lincoln, where George Bush scooped up 89 percent of the vote. Over the past few years, 7 percent of the population has drifted away, searching for better opportunities. In 2002 the county's seven hundred residents who remained shared roughly $3.1 million in federal spending. That's more than the combined value of all local retail sales.

Roughly one in four Grant County workers draws a paycheck directly from federal, state, or local government agencies. In urban Lincoln, Nebraska, by contrast, only one in twelve workers relies on the taxpayer's dime.

Grant County isn't unique. In northern New York, Republicans talk earnestly about cutting taxes while also struggling mightily to expand every conceivable government program that will funnel a paycheck into the region. They fund new museums and build parks and bike paths. They bankroll tourist trains and operate ski resorts that lose millions of dollars a year. In Hamilton County, the most Republican place in New York state, fifteen of the top twenty employers are in the public sector.

Remember Ochiltree County, Texas, the most Republican place in America? Despite all the drown-the-government-in-the-bathtub rhetoric, the county's nine thousand residents gobbled up nearly fifty-three million dollars in federal spending in 2003 alone. That's 10 percent higher than the per capita average for Texas — and a whopping 25 percent higher than per capita spending in urban Dallas.

According to an analysis of government spending patterns compiled by the University of Texas at Austin, "Governments employ much larger portions of the population in more western and rural counties [of Texas]. Government employment is more important proportionally to western and rural counties across the state than to major urban centers."

It's not only Bush's massive federal bureaucracy that's creating New Deal–style public works programs in small towns. Rural states are also putting as many homelanders as possible on the payroll. In Alaska and Wyoming one out of every six workers is directly employed by a state or local government agency. In Dick Cheney's home state, sixty-seven thousand people draw a taxpayer-funded salary. That's five times the number of Wyomians working on farms or ranches. It's also twice the level of government employment that you will find in metro Massachusetts or Maryland.

"Some of the other states with big bureaucracies also lean conservative in their politics, including Mississippi and Alabama," notes Chris Edwards, in a 2006 report published by the conservative Cato Institute.

If homelander America's public sector is bloated, the private sector isn't much better. Many rural industries are lavishly subsidized, either in direct cash payments from taxpayers or through donations of publicly owned land and resource rights. Ranchers depend directly on federal pasturelands leased well below market value. Mining corporations lay claim to lucrative mineral deposits on public property (some smack in the middle of our national parks) and pay a fraction of the ore's value.

In Alaska's Tongass National Forest, where I grew up, the Forest Service has spent more than eight hundred million dollars since 1982 building logging roads and "infrastructure" for a timber industry that has dwindled to fewer than three hundred workers. According to a study by Taxpayers for Common Sense, the federal government spent forty-eight million dollars supporting Tongass loggers in 2004 alone. In return for its investment, the Forest Service earned back "user fees" worth roughly eight hundred thousand dollars.

American taxpayers are shelling out $157,000 a year for every logger, truck driver, and camp cook who goes into the publicly owned forests to cut down old-growth Sitka spruce. Of course, most of the money doesn't go to the loggers; it goes to hundreds of U.S. Forest Service workers who live in the towns that surround the forest. Their paychecks buttress the local economy.

Farmers pocket even more money. Nearly two million homelanders now receive direct payments of one kind or another each year from the U.S. Department of Agriculture (USDA). That's a remarkable figure when you consider that only about six million Americans now work in agriculture.

During the same period that we were weaning welfare moms off their unwholesome government dependency, payments to farmers and rural-based agricultural corporations more than doubled, from $7.2 billion in 1995 to $16.4 billion in 2003. "The federal subsidies are bad," Vickie Lippelmann, a farmer in Oberlin, Kansas, told the *Kansas City Star*, "but we're very dependent on them now. Without them, many of us would go out of business."

Not surprisingly, sixteen of the twenty states most heavily subsidized by the USDA voted for George Bush in 2004. The biggest drain of them all was Texas, which absorbed roughly $1.8 billion in federal farm aid in 2003 alone.

Commodity subsidies are a long-standing tradition in American politics, but under the Republican Congress the big growth sector has been pure, undiluted pork. Between 1998 and 2004, the value of congressional "member items" larded onto federal budget bills jumped threefold — to an astonishing $32.7 billion.

A survey by *Harper's Magazine* in July 2005 found more than eleven thousand earmarks in one spending bill alone. The largesse included a one hundred thousand dollar payment for goat meat research in Texas, half a million dollars for "future foods" studies in Illinois, and another half-million dollars for "cool season legume" research in Idaho and Washington state.

This surge in political spending reflects a brilliant electoral strategy devised by former House majority whip Tom DeLay. Under his leadership, Republicans scrapped the old seniority ranking system, used for decades to dole out coveted appropriations committee assignments. Those seats now go to GOP members who are considered weak or vulnerable. "This lent wobbly new lawmakers two vital assets," wrote Ken Silverstein, in a *Harper's* article titled "The Great American Pork Barrel." "[F]irst, the ability to direct pork projects to their home districts, thereby impressing constituents with their ability to bring home federal monies; second, a fail-safe method of filling campaign war chests — namely, by tapping earmark seekers for donations."

The rural feeding frenzy reached a new pinnacle with the 2005 Transportation Bill. Alaska congressman Don Young, chairman of the House Committee on Transportation and Infrastructure, has come to be seen as something of a homelander Robin Hood, robbing money from highly productive blue states and funneling it to red states.

Young scored more than nine hundred million dollars in projects for Alaska, the third-largest haul of any state, despite the fact that he represents a total population smaller than San Francisco. Thanks to his influence, the federal treasury will bankroll not one but two massive and equally unnecessary bridge projects.

The most notorious folly is a $223 million span taller than the Brooklyn Bridge that will connect the village of Ketchikan (population eight thousand) to a largely uninhabited island. It's true that the local airport sits on the far side of the channel, but only half a dozen flights land and depart each day. Travelers can already catch a convenient ferry that departs every half hour.

Alaska's stunning porkfest made for great headlines, with per capita spending from that one piece of legislation topping $1,800. The conservative *Weekly Standard* weighed in with a rare note of outrage, calling Young the "head hog" in the Republican Congress. But Young found himself in good company. The top ten recipients of transportation money, per capita, were all rural states. Seven out of ten were Republican strongholds.

In Montana the haul was $440 per person — not quite Youngian largesse, but pretty respectable. In North and South Dakota, homelanders bagged roughly $350 per person. How did the big urban states fare? The places where the vast majority of Americans live? California pulled in a meager $78 per capita. Texas and Florida both received a measly $40 per person.

Even those numbers hide the degree of small-town gluttony. In many metro states, Republicans from rural-exurban districts were often able to suck up the lion's share of federal spending. Nearly a third of California's $2.6 billion went to projects sponsored by one lawmaker, former Republican House Ways and Means Committee chairman Bill Thomas, who represents a bustling exurban district around Bakersfield. (The primary industries are agriculture and oil.) The same story played out in Illinois, where more than one-third of the $1.2 billion in transportation spending went to projects sponsored by House Speaker Dennis Hastert.

In some instances, the homelander all-you-can-eat federal buffet isn't just unsavory — it's downright dangerous. When the Department of Homeland Security was created, Republicans agreed chastely to deny themselves line-item pork add-ons. But they also established a marvelous formula for dispersing the money, guaranteeing that each state would receive just under 1 percent of the total allotment. As a consequence, more than one-third of the entire Homeland defense appropriation was parceled out without any assessment of actual need or threat.

Low-population states such as Wyoming and North Dakota received forty dollars per person to arm themselves against the impending al-Qaeda menace. Meanwhile, the big I-have-a-bulls-eye-on-my-forehead states like California and New York managed to pocket about five dollars per capita. This has real-world consequences. In tiny towns in Alabama you can find volunteer fire squads with expensive bio-terror equipment; meanwhile, our major ports remain vulnerable owing to a lack of funding. In May 2004, New York City's Republican mayor, Michael Bloomberg, complained to CBS News that his citizens remained firmly "in the crosshairs."

The growing reliance on government has led homelander politicians to tolerate record-level budget deficits. Speaking privately, some rural analysts worry that a kind of "small-town socialism" has emerged that will be painfully difficult to dislodge. New businesses that do move into rural counties often do so only because they're bribed with government subsidies or lucrative public sector contracts. Homelander politicians have taken to calling this practice "public entrepreneurship."

The lavishness of this arrangement confuses critics on both the right and the left, who expected at least some modicum of fiscal conservatism from a Republican Congress and a right-leaning White House. In fact, the GOP has embraced massive federal programs and deficit spending as an integral part of its homelander strategy. Rural Americans have been integrated into an airtight patronage system.

Metros still wring their hands over the quaint notion that Republicans plan to dismantle the social safety net, but according to a study prepared by the Cato Institute, non-defense discretionary spending rose 36 percent during Bush's first term, a spree that topped Lyndon Johnson's during the era of the Great Society. The big-ticket item was a budget-busting new Medicare drug entitlement program that will cost taxpayers $72.4 million a year. Overall, wrote Brian Riedl, with the conservative Heritage Foundation,

"Federal spending has grown twice as fast under President Bush as under President Clinton."

It's worth noting that whenever the White House has threatened rural funding, homelanders have rebelled at once. The small-town voters who backed Bush's second term in huge numbers also helped to kill his campaign to reform Social Security. Despite months of heavy lifting by the president and the right-wing media, polls found that only one in three Americans approved of the privatization plan. Once again, the people portrayed by metros as lapdogs and authority puppets gave a collective thumbs-down to one of the administration's pet projects. And once again, Bush backed off.

One reason for Bush's willingness to spend money like a lunatic is that it doesn't come out of his constituents' pockets. The vast majority of federal tax dollars flow out of highly urbanized blue states, such as California, Illinois, Massachusetts, New York, and New Jersey. Meanwhile, nine of the ten states that gobble the most money from the federal treasury voted for George Bush. All are rural or low population states, including Montana and North and South Dakota.

Consider the state of Alabama. This bedrock homelander stronghold ranks forty-ninth in terms of annual contributions to the federal treasury, paying only about $3.9 billion in 2003. But the state received back about $7.8 billion in federal programs. For every dollar that Alabama's right-leaning voters shelled out, they received $1.82 back — not a bad return. According to a report compiled by the Tax Foundation, that amounts to an annual stipend of $899 for every man, woman, and child in the state.

Mississippi, New Mexico, and West Virginia did just as well, nearly doubling the return on their federal tax payments. And once again, Alaska deserves a special mention. The state that used to be known as Seward's Folly still acts as a powerful drain on U.S. taxpayers. The residents of that state pay no state income tax and contribute a measly six thousand dollars per person on average in federal taxes.

But they receive roughly twelve thousand dollars per person from Washington every year.

Thomas Frank blasts Kansans for being oafish enough to support Republicans, but when you look at the numbers, this homelander "derangement" begins to look more like sheer cunning. In 2000, when George Bush was elected, taxpayers in Kansas were shelling out $16.6 billion to the IRS and receiving back only $14.2 billion. They were losing more than $2 billion a year — nearly a thousand bucks for every man, woman, and child in the state. Now *that's* truly stupid. By 2003, however, the situation had reversed dramatically. Kansans paid only $14.4 billion and received a tidy $18.2 billion back from the federal treasury — a sweet profit of $1,200 per person.

If homelanders are the big winners in the federal pork game, metro Americans are the big losers, bleeding tens of billions of dollars each year. Eight of the ten states with the biggest net loss in federal tax dollars voted for John Kerry in 2004. Urbanites in New Jersey lose an astonishing forty-three cents out of every dollar paid in Federal taxes.

The most generous Americans, in real dollar terms, live in California, Illinois, and New York. Metros lose an average of twenty-five cents out of every dollar they pay to the IRS. Because their economies are enormous, the total outflow is astronomical. According to the California Institute, a policy think tank based in Washington, D.C., taxpayers in California underwrote the national porkfest to the tune of fifty billion dollars in 2003. Illinois, meanwhile, chipped in another ten billion dollars, while New York state added seven billion.

And poor John Kerry. Homelanders not only beat him at the ballot box; they also picked his state's pockets to the tune of $3.1 billion.

A few weeks after I raised this issue with Allen, we were driving through eastern Kansas, looking at some of the old farmsteads and ranches where we lived as children.

The towns were dusty and hollow looking. Alfalfa and soybeans stretched in every direction, but many of the main streets were boarded up, the sidewalks empty. Most of the commercial activity seemed to be going on at gas stations and convenience stores sprinkled along the county highway. A little hamlet called Elk Falls billed itself as "a living ghost town" and featured an outhouse museum on the main square. But time and again we cruised past new, state-of-the-art public schools with expansive, manicured sports fields.

Looking out the window of the truck, Allen smiled wryly and said, "I wonder who's paying for all those new buildings?"

## 16

# Breaking with Tradition

The Republican Party's homelander strategy would crumble overnight if Democrats weren't such pariahs outside the urban beltway. They don't have to *win* small-town votes; they just need to narrow the gap, so that rural counties don't feed such large surpluses of votes to GOP candidates.

There was a time not so long ago when the Democratic Party was *the* political choice for rural America, from the populist Great Plains to the Rocky Mountain West to the back roads of the South. As recently as 1980, rural counties were as likely to swing Democrat as Republican. Small-town progressives from states like Montana and Oklahoma helped push through some of the twentieth century's most important progressive legislation. Go back a little further and you find many small-town societies that were downright left wing — far more radical and experimental than the cities.

So what happened? How did liberals lose rural America? By far the most common explanation for the Democratic retreat is that the party leaders fell on the sword of racial justice, sacrificing their southern base in the 1960s when Lyndon Johnson signed the Civil Rights Act. Johnson's former press secretary, Bill Moyers, tells the story of finding Johnson late one night sitting in his pajamas "in a melancholy mood" while reading the day's papers.

"I asked what was troubling him," Moyers said. "'I think we just delivered the South to the Republican Party for a long time to come,' he said. Even as his own popularity soared in that heady year, the President saw the gathering storm of a backlash."

In conversations with rural Democrats across America, you hear this anecdote recounted again and again. The subtext is clear: We did the right thing; we took a bullet for racial equality. "You had a whole string of civil rights laws that were enacted in the 1960s," John Watson tells me one afternoon, as we sit on a friend's porch drinking a beer.

Watson is the Democratic Chairman of Blanco County, Texas, where Lyndon Johnson grew up. That part of Texas is now a Republican stronghold. "Barry Goldwater announced his so-called southern strategy, which said a lot of things that white people in the south, who were either overtly or covertly racist, found comforting."

There's no doubt that racial politics helped to uproot the Democratic Party in the South, providing a useful wedge for Republican politicians. But the race theory alone doesn't explain one of the most remarkable political realignments in American history. For one thing, it rests on the dubious notion that bigotry was limited to the South. To be sure, Jim Crow was a different animal than northern racism, more virulent and more institutional. But racial hatred has also shamed and bloodied many of our northern cities and suburbs, where Democrats continue to prosper.

The race argument also fails to explain the collapse of progressivism in small towns north of the Mason-Dixon line. Democrats didn't just lose the South; they lost most of rural America. Kansas, Maine, and Oklahoma sent thousands of boys to die fighting the Confederacy. Now they're bright red Republican strongholds. "I think it was a combination of a lot of factors," Watson says. "After Goldwater the whole sixties thing came along, and Vietnam. The South has always been militaristic and sends more people to the armed services than other areas of the country. Then in the early seventies abortion came on the scene and gun rights became a contentious issue and Republicans were seen to be better on that, though southern Democrats certainly don't advocate taking guns away."

Republicans continue to win enormous loyalty in homelander America, despite their opening the party to far more people of color.

Obviously, the Republican record on race is mixed. Ronald Reagan launched his 1980 presidential campaign in Philadelphia, Mississippi, the tiny town where three civil rights workers were murdered in 1964. He gave his first campaign speech the day before the anniversary of the killings but never mentioned the victims or the crime. Instead, he talked about states' rights.

More recently, Republican strategists have worked aggressively to suppress the black vote in battleground states such as Florida and Ohio. There are signs that some conservatives hope to quietly gut provisions of the Voting Rights Act. But it's also true that over the past quarter century the GOP has elevated more people of color to positions of real power than has the Democratic Party. Republican Clarence Thomas, a movement conservative, is the only African American currently seated on the Supreme Court. Colin Powell, the son of Jamaican immigrants, was appointed by the first President Bush to head the Joint Chiefs of Staff. The second President Bush named him to serve as America's first black secretary of state. Powell was succeeded in the post by Condoleeza Rice, the first African American woman to hold the country's top diplomatic job. Bush also named Alberto Gonzales to serve as the nation's first Hispanic attorney general.

Republicans may be the party of white Protestants — the American Theocracy, as Kevin Phillips describes it — but they have cheerfully crafted a Supreme Court dominated by Roman Catholics. Ken Mehlman, head of the Republican National Committee, is Jewish. Grover Norquist, one of the GOP's most powerful appa- ratchiks, is married to Samah Alrayyes, a prominent Palestinian Islamic activist. It's hardly the sort of roster you'd expect to find in a party that hopes to build a coalition of rubes and crackers and Christian cultists.

The truth is that Republicans are too smart for that sort of thing. Karl Rove knows that conservatives will need the Hispanic vote if they hope to thrive in the coming decades. That's why the Bush administration is pushing a liberal immigration policy that many homelanders loathe. The GOP needs partnerships with Roman Catholic and Jewish organizations — not to mention corporate leaders — groups that won't associate themselves with racial or religious bigotry.

I'm not suggesting that pockets of fierce prejudice don't remain in parts of rural America. But it's simply no longer possible to claim that Republicans are winning homelander support based on the sly wink of racial or ethnic intolerance. This myth has prevented Democrats from examining their own failure to connect with small-town voters.

So if it wasn't race — or not race alone — what was it? What triggered the progressive movement's rural collapse? Put bluntly, the Democratic Party's urban wing decided over a period of decades that its agenda could move faster and further without interference from homelanders. These Democrats shifted their loyalty from a small-town base (white, socially conservative, politically and economically liberal) to an urban base (ethnically mixed, socially progressive, and economically moderate). In the process, they rejected a particular brand of rural populism that had shaped the party's agenda for half a century. They also abandoned hundreds of rural politicians, whose popularity once helped to anchor the Democratic Party's majority in Congress.

Bear with me for another bit of history. In the 1800s, America's East Coast cities were conservative, even aristocratic, places. The frontier was where you went to reinvent yourself and to make your fortune. The hardships of rural life often forced people to play by different rules. As a consequence, homelanders were often political and social innovators.

Western prairie towns were the first to elect women to public office. Communities on the northern plains adopted communal or even socialist economic models. Granges and farm cooperatives were an accepted part of small-town life. Labor unions were active in hundreds of mining and factory towns. Utopian communities, most based on idealistic interpretations of Christian Scripture, sprouted in the new territories.

This rural progressivism makes conservatives itch and tug at their collars. They prefer to remember our small-town past as a golden age of picket fences, church steeples, and girls in gingham dresses pushing hoops down country lanes. They summon up visions of coherent families with strong fathers, nurturing mothers, and obedient, well-mannered children, all getting by on their own gumption. The real story is more nuanced and often more radical.

In 1878 a group of uppity farmers known as the Greenbackers hooked up with certain labor organizations to form the Greenback-Labor Party, which won more than a million votes in congressional races nationwide. The fight wasn't just symbolic; they managed to send fourteen congressmen to Washington, D.C. The group demanded the vote for women at a time when that notion was still considered extreme. They pioneered the idea of federal regulation of interstate commerce and even campaigned for a progressive income tax.

The Greenbackers morphed into the Populist Party, a coalition of progressive farmers and workers that won control of the Kansas legislature in 1880. In 1892 a frontiersman from Ohio named Jim Weaver ran for president on the Populist ticket and won twenty-two electoral college votes, every one of them in rural states. His popular support in urban states such as Massachusetts and New York languished in single digits, but in Georgia, North Dakota, and Wyoming, Weaver was a force to be reckoned with.

At about the same time, a rural Republican named Colonel Robert Ingersoll was barnstorming around the country, urging the rigid separation of church and state. "Religion should have the influence upon mankind that its goodness and its argument give it, and no more," Ingersoll argued. "The religious argument that has to be supported by law is not only without value, but a fraud and a curse."

These same rural progressives helped to engineer the political rise of William Jennings Bryan. Bryan was the Howard Dean of his day — capable of howling with the best of them — and he ruled the Democratic Party from 1896 until 1908. He was a washout as a presidential candidate, but he reinvented his party, inviting in blue-collar workers, farmers, and the nation's growing pool of European immigrants.

In those days, progressives were deeply wedded to traditional ideas about American life and culture. Faith and activism intertwined in ways that would echo during the 1950s and 1960s in the black churches of the civil rights era. Homelander liberals drew their idealism not from academic theory but from the Gospels and the example of Jesus Christ. This mingling of faith and progressive politics defined the Democratic Party from the end of the Civil War right up through the early 1930s.

"If we have to give up either religion or education," Bryan declared, "we should give up education." These days, his mingling of progressive politics and missionary zeal strikes metros as problematic. "Some biographers saw Bryan's stand [against evolution] as a contradiction of the progressive goals he fought for during most of his life," wrote Doug Lindon, in an essay for the University of Missouri Law School's history of the Scopes trial.

In Bryan's day, however, people saw no contradiction at all. It's not that they were closed-minded or ignorant; homelander culture could be remarkably sophisticated. Starting in the 1870s, traveling Chautauquas brought lecturers, classic theater, Metropolitan Opera performances, book clubs, and intellectual debate to thousands of hamlets and county seats across the country. By some estimates, the audiences reached forty million people a year, nearly half the nation's population.

Founded in rural western New York by a Methodist minister, the circuit fostered revival-style gatherings for people who believed that well-rounded Americans needed a dose of Gounod and Goethe along with their Genesis. The English actor Ben Greet, a star of the Bible Belt stage just before the First World War, declared that his audiences were "God-fearing, God-loving, and know their Bible and their Shakespeare."

This is the great American civilization that rural conservatives still dream of, a place where a life of the mind exists that is tolerant and courteous and full of rigor but also firmly shaped by the Christian values of modesty, decency, and hard work.

You might think it difficult to imagine modern evangelical churches urging high culture on parishioners; but go to the Bob Jones University Web site, which describes the university as "a liberal arts nondenominational Christian university [which] stands without apology for old-time religion and the absolute authority of the Bible," and you will find advertisements for this year's opera and drama series featuring Shakespeare's *King Lear* and *Twelfth Night* and Arrigo Boito's *Mefistofele*.

But if rural Americans in Bryan's day were open to a certain type of refinement, they were hostile to the nation's increasingly modernist city-centered life. The first great homelander backlash was led by the Democratic Party, whose leaders clung to the ideals of Jeffersonian democracy, with its focus on individualism, small government, and Christian virtue. During Bryan's first presidential campaign, his speeches were the stuff of an American Moses, promising to lead the people back into a sort of agricultural promised land:

> The great cities rest upon our broad and fertile prairies. Burn down your cities and leave our farms, and your cities will spring up again as if by magic; but destroy our farms and the grass will grow in the streets of every city in the country.

The Republicans of that era were far more metro in their orientation. Their candidate in 1896 was William McKinley, governor of
Ohio and a proxy for the East Coast establishment. When the votes
were counted, Bryan captured most of the homelander states that are
now bright red Republican territory, but McKinley connected well in
cities and prevailed with just over 50 percent of the popular vote.

> With urban populations swelling, ruralist Democrats found
> themselves on the losing side of history. It was a theme that
> would repeat over the next twelve years as Bryan's homelander
> rhetoric was narrowly rejected again and again.

In 1912 the Democrats nominated Woodrow Wilson. He was a
transitional figure, a rural-urban hybrid not unlike Bill Clinton eight
decades later. The governor of New Jersey and the president of
Princeton University, Wilson was also a native southerner and a
devout Presbyterian. Also like Clinton, he managed to attract less
than half the popular vote, not even quite matching Bryan's tired
popularity. He won the White House only because Teddy Roosevelt's
"Bull Moose" (Progressive) Party split the Republican base.

In the slow rupture between Democrats and rural culture, Wilson is
distinguished by being an appealing figure to almost no one. He was a
cold fish, an intellectual and a scholar, hardly the sort of guy homelanders would ask in for a beer. His personal convictions were distinctly traditional, far more in line with the Pat Robertsons and James
Dobsons of today than metros are comfortable acknowledging. After
his election, Wilson confided to his campaign manager that "God
ordained that I should be the next president of the United States."

Wilson believed in America as a Christian republic, a nation
imbued with divine purpose and responsibility. His idealism wasn't
modern or rationalistic; it was a direct articulation of faith: "My life
would not be worth living if it were not for the driving power of religion," he wrote in 1915. "Never for a moment have I had one doubt

about my religious beliefs. There are people who believe only so far as they understand — that seems to me presumptuous and I am sorry for such people."

During his eight years in office, Wilson was often a daring progressive. He endorsed women's suffrage and fought to end government corruption; he developed a radical new finance system that is credited with saving thousands of family farms; and he appointed Louis Brandeis, the first Jewish American to sit on the U.S. Supreme Court.

But like many homelanders today, Wilson also harbored deep reservations about the extent and quality of American inclusiveness. He spoke bitterly of German, Irish, and Italian immigrants, who wished to retain their languages and their cultural identity. He worked infamously to segregate the federal government and endorsed the activities of the Ku Klux Klan, which had been in decline. "The white men were roused by a mere instinct of self-preservation," Wilson wrote, in his *History of the American People,* "until at last there had sprung into existence a great Ku Klux Klan, a veritable empire of the South, to protect the Southern Country."

Under Wilson, the Democrats were still deeply wedded to the small-town principles of social tradition and racial insularity, but they were also experimenting with big-government ideas, including the creation of the Federal Reserve Board and the national War Finance Corporation. The party's northeastern wing embraced futuristic metro concepts such as the League of Nations. Urban thinkers also began to introduce new ways of thinking about the federal government's role in everyday life.

Thomas Jefferson had argued famously that "government is best that governs least," a principle that shaped American society and Democratic policy for more than a century. But in 1915, Louis Brandeis suggested that a new set of problems had arisen — "industrial despotism," he called it— that might require greater federal intervention.

We are as free politically, perhaps, as free as it is possible for us to be. On the other hand, in dealing with industrial problems the position of the ordinary worker is exactly the opposite. The individual employee has no effective voice or vote. [Corporations have developed] within the State so powerful that the ordinary social and industrial forces existing are insufficient to cope with it.

These ideas wouldn't come to fruition for another decade. In 1920, as the Jazz Age dawned, the Democrats pulled off one of the great electoral self-immolations in American history. (By comparison, the Republican Revolution of 1994 looks like a tap on the chin.) Ohio governor James Cox led the Democratic ticket with thirty-seven-year-old Franklin Roosevelt as his running mate. They won just 34 percent of the popular vote.

Eight years later, New York governor Al Smith was the Democratic standard-bearer. He was the first true metro to lead the party, a product of the Tammany Hall political machine and a Roman Catholic. He also opposed prohibition, the big "family values" issue of the day. Homelanders turned away in droves. Smith managed to carry a dozen of the nation's big cities, but he still lost the popular vote by an overwhelming margin.

Even the supposedly "Solid South" rebelled, with Florida, North Carolina, Tennessee, Texas, and Virginia giving their electoral votes to California Republican Herbert Hoover.

That same year, Franklin Roosevelt struck a deal with his enemies in the Tammany machine and got himself elected governor of New York. Following his humiliation in 1920, Roosevelt had watched his party's southern and rural base fail to produce any semblance of victory. Democrats had lost control of Congress in 1915. With the exception of Wilson's eight years, Republicans had occupied the White House since 1897. With America's urban populations continuing to swell, the Democratic reliance on fickle homelander voters seemed quixotic at best.

As governor, Roosevelt began to test some of the big metro ideas that would later reshape American society. He developed a massive hydroelectric project on the St. Lawrence River, bringing industry and electricity to rural parts of the state. He recruited a team of urban intellectuals, who would later follow him to Washington. After the stock market crash in 1929, he talked New York's legislature into spending twenty million dollars on public works projects to spur employment.

In the early 1930s the nation was a clumsy hybrid. We were a modern industrial and urban society equipped with little of the bureaucratic and institutional apparatus now considered essential for running a vast and complex economy. Despite the progressive reforms of Teddy Roosevelt and a half-dozen new programs created by Woodrow Wilson during the First World War, the federal government remained ill-prepared to deal with a domestic crisis on the scale of the Great Depression.

When the 1932 presidential campaign got under way, America's economy was imploding, especially in rural communities. Farmers were drowning under huge surpluses of grain and other commodities, which in turn triggered historically low prices. With revenue crashing, farmers couldn't pay their bills. There were twenty thousand farm foreclosures every month. Violent protest marches erupted in state capitals across the country. A little more than a century after his death, Jefferson's prophecy that the country would endure as a sort of yeomanry of farmers, orchard keepers, and plantation owners was unraveling.

Roosevelt was the first politician to offer a coherent alternative, a new vision of what the United States might look like. "I pledge you, I pledge myself," he said, "to a new deal for the American people." He wasn't just promising a chicken in every pot. He meant to create a different kind of American society, framed by what he would eventually describe as a second Bill of Rights. "We have come to a clear realization of the fact that true individual freedom cannot exist without economic security and independence," Roosevelt argued in a later speech delivered in 1944. "People who are hungry and out of a job are the stuff of which dictatorships are made. In our day these economic truths have become accepted as self-evident."

Disgust with Herbert Hoover was widespread even among Republicans, and Roosevelt won by a landslide. He scooped up 57 percent of the popular vote and dominated in every part of the country. He was the first Democratic president in history who didn't owe his election to rural or southern voters. His coattails also helped Democrats claim control of Congress, and here again the gains came mostly outside the South. Democratic candidates upset incumbents in Connecticut and New Hampshire, helping to build an eleven-seat Senate majority. In the House the victory was even more complete: Democrats picked up a total of ninety-seven seats and the Farmer-Labor Party gained another four, leaving the GOP in tatters.

Few understood it yet, but the umbilical chord between Democrats and their homelander base had been stretched to the breaking point. The party's center of gravity had shifted northward toward the teeming industrial churn of America's cities. Over the next half-century, southerners and ruralists would continue to carry the Democratic Party's banner, but they would often be marching in the opposite direction, aligning themselves with conservative Republicans in an effort to block metro programs, from the New Deal to the Fair Deal to the Great Society.

It's important to note that Roosevelt wasn't only a metro by political calculation. Unlike Bryan or Wilson, the new president was urban in spirit and personal experience. He had deep cultural ties to Europe. He had a progressive, outspoken wife in Eleanor Roosevelt. Through his life, he sustained a marriage of convenience while also carrying on a series of romantic affairs with other women, including his personal secretaries.

In his Four Freedoms speech, delivered in January 1941, Roosevelt spoke about religious faith in a new way that sounds essentially modern.

> The first is freedom of speech and expression everywhere in the world. The second is freedom of every person to worship God in his own way everywhere in the world. The third is freedom from want, which, translated into world terms, means economic understandings, which will secure to every nation a healthy peacetime life for its inhabitants everywhere in the world. The fourth is freedom from fear, which, translated into world terms, means a worldwide reduction of armaments.

This Democrat wasn't taking his progressive ideas from the New Testament; his mentors were urban theorists from Harvard and Columbia University. They were men willing to experiment with basic tenets of American society in ways that more traditional politicians found shocking. "It is common sense to take a method and try it; if it fails, admit it frankly and try another," Roosevelt said. "But above all, try something."

During his first hundred days in office, he did just that. His team pushed through a remarkable wave of legislation, raising the girders of a modern industrialized superstate, with a centrally coordinated economy. With the Depression deepening, Roosevelt demanded that every American be mobilized into a kind of national collective, with himself as the great leader.

> We must move as a trained and loyal army willing to sacrifice for the good of a common discipline, because without such discipline no progress can be made, no leadership becomes effective. We are, I know, ready and willing to submit our lives and our property to such discipline, because it makes possible

a leadership which aims at the larger good. This, I propose to offer, pledging that the larger purposes will bind upon us, bind upon us all as a sacred obligation with a unity of duty hitherto evoked only in times of armed strife.

Nothing like it had ever been seen before in America, even in wartime. In the course of a few short months, Roosevelt placed new restrictions on industry. He created the Agricultural Adjustment Administration, the Civilian Conservation Corps, the Emergency Relief Administration, the Federal Deposit Insurance Corporation (FDIC), the Tennessee Valley Authority (TVA), and the Works Progress Administration (WPA). Some advisers were urging even more radical steps. "You may have no alternative," declared progressive theorist and columnist Walter Lippman, "but to assume dictatorial power."

Given Roosevelt's present-day mythical status (especially among metros, but also with many homelanders), it's hard to imagine the outrage and fear that his vision inspired among rural politicians. We see the breadlines, the Dust Bowl shacks, the hungry faces peering out of Walker Evans's photographs, and we imagine that any opposition to the New Deal must have been purely reactionary. During the civil rights era, those who supported states' rights and decentralized political power became associated with veiled racism and bigotry.

But Roosevelt's promise of concentrated and benevolent federal power meant a profound break with his own party's tradition. It was a direct repudiation of Democratic leaders who still embraced a different ideal of what America should look like. They wanted a nation of small farmers and independent entrepreneurs. They wanted a government small enough that it would never challenge the freedom of its own citizens.

To make matters worse, Roosevelt's imperial presidency emerged at a time when other centralized governments — in Italy, Germany, and Japan — were sliding into dictatorship. Historian Michael Ybarra describes the anxiety inspired by Roosevelt's new, working-class "army."

> In September, more than a quarter million people paraded down Fifth Avenue behind the lofted banners of the Blue Eagle, the symbol of the [National Recovery Administration]. Some watching the biggest demonstration in New York's history, with platoons of young men in the olive-drab uniforms of the Civilian Conservation Corps, thought they saw disturbing parallels with Germans marching behind their new bent-cross symbol.

When opposition to Roosevelt's agenda first surfaced, it didn't come from Republicans. The GOP was crippled and rudderless, but almost from the beginning rural Democrats began to drag their heels. The year Roosevelt came to office, freshman senator Pat McCarran, a Democrat from Nevada, accused the White House of a dangerous power grab. "In all the history of legislation, when was there more drastic power demanded?" he asked. "When was the individual struck at more seriously?"

Other rural Senate Democrats, including Bennett Champ Clark of Missouri and Louisiana's Huey Long, were early critics of the New Deal. In the House of Representatives, they were joined by Alabama congressman George Huddleston, a populist who had daringly campaigned against American involvement in the First World War. "I have called myself a Democrat, an old-fashioned, southern, Jeffersonian Democrat," Huddleston declared.

> It is not my fault that I am unable to accompany these courageous gentlemen to the extremes of radicalism and that variety of "liberalism" — the "liberalism" of Mussolini and of Stalin and of Hitler — which they support upon the floor of the House.

Over the next few years, more and more rural Democrats would break away, a revolt that widened when Roosevelt tried to expand the size of the Supreme Court and pack it with his own cronies in 1937. It was a power grab of almost unprecedented hubris, the sort of thing that makes George Bush look like a choirboy. Senator Burton Wheeler, a former Progressive Party candidate for vice president and a Democrat from Montana, led the successful fight to block the move. "It is an easy step," Wheeler wrote, "from the control of a subservient Congress and the control of a Supreme Court, to a Hitler or a Mussolini."

Senate Democrats such as James Byrne from South Carolina, Joe O'Mahoney from Wyoming, and Pat McCarran from Nevada were in constant rebellion against Roosevelt, even allying themselves with the Republican opposition. "The time has come for the people of this country to rise in defense of their own country," McCarran declared.

Metros — and the vast majority of Americans — now see the New Deal as the political norm. Programs like Social Security, Medicare, and food stamps enjoy immense popular support and are accepted as a necessary "safety net," without which society couldn't function.

But in the 1930s hundreds of populists and reformers and idealists were deeply troubled by the big-government infrastructure taking shape around them. "The difference between attacking J. P. Morgan in the name of labor and Franklin Roosevelt in the name of the individual is not as large as we might think," wrote George Packer (grandson of George Huddleston), in his family history *Blood of the Liberals*.

In 1938 the simmering rift between Roosevelt's urban agenda and his homelander detractors burst into open warfare. After six years in the White House, Roosevelt was at the height of his power. He had cowed the Supreme Court into approving his most far-reaching legislation. He might well have been able to use his authority (and popularity) to rebuild support among political elites in rural America, even in the South.

But Roosevelt was angry and impatient. In a sign of things to come, he decided that if small-town politicians wouldn't join his "loyal and trained army," they would have to go. "Government cannot take a holiday of a year, or a month, or even a day," Roosevelt declared in a radio address in June 1938, only a few months before the midterm elections, "just because a few people are tired or frightened by the inescapable pace, fast pace, of this modern world in which we live."

He set out to campaign openly against congressional opponents within his own party — mostly in the South but also in New York and Nevada. Roosevelt hoped to elect a new slate of candidates loyal to the Democratic Party's "definitely liberal" principles. "I feel that I have every right to speak," he said, "in those few instances where there may be a clear-cut issue between candidates for a Democratic nomination involving these principles."

It was a violent break with political tradition, the first overt rupture between the Democratic Party's new urban-progressive wing and the traditional rural-conservative base. During a whistle stop tour through Nevada, Roosevelt appeared with Senator McCarran's opponent in the Democratic primary, calling him "brother" and embracing him in front of a crowd. The move came to be known as "Roosevelt's purge," and critics saw it as another sign of the president's growing despotism.

When the dust settled, it became clear that Roosevelt had overreached. "Every conservative Democrat on the President's hit list was reelected in triumph as a Democrat," noted Walter Cronkite, who wrote about the 1938 election in an essay for NPR. "[But] over the next twenty-five years, the South grew increasingly restless in the Democratic Party."

In addition to those from the South, rural voters from eastern Oregon to the north country of New York state had begun looking for different ideas and different leadership to better reflect their values. The schism between rural and urban values, long present in America's cultural life, had begun to twist the nation's politics.

After 1940 it seemed to many progressives that metro culture had come of age politically, eclipsing small towns for good. Democrats could win elections and reshape American society by appealing to a new coalition of urban Jews and Roman Catholics, African Americans, women, young people, and educated professionals. "These are without doubt the years of the liberal," declared metro icon John Kenneth Galbraith. "Almost everyone so describes himself."

The agenda was ambitious. Poverty and civil rights came first, but the list of goals and demands seemed to grow every year. After the Second World War, a new political generation came of age, the first in American history to grow up in metro culture. Progressive activists were outraged by the escalating war in Vietnam. Modern feminism emerged, and liberals began calling for the legalization of abortion. After the 1969 Stonewall Riots in New York City, gay and lesbian issues moved onto the front pages of American newspapers for the first time.

Roosevelt's vision of a large, benevolent federal bureaucracy flourished for decades under Democratic and Republican administrations alike. Efforts to roll back major programs were defeated easily. As noted earlier, Barry Goldwater challenged Lyndon Johnson in 1964 and was crushed. But this metro victory served to only embolden progressives, suggesting that the real fight was between those who wanted incremental progress and those who wanted radical change.

"1968 was sort of the culmination of a lot of things when you talk about urban and rural," says cultural historian Mark Kurlansky. "Everybody was either scared or tremendously excited about the revolution that was about to happen. There was this belief that things were going to be drastically reordered. People were afraid of the movement. They were afraid of disorder. The whole thing that [Richard] Nixon seized on was that the progressive politics of America were alien to a lot of people."

But it wasn't just Nixon's propaganda. The truth is that a new generation of metro activists were moving in cultural and political directions that *were* alien to most homelander Americans. Many urban activists were increasingly radicalized. They were willing to forgo the ballot box, trading peaceful protest and debate for violence and disruption. The New Deal's buttoned-down brain trust had been replaced by yippies, Black Panthers, and Weathermen. Where Roosevelt had promised a broader pact between the government and its citizens, provocateurs like Abbie Hoffman and Eldridge Cleaver seemed to think that democracy itself had failed, that social structure of almost any kind was absurd and corrupt.

Cleaver, the Black Panther's "minister of information," was a poet and an ex-con who served time for drug and rape convictions. He gave a speech at Stanford in 1968 calling for a "pussy power" revolution and challenging California governor Ronald Reagan to a duel to the death. "I give him a choice of weapons," Cleaver said, "a gun, a knife, a baseball bat, or marshmallows."

"The Black Panthers were moving away from the civil rights movement and the Weathermen were taking over the SDS [Students for a Democratic Society]," Kurlansky acknowledges. "The police and the FBI kept provoking them. Somebody hits you, you want to hit back. That was the moral failure of the left."

As Kurlansky suggests, this metro fury had more than a little justification. The massive black migrations of the 1940s and 1950s had spawned vast slums. Poverty and crime were epidemic. Meanwhile, great progressive icons were being murdered: John Kennedy in 1963, Malcolm X in 1965, Bobby Kennedy and Martin Luther King, Jr., in 1968. Month by month, the war in Vietnam slaughtered more American kids. On the home front, police violence against protestors and activists was escalating.

If homelanders felt increasingly isolated from the political establishment, so too did thousands of young urbanites. By almost any measure, American society was spinning out of control. Race riots ripped through Newark and Oakland and Detroit. Students occupied college campuses. "Our young people, in disturbing numbers, appear to reject all forms of authority from whatever source," complained Grayson Kirk, president of Columbia University, "and they have taken refuge in a turbulent and inchoate nihilism whose sole objectives are destructive."

One of the more remarkable aspects of Roosevelt's metro revolution was that he convinced average people that there were other models for American life, other ways of doing things that would still protect the nation's essential values. Each generation would be more prosperous, more tolerant, freer, but there would also be order. There would be a new framework, based on free trade and democracy.

But as philosopher and educator Thomas Dewey acknowledged as early 1935, there was real tension among metro progressives, between those advocating reform and those seeking revolution.

> Liberalism has long been accustomed to onslaughts proceeding from those who oppose social change. But today those attacks are mild in comparison with indictments proceeding from those who want drastic social changes effected in the twinkling of an eye, and who believe that violent overthrow of existing institutions is the right method of achieving the required change.

For nearly forty years, Democrats, like their Republican counterparts, held the fringes at bay. But in 1968, Nelson Rockefeller (under attack from Richard Nixon's right-wing supporters) and Lyndon Johnson (besieged by metro progressives) both collapsed. The center couldn't hold. It was Johnson's capitulation as much as his endorsement of civil rights that poisoned the Democratic Party's fortunes in rural America.

Metro radicals were emboldened even further by Johnson's withdrawal. They descended on the Democratic National Convention in

Chicago, and for a week images of rioting protestors were beamed into America's homes. Most television viewers were appalled, but the reaction in homelander country was pure disgust. If this was the future that urban progressives were offering, they didn't want it. At the end of the convention, Democratic nominee Vice President Hubert Humphrey, a South Dakota native and former senator of Minnesota, gave a bitter statement to CBS's Roger Mudd:

> I know what caused these demonstrations. They were planned, premeditated by certain people in this country that feel that all they have to do is riot and they'll get their way. They don't want to work through the peaceful process. I have no time for them. The obscenity, the profanity, the filth that was uttered night after night in front of the hotels was an insult to every woman, every mother, every daughter, indeed, every human being, the kind of language that no one would tolerate at all.

Leftists were perfectly happy to be intolerable. They had no interest in sustaining Roosevelt's legacy, or in rebuilding popular support for progressive programs in small towns. They had inherited a massive, modern bureaucracy and a laundry list of social programs, all designed to foster new levels of equality, opportunity, and prosperity, and they wanted none of it. It was Abbie Hoffman who boasted cheerfully, "Because of our actions in Chicago, Richard Nixon will be elected president."

In hindsight, it's hard to see the protests as anything but a self-indulgent tantrum. They represented the maturing of a political sensibility that is profoundly and essentially modernist. For many metros, civil life had become a kind of theater, a social ritual, and a form of self-expression. Rebellion is an accepted part of youth culture, a form of experimentation, one of the many identities that young urbanites adopt and throw off like fashion.

This lack of seriousness and civility may have been a final wedge, separating Democrats from their traditional rural base. If progressive metros weren't prepared to lead, homelanders would look elsewhere. Because of the rural bias in our political system, the Democratic Party has been crippled by this loss. Since 1968, they have held the White House for a grand total of twelve years. In a nation where 80 percent of the population lives in cities and suburbs, John Kennedy was the last true metro Democrat to win the presidency.

# ⑰
# Let's Hear It for Rural Democrats!

A year before the 2004 elections, I stood in a big convention hall in Lake Placid, New York, watching Senator Chuck Schumer pump his fist in the air. "So stand up everybody and applaud your-selves!" he crooned. "This big room is full of rural Democrats! Let's hear it for the rural Democrats! No longer an oxymoron!"

The crowd cheered a little uncertainly. Even here, at a pep rally for the party's rural base, the metro leadership couldn't shed that little twist of urban irony. Despite Schumer's cheerleading, the folks gath-ered here in the old Olympic skating rink knew the truth better than anybody: Their rural organization was in shambles, even in much of the "blue" Northeast.

The lack of a solid local base is devastating. Metro politicians know instinctively that when dealing with black or Hispanic communities they need on-the-ground ambassadors who can introduce them into the culture and lend them credibility. But Democratic ties to rural America have atrophied to such a degree that they often have to start from scratch.

"What has happened is that we have ceded the politics of rural America to the Republican Party," said New York's Senator Clinton. "We shouldn't write off any part of the country; I'm not willing to do that anymore."

That may sound disingenuous, coming from a woman deeply reviled by tens of millions of homelanders. When I mention her name to Allen, and raise the specter of another Clinton running for the White House, he hunches his shoulders. "It would be a *disaster*," he says. "She is hated in my part of the country." But in 2000, Clinton

campaigned hard across rural New York. I followed her one afternoon (along with a bedraggled group of urban reporters) down a
rutted dirt road that led to Big Moose Lake, in the wildest corner of
the western Adirondacks. The mud was so deep in places that one of
the Secret Service cars sank to its axles. The collection of cabins and
trailers boasts a year-round population of forty-three.

The crowd waiting for her at the local tavern numbered less than a
dozen, most registered Republicans, but Clinton worked the room tire-
lessly, and it paid off. Despite her carpetbagger reputation (and eight
years of White House scandal), Clinton actually managed to win two
conservative northern counties; she nearly picked off a couple more. In
the years since, she has made it a point to visit rural New York regularly,
funneling money and encouragement to local Democratic leaders.

Partly as a consequence, St. Lawrence County (so far north that it
hugs the Canadian border) sent a Democrat to the state assembly for
the first time in twenty-three years. "She's smart enough to know
that rather than just ignore the areas that don't traditionally vote
Democratic, it's better to try and win them over," says Joseph Butler,
the Republican mayor of Watertown, a small conservative city
anchored by the Fort Drum Army Base. "I think she's doing it."

Unfortunately, Clinton is a rare exception. For decades, metro
Democrats have allowed the party's small-town grass roots to wither,
starved by weak fund-raising, an unpopular message, and a shortage
of viable local candidates. "We're not strong at all," said Stephanie
Sterling, party chair in Essex County, Vermont. She gave a weary smile.
"The Republicans far outweigh the Democrats and Independents out
my way. I don't know why."

"In order to get my petition filled out and filed, I only needed thirteen names," grumbled Jeannie Ashworth, town supervisor in the
tiny New York town of Wilmington, where Republicans outnumber
Democrats three to one. (Statewide, Democrats outnumber
Republicans two to one.) "So that tells you how many Democrats are
registered in my area."

According to Ashworth, the only way she could get herself elected was by convincing locals that party affiliation didn't matter very much. It turns out this is an increasingly common strategy among rural Democrats nationwide. They run against their own party's national leadership or disavow party loyalties altogether, running essentially as independents.

Nebraska senator Ben Nelson's Web home page is splashed with a big red banner, and the word *Democrat* is nowhere to be found.

Kansas governor Kathleen Sebelius is another leading Democrat (she's policy chair for the Democratic Governors' Association) who avoids unnecessary mention of her party affiliation. Even former Virginia governor Mark Warner's home page downplayed his party loyalties. A possible presidential candidate in 2008, his Web biography offered only a single terse line that reads *affiliation: Democrat.*

This blurring of party lines may be a necessary survival strategy, but it's hardly a blueprint for rebuilding a powerful Democratic brand in rural America. "People want to know why it is that folks in rural places tend to vote in a conservative manner," says Amy Glassmeier, an analyst at Pennsylvania State University. "It's a philosophical question, but it's also an empirical question. You can look at where people are, their objective circumstances, what options they have — which are often very few."

John Kerry was the most metro-centric Democratic presidential candidate since Michael Dukakis. In a sign of things to come, his campaign speech in Lake Placid was awkward and flavorless, with few references to small towns or the issues that rural voters care about. He talked about boilerplate stuff, education and the economy. His suit jacket stayed on. He gave the distinct impression of a politician who wasn't really there, not really talking to this crowd.

When the address was over, the event's organizer, Stuart Brody, then head of New York's Democratic Rural Caucus, didn't hide his disappointment. "Our candidates' speeches have to be torn up," he groused. "You can't talk in generalities. You have to come in here and say here's how we're going to affect your life." He described the Lake Placid gathering as a timid start: "This is the first time in years that our party is making a concerted effort to go into rural areas," he said. "A whole new infrastructure is being put into place."

But even Brody couldn't help swatting aside the hot-button issues that preoccupy many of his neighbors. "Prayer in the public schools, flag burning, capital punishment, pro-choice and pro-life," he said, ticking the list off on his fingers with a tone of exasperation. "They're used by Republicans to divide America. They divert attention from critical issues."

"It seems to me that a lot of rural folks really care about that stuff," I said. "They're worried enough about values and moral issues that they're willing to put aside some of the pocketbook things that Democrats prefer talking about."

"I know those people," Brody conceded, nodding slowly. "And what I try to say to them is that America was founded on the principle that you can do what you want to do, so long as you don't impose it on other people. That's why we are America. So why should we start imposing our moral views on others? I say let people live."

Not a bad message, if you're talking to voters in Chicago or Detroit or Manhattan, but there's not much there that will win over folks in Georgia, Kansas, or South Dakota. Speaking privately, many Democratic politicians and strategists concede that they're just not comfortable "out there" in rural America.

Occasionally, this alienation bubbles to the surface. In 1982, New York City mayor Ed Koch torpedoed his chances in the governor's race by slamming homelander culture in an interview with *Playboy*. "This rural America thing — I'm telling you it's a joke," he babbled. "You have to drive 20 miles to buy a gingham dress or a Sears Roebuck suit."

Democrats aren't usually quite as stupid as that, but they are visibly uncomfortable with the rhythms and the pace of small-town life. It's so easy to make gaffes. One false word and you look like a poser or a fake. Poor John Kerry casually misnamed the Green Bay Packer's shrinclikc football stadium — calling it Lambert Field, instead of Lambeau — and the fumble echoed in the media for weeks. Even when things go reasonably well, Democratic candidates can be sure that pundits will mock them savagely for reaching out to homelanders.

In a typical salvo, the *New York Times*'s Maureen Dowd wrote that Kerry's hunting trip was a stab at convincing middle America that he wasn't "a merlot-loving, brie-eating, chatelaine-marrying dilettante." Balancing the two worlds is brutally complicated, especially for urban politicians who are constantly vulnerable to accusations of waffling and flip-flopping.

In 2006, Hillary Clinton endorsed a constitutional ban on flag burning, a symbolic nod to homelanders roughly as meaningful as George W. Bush's embrace of "compassionate" conservatism, but metros weren't having it. The progressive blogosphere exploded with rage as urban pundits declared Clinton a Judas and a quisling. Florida's *St. Petersburg Times* described the measure as "political pandering of the worst kind. She was against outlawing flag-burning before she was for it."

Perhaps as a consequence, some party leaders have begun to dream of a day when they can avoid or ignore homelander culture altogether. In a speech just before the New Hampshire primary, John Kerry observed that Al Gore had "proved that he could have been president without winning one southern state, including his own." The comment suggests one possible future for America, where the two political parties are geographically and culturally segregated.

In his book *A National Party No More*, Democrat Zell Miller claimed that his party's leadership has already traveled a considerable distance down that road, alienating small-town politicians. "If you are only an individual with some rural route address, then forget it, Bubba," Miller wrote. "The politicians won't even blow you a kiss, much less romance you."

In fact, the Democratic Party still boasts a small but increasingly influential rural bloc. Senators such as Jeff Bingaman from New Mexico, Tim Johnson from South Dakota, and Mark Pryor from Arkansas have managed the remarkable feat of getting themselves elected in homelander states where their party's national platform is deeply unpopular.

In 2004, John Kerry won a majority of votes in only 13 percent of the country's most rural congressional districts, but homelander Democrats won House seats in those same districts 44 percent of the time. "The success of these rural-district Democrats at avoiding [Bush's] presidential coattails is a big reason why their party remains within striking distance — fifteen seats — of winning control of the House," notes *Congressional Quarterly*'s Gregory Giroux.

Rural leaders hope to expand their success by tugging the party to the right. "Sometimes I don't think my leadership gets it," Representative Bud Cramer, a Democrat from Alabama, told the Associated Press. "If they're to really stand the chance to take the House back, they've got to leave those members plenty of room to vote where their district is coming from rather than where the national party is coming from."

Homelander Democrats also hope to reshape the party's message before 2008, staking out a more rural-friendly position on social issues. In the *Washington Post*'s post-mortem of the 2004 election, West Virginia governor Joe Mahchin (a pro-life, pro-gun, anti–same sex marriage Democrat) declared unequivocally, "It's the values — my goodness, it's the values."

"It's not necessarily our ability or inability to speak about our faith," Iowa's Democratic governor Tom Vilsack told *Salon*. "It's the perception that the Democratic Party is a party of elites, whether intellectual or Hollywood, and that as a result perhaps it's more difficult for Democrats to understand where common folks are coming from."

———  ———  ———

It's undeniable that rural voters will be key to the Democratic Party's chances in 2006 and 2008. Jimmy Carter and Bill Clinton reached the White House by winning homelander support. Democrats who have failed to connect in small towns have fallen short. Without a small-town revival, it's also hard to see how the party can reclaim control of the Senate.

But many urban Democrats squirm at the idea of being forced to embrace a Bible-and-guns platform. "I don't subscribe to any of these notions that we have to examine our conscience as to who we are," grumbled San Francisco congresswoman Nancy Pelosi to the *Washington Post.* "We know who we are. We know what we stand for."

This intraparty rift has made it nearly impossible for Democratic leaders to craft a coherent message. Ten years after the Republican Revolution, they have yet to find a unifying vision along the lines of the GOP's Contract with America. Critics accuse the party's leaders of being irresolute and cowardly, but the muddle is far more structural and ideological.

Put bluntly, many of the rural Democrats remaining in the House and Senate simply don't agree with core metro supporters. They're not cowardly or wishy-washy; they just don't share the same values. "In most cases, rural-district Democrats have voting records in line with their conservative-leaning constituencies but at odds with their party's more liberal leaders," noted Giroux.

This metro-homelander rift has been starkly visible in the Democratic Party's opposition to the Bush agenda. Urban leaders such as Ted Kennedy, Chuck Schumer, and Nancy Pelosi have pushed for open confrontation, while rural leaders such as Harry Reid and Ben Nelson have usually avoided open fights. (In 2005 and 2006 Reid began to toughen his stance, under pressure from the Democratic Party's metro wing and from progressive blog and Web sites.)

This internal split made headlines during the Supreme Court confirmation hearings for Justices Roberts and Alito. Most of the

Democrats who crossed over to vote in favor of John Roberts as chief justice came from homelander-dominant states. White House strategists openly courted rural Democrats. Even before Alito met with members of the Judiciary Committee, he sat down with Tim Johnson of South Dakota, Ben Nelson of Nebraska, and Mark Pryor of Arkansas. All three became staunch supporters of Bush's nominees.

Democratic leaders find themselves at a peculiar and dangerous crossroads. Since the election of Franklin Roosevelt, urban voters have seen the Democratic Party as *their* political movement, personified by progressive icons such as John and Bobby Kennedy and more recent leaders such as John Kerry, Hillary Rodham Clinton, and Barak Obama. But top Democrats have learned from painful experience that they can't win without homelander support.

The question, of course, is how to straddle these two worlds. Hillary Clinton has worked hard to prove that she can compete outside the urban beltway, or at least keep her homelander deficit to a survivable level. But she also has to satisfy her political base. So far, Clinton's approval ratings remain strong among core Democratic voters, but many of her one-time supporters are skeptical. High-profile metro activists like Arianna Huffington and Susan Sarandon have declared Clinton a traitor for staking out symbolic center-right positions on issues like flag burning and the Iraq War.

The bigger question faced by metro candidates like Clinton is whether they can win. Her candidacy might trigger a rural surge even more powerful than the tidal wave that swamped Kerry in 2004. There is growing pressure within the party to choose a more rural-friendly candidate, a politician who hasn't alienated quite so many small-town voters.

Politicians like former Virginia governor Mark Warner and Iowa governor Tom Vilsack are positioning themselves to step into the leadership role if Clinton should stumble. Both have brilliant track records appealing to rural and exurban voters. Warner is famous for sponsoring a NASCAR team and for winning red-state elections at a time when Republicans seemed all but unbeatable. He's the sort of candidate who might bring the party back to its rural roots, reviving the tradition of small-town populism that energized it through its first hundred years.

Republican strategist Bill Greener is convinced that this sort of homelander candidate could break through in much the same way Bill Clinton did in 1992. "Despite the sort of divide that exists between things that have a Democratic label and the communities that constitute rural America, all it takes is somebody who's able to connect at a very human level."

Still, it's hard to imagine those pro-life, pro-gun candidates playing well in America's blue cities. Metros are desperate to retake the White House, but after nearly twelve years of a Republican Congress and two terms of George Bush in the White House, they're also furious. They're tired of the Democratic Party rolling over. They want a candidate who reflects their values, who shares their sense of tolerance and moral nuance. Above all else, they want someone who embraces their urban values.

Put simply, it's increasingly difficult to imagine the candidate who satisfies both tribes. When I ask my brother about the appeal of Democrats with social conservative values, Allen says, "Sure, I'd vote for them. If they're right on my issues, they'll get my vote. I like Joe Lieberman. At times Joe Biden can be tolerable. But aren't those guys despised by the members of your party?"

# One Nation, Two Tribes

This journey through rural America began with an accidental discovery. Presidential voting returns after 2000 and 2004 — and
congressional elections over the last decade — show that the nation's
culture war is being fought on a starkly urban-rural axis. It's no
longer the Mason-Dixon line that divides one tribe from another; it's
the metro beltway that runs between our cities and inner suburbs
and the sprawling exurbs and small towns of the homeland. This rift
often transcends the old divisions of race and class, North and South.

Homelander culture isn't confined to red states in the South or the
Midwest. Rural values remain deeply entrenched in much of small-
town America, from California to Massachusetts to Florida. As a
consequence, the rural-conservative movement is more broad-based
and resilient than metros have understood. It's not only Bible
thumpers in Georgia and wild-eyed Kansans; some of the nation's
most influential traditionalist thinkers and activists have come from
Illinois, Indiana, New Jersey, New York, and Pennsylvania.

In many instances, small-town insurgents have proved far more
politically astute and aggressive than have their urban neighbors.
They have dominated the national agenda by organizing, volunteering, and donating. Metros mutter about rubes, theocrats, and
Limbaugh-listening dittoheads. They complain about stolen elections
and dirty tricks. But for the most part homelanders have won their
fights fair and square. For all the hand-wringing about an evangelical
jihad, rural conservatives have won the lion's share of their battles
honestly, by turning out in record numbers and filling ballot boxes.
Indeed, compared with the often turbulent progressive movements of

the 1960s and 1970s, the homelander movement has been remarkably peaceful and law-abiding.

Of course, it doesn't hurt that many of the states controlled by rural conservative activists enjoy huge structural advantages in national politics. The electoral college strips our most populous urban states of roughly 20 percent of their voting power. That's more than enough to sway close presidential campaigns. The bias in the U.S. Senate is even more profound, effectively guaranteeing rural conservatives a permanent role in American politics, even as our small-town population dwindles. Rural leaders have capitalized on those advantages to remarkable effect. They have also used congressional redistricting to hard-wire a similar homelander tilt into the House of Representatives.

Let's pause a moment to give due credit. The rural insurgency represents one of the most remarkable political comebacks in American history. Tradition-minded conservatives have bucked a trend toward urban liberalization that has swept every other modern industrial society in the world. Driven by a conviction that their vision of society is superior and more wholesome, homelanders have organized a far-flung swath of small-town America (much of it economically depressed, with a stagnant population) into a dominant national movement.

Men like George Bush, Tom DeLay, Dennis Hastert, and Roy Blunt translated razor-thin electoral victories — and fragile congressional majorities — into a daringly conservative agenda that conflicts with the urban values of most Americans. In order to pull it off, they manipulated an entrenched political system, and engineered new alliances with groups that had viewed rural evangelicals with deep distrust, like the Roman Catholic Church. They also co-opted the urban media in ways that left their supposedly more sophisticated Democratic opponents spluttering with impotent rage.

Small-town elites also cemented control over the Republican Party's internal machinery. They rewrote the rules of engagement in the

House and the Senate, neutralizing metro Republican moderates. Rural conservatives thrashed John Kerry, but his drubbing was mild compared with the rough treatment meted out to centrist Republican leaders like Rudy Giuliani, Jim Jeffords, John McCain, William Weld, and Christine Whitman.

In a final turn of the screw, rural leaders proved their skill (and their worldliness) at gaming the federal budget, enriching their communities and their constituents. Thomas Frank laments the "penchant for martyrdom" that has led rural folks to vote against their self-interest, but those misguided rubes have gobbled up hundreds of billions of dollars in New Deal–style subsidies funded almost entirely by metro taxpayers. This achievement makes it hard for Democratic politicians to woo homelanders back into the progressive fold with economic promises and talk of pocketbook issues.

Small-town voters also deserve a little respect. Folks like Allen have a sophisticated sense of what they want from their government. Millions of social conservatives are intelligent, well read, and politically astute. They don't see issues like traditional marriage, abortion, and gun rights as cynical wedge strategies but as part of an idealistic grassroots movement, on a par with the battle for civil rights and the campaign for civil liberties, which motivate urban voters.

Rural folks aren't mindless followers. When they don't get what they want, they speak up aggressively and demand their pound of flesh. It's worth noting that during George W. Bush's first six years in office urban liberals didn't win a single major fight. But homelander activists have handed Bush four stunning political defeats, derailing Harriet Miers's nomination, panning the administration's scheme to partially privatize Social Security, shredding the Dubai ports deal, and flatly rejecting the administration's liberal immigration reforms.

Despite this track record of independence and success, tens of millions of metros continue to dismiss their small-town neighbors as ignorant, pathologically deluded rubes. Conservative leaders are portrayed as tongue-tied, pomade-wearing, Bible-thumping cretins. In April 2006, *Rolling Stone* magazine published a cover story asking bluntly whether George Bush was the worst president in American history. On the cover he was caricatured as a monkey in a dunce's cap. This sort of cultural blindness is pervasive in urban America and extends deep into the heart of the Democratic Party.

It's not just a matter of Howard Dean dismissing Republican voters as lazy, white Christians. While researching this book, I sat in on a discussion between two political operatives, a Republican and a Democrat, both considered experts on rural campaigns. The Democrat seemed like a rank amateur. His ideas about rural values were anecdotal and clichéd. His strategies — which boiled down to more Democrats talking more often about God and NASCAR — sounded shallow and clumsy.

The Republican, by contrast, came equipped with sophisticated marketing research. His candidates were able to use complex mapping and demographic software to study the needs and values of particular rural communities. They were deploying micromedia campaigns, delivering tailored political messages that were often refined to the sensibilities and issues of particular small towns. After listening to them debate for half an hour, I realized there could be little doubt about which side was more sophisticated, more thoughtful, and more professional.

Why do metros and their political leaders refuse to take rural voters seriously? In part it's because many of the nineteenth-century values that homelanders embrace appear deeply misguided, intolerant, and even un-American when viewed from inside the urban beltway. To borrow a phrase from my ten-year-old son, Nicholas, small-town culture just doesn't "scan." Depending on your point of view, rural life may be quaint or creepy, but it sure isn't significant.

As a result of this myopia, metros have been declaring victory over the social conservative menace for forty years. Progressives crowed triumphantly following Barry Goldwater's defeat in 1964. They laughed and japed when evangelical leaders Jimmy Swaggart and Jim Bakker fell to scandal in the 1980s. They breathed a sigh of relief after Ronald Reagan left office in 1988. Bill Clinton's election in 1992 was heralded as a turning point, the long-awaited rise of the post-sixties baby boom generation. Newt Gingrich's ouster in 1998 was celebrated as the end of an era.

Not surprisingly, metros greeted Tom DeLay's downfall in 2006 with the same gloating triumphalism. The Hammer had fallen; he'd been brought low by ethics scandals, indictments, and sagging popularity in his exurban Texas district. DeLay wasn't the only homelander under fire. George Bush's popularity was tanking. Newspapers were running stories about the fall of the Moral Majority and the sharp decline of the Christian Coalition.

Without winning a single election, many of my metro friends were giddily declaring victory. Even some conservative leaders were distancing themselves from the debacle. Newt Gingrich had retreated into professorial psychobabble. "The system's broken," he said, in a speech at Ohio's Mount Union College. "It cannot be repaired. This next generation had better be thinking about how you're going to replace this model [of government] with a twenty-first-century, intelligent, effective system that resembles UPS and FedEx and eBay and Google."

Kevin Phillips, the conservative sage who predicted the rise of a rural-based Republican majority in the 1960s, publicly denounced the GOP as a theocratic movement led by Christian mullahs. "[T]he coming together of a heartland — across fading Civil War lines — would determine control of Washington," Phillips wrote in a 2006 essay for the *Washington Post*. "These developments have warped the Republican Party and its electoral coalition . . . and become a gathering threat to America's future."

All the handwringing on the part of Republicans (and the *schadenfreude* on the part of urban Democrats) has obscured the fact that homelanders are still firmly in power. Despite one of the most scandal-ridden years in American history, Dennis Hastert (a DeLay protégé from rural-exurban Illinois) has remained firmly entrenched as House Speaker. John Boehner, a social conservative from exurban Ohio, replaced DeLay as majority leader. (Boehner's great claim to fame was an episode in 1995 when he handed out tobacco industry checks on the House floor.) The newly crowned majority whip is Roy Blunt, an evangelical Christian from rural Missouri and the former head of Southwest Baptist University.

Outside Washington, meanwhile, the grassroots machine is still running at full throttle. The Christian Coalition and the Moral Majority may have foundered, but new institutions are thriving, building membership and constructing even more sophisticated political networks. Groups like the Southern Baptist Convention, the Family Research Council, Vision America (and its Patriot Pastors component), and Focus on the Family are more influential than ever. With the 2006 midterm elections looming, Republican leaders show little interest in wooing back disgruntled centrist metros. They focus instead on satisfying their conservative rural-exurban base. Here's how Associated Press political writer Laurie Kellman summed up the GOP's strategy:

> Protection of marriage amendment? Check. Anti-flagburning legislation? Check. New abortion limits? Check. Between now and the November elections, Republicans are penciling in plans to take action on social issues important to religious conservatives, the foundation of the GOP base, as they defend their congressional majority. In a year where an unpopular war in Iraq has helped drive President Bush's approval ratings below 40 percent, core conservatives whose turnout in November is vital to the party want assurances that they are not being taken for granted.

Homelanders are still the darlings of the ball. Even John McCain, long heralded as one of the GOP's last great independents, finds himself scrambling to court social conservatives and evangelicals, whom he once condemned as "agents of intolerance." He made headlines (and drew metro raspberries) for agreeing to speak at Liberty University, Jerry Falwell's college in southern Virginia. Asked by the *Daily Show*'s Jon Stewart if he was "going into crazy-base world," McCain answered, with a nervous laugh, "I'm afraid so."

Rural elites were so confident in their stature that even these overtures didn't suffice; the mountain had come to Mohammad, and Mohammad was unimpressed. "There's no support for McCain in this constituency," declared Steve Scheffler, head of the Iowa Christian Alliance, in an interview with the Associated Press. "And I don't see how you can make a scenario where you can bypass us."

In the short term Scheffler is almost certainly correct. Homelanders helped Republicans conquer Washington, and in the process they claimed pride of place as kingmakers and gatekeepers. They won't relinquish that power and influence without a fight. But there are growing signs of discontent within the GOP, rumblings of concern that in the long run their small town strategy may prove disastrously shortsighted.

The reason is simple demographics. For all the talk about rural values, urbanization continues at a dizzying pace. Every year two million more people crowd into America's densely populated metro neighborhoods and inner suburbs. Those blue islands are getting bigger. Some conservatives have begun to acknowledge the nervous reality that many of the country's best and brightest are gravitating to the kinds of communities that vote reliably Democratic.

"When people in their twenties are surveyed on where they want to live," wrote David Brooks in *On Paradise Drive*, "more of them answer inner-ring suburbs than any other place. It's easy to see why. These places combine the sophistication of the city with the child-friendly greenery of the suburbs. The people here are well educated, lively, and tolerant."

Meanwhile, many of the rural counties that vote reliably Republican are stagnating and emptying out. Some of the constituencies that help paint small towns red are dwindling with remarkable speed. Military veterans swung for George Bush by 57–41 percent margins, a landslide in national politics, but the "greatest generation" that fought in World War II and Korea is declining rapidly. In 2000, when Bush was first elected there were 26.4 million vets. By 2008 their numbers will have contracted to roughly 23 million, according to forecasts prepared by the Department of Veterans Affairs. That's the political equivalent of losing an entire red state the size of Utah.

This one cultural change will redefine American elections and diminish the power of the homelander vote. Even if veterans offer the next Republican presidential candidate the same level of loyalty that they gave to George W. Bush, the GOP will have to reckon on roughly one hundred seventy thousand fewer votes in Florida and seventy thousand fewer votes in Ohio. All other factors being equal, that's more than enough to flip both states to the Democratic Party.

But all other factors won't be equal. By 2008, America's rural population will have slipped to about fifty-six million, roughly the level of the mid-1970s. Meanwhile, the nation's metro population will have grown (over census 2000 levels) by another thirty million people. Already, the GOP faces troubling signs that it has spread its homelander base too thinly. Tom DeLay was vulnerable in 2006 in part because of scandals and indictments; but he had also diluted his district's rural-exurban base with so many rebellious metros that his margin for error had shrunk dramatically.

DeLay's not alone. Dozens of Republican lawmakers have stretched their districts, swallowing up as many blue-leaning voters as possible. But every year, the metro tide continues to rise. Unless conservative leaders can broaden their appeal — bringing in more Hispanics and winning back urban moderates — the GOP will be swamped.

Marketing the homelander agenda to mainstream America won't be easy. Not so long ago, rural conservatives could fly under the radar, obscuring the seriousness of their goals and couching their agenda in codespeak. "I paint my face and travel at night," boasted Ralph Reed, former head of the Christian Coalition. "You don't know it's over until you're in a body bag. You don't know it's over until election night."

But the days when Pat Robertson could mutter assassination threats and describe secular-humanist college professors as "killers" on his *700 Club* television program while still appearing as a moderate spokesman for Christian values are over. The era when a politician like John McCain could embrace Jerry Falwell while still portraying himself as a centrist maverick has ended.

The change reflects a growing awareness in metro circles that this version of the Republican Party is profoundly different. Even the most casual voter understands that the GOP is no longer the low-taxes, balanced-budget, small-government movement of Dwight Eisenhower or Gerald Ford. In a way, homelanders are victims of their own success. They have won so much power and claimed victory in so many battles that the enormity of their agenda is hard to conceal. You can't try to remake American society without eventually showing your hand.

But metros are also wising up. They're paying closer attention. Reporters are picking nervously around the edges of homelander culture. There is also a new brand of fiercely urbanist media that is frankly outraged by the social conservative agenda. Partisan cultural observers like Stephen Colbert, Al Franken, Bill Maher, Michael Moore, Bill Moyers, and Jon Stewart have taken up the gauntlet thrown down by Rush Limbaugh and Bill O'Reilly. Outlets like the MediaMatters Web site, Air America radio network, and *Salon* magazine are cranked up and combative. If a Republican lawmaker praises a segregationist leader, you can bet the comments won't be buried below the fold. When an investigation turns up Ralph Reed's seedy e-mails ("I need to start humping in corporate accounts!"), the news flashes gleefully across a hundred blog sites.

Significantly, these metro pundits are challenging directly the notion that rural-traditional values are superior to their own moral framework. "[Bill O'Reilly] is a huge hypocrite," Al Franken jabbed on *The Colbert Report* in March 2006. "He keeps talking about [our] secular liberal value as opposed to [his] traditional values. I didn't know that phone sex was a traditional value. Maybe telegraph sex could be a traditional value, but not phone sex."

But homelanders haven't angered only urban liberals and moderates; they've also managed to alienate millions of Hispanics, who were once seen as the keystone of the Republican Party's permanent ruling majority. Their conservative Roman Catholic values — pro-family, anti-homosexual and pro-life — were seen as a natural fit with rural conservatism. Their exploding numbers would replace the diminishing pool of small-town voters.

George Bush worked hard to woo the Hispanic community in 2004 and succeeded in capturing 40 percent of its vote. In 2006 he proposed a center-left immigration initiative that included a guest-worker program and a system that would allow undocumented immigrants to earn citizenship. His party's corporate establishment loved the plan, which could insure a continued supply of cheap labor, but rural Republicans rebelled and pushed instead for a giant Berlin Wall–style fence to be erected along the U.S.–Mexico border. "Anybody that votes for an amnesty bill deserves to be branded with a scarlet letter, 'A' for amnesty," thundered Iowa representative Steve King, "and they need to pay for it at the ballot box in November."

California representative Dana Rohrabacher described the Bush plan as a "foul odor" and argued that menial jobs currently filled by illegal immigrants should go instead to "the millions of young men who are prisoners around our country. . . . I say, let the prisoners pick the fruits."

It's hard to welcome Hispanics under the Republican Party's "big tent" when homelanders insist on describing them as "a scourge" of law breakers. Because rural activists control his party's primaries, Senate majority leader, and presidential hopeful Bill Frist capitulated. He shelved Bush's bill and agreed to focus his energies on law enforcement and border interdiction rather than worker-legalization programs. Mexican Americans were outraged, and Republican strategists were horrified.

"Most Republican officeholders know that the political — and moral — cost of turning the GOP into an anti-immigration, Know Nothing party would be very great," fretted William Kristol in the *Weekly Standard.* "It could easily dash Republican hopes of becoming a long-term governing party. How many Republicans will have the courage to stand up and prevent the yahoos from driving the party off a cliff?"

It wasn't supposed to be this way. Over the decades, many rural conservatives believed devoutly that they could convince the rest of America to share their values. If they could only speak directly to people, bypassing liberal media and neutralizing the Democratic Party, their agenda would take hold with enough voters to build a broad-based political movement. But if the Republican Revolution has brought some big wins, the "hearts-and-minds" campaign has been a disaster. Despite the success of Fox News, the popularity of Rush Limbaugh's radio program, and the rise of sophisticated new publishing and entertainment outlets, the homelander vision simply hasn't gained traction.

Indeed, just the opposite. The sleeping giant of urban-suburban America has begun to stir, and Republican leaders are justifiably nervous. For all their rhetoric, they understand that metro voters have little interest in a movement that meddles with their churches or their bedrooms. The Terry Schiavo affair scared people, as did the draconian abortion ban in South Dakota. America may still be a nation of Christians, but we don't want to live in a Christian nation. We don't want our morality (or our medical care) dictated to us by lawmakers or politically powerful preachers.

We don't even want to live in small towns. If we did, we wouldn't be leaving them behind for the cities and suburbs.

These aren't subtle trends. In spring 2006, George Bush's approval rating in urban and suburban America had collapsed to 29 percent, a record low for a second-term president. Nationwide, nearly half the voters polled by ABC and the *Washington Post* strongly disapproved of the president's performance, compared with only 20 percent who strongly approved. Support for the Republican Congress, according to a Fox News poll, was even lower, crashing to 25 percent.

Obviously, George Bush isn't solely to blame for the lack of converts in urban America. In the 1990s, Newt Gingrich alienated millions of urban voters with his combative rhetoric and his government shutdown. After 1994, when the Republican Party might have been legitimizing and mainstreaming its big ideas, the party instead went negative, helping to create one of the nastiest and most venomous political climates our country has ever seen. Its secretiveness and win-at-any-cost values also led to remarkable levels of venality and corruption.

Bush's election in 2000 offered a fresh start. Ironically (and tragically), so did the terror attacks in 2001. That was the moment when homelanders might have shown the rest of America that they were the grown-ups. Their small-town ethic would bring us together. The tired liberalism of the New Deal would be replaced by something better and more practical. Their toughness and moral rectitude would bring us back to our national roots, to a time when our leaders were more straightforward and more honest.

It didn't turn out that way. Bush's legacy will be haunted primarily by the disastrous Iraq campaign, but in the context of America's culture war, he will also be remembered as the man who discredited rural conservatism. His bunglers couldn't find a way to keep the lights on in Baghdad after the invasion. They couldn't deliver food supplies to New Orleans after Hurricane Katrina. They couldn't craft a decent Medicare bill or think seriously about climate change or balance a budget.

When Wyoming's Dick Cheney held secret energy policy talks with the oil and gas lobbyists, many assumed that there would be cozy backroom deals (the oil and gas industry has enjoyed historic profits since 2000), but we also assumed that those steely eyed pragmatists would guarantee a reliable flow of oil, gas, and electricity to our nation's industries. Instead, we experienced a major energy crisis in California that disrupted a big chunk of the national economy. We saw the power grid collapse across the entire Northeast and parts of the Midwest. Gasoline shortages triggered historic price spikes at the pumps. The cost for home-heating oil surged.

Metro Americans have come to believe that this administration represents the worst of rural American values, not the best. Homelander apparatchiks like Oklahoma's Michael Brown (former head of the Arabian Horse Show Association) symbolize a kind of soft-bellied, smalltown ineptitude that urbanites find really shocking. A survey released by the Pew Research Center in March 2006 found that the most common adjective for George Bush was "incompetent." Only 28 percent of Americans used positive homelander terms like "Christian," "good," or "honest."

In that other America, outside the urban beltway, things still looked very different. If anything, the gap in perceptions had widened. One afternoon, I stood in a windswept grocery store parking lot in the tiny mountain village of Elizabethtown, New York, interviewing people about an effort in Congress to censure George Bush. "It's absolute nonsense," a guy named Tom Haley told me. He shoved his hands into his jacket pockets, face tense with disgust. "I think Bush is doing a wonderful job. I mean, this man is under enormous pressure."

"You think the president is leading the country in the right direction?" I said, doing my level best to keep the incredulity out of my voice. "Polls show that most Americans, especially in cities, don't like the job he's doing."

"You have to understand that I'm a Christian," he said, "and the president is as well. He's being led by the Lord. He's doing the best he can."

Haley wasn't alone. Bush's approval ratings in homelander country still hovered at a respectable 50 percent. Rural folks weren't blindly stubborn or obedient; they just had different priorities. For many small-town folks, the Republican Party's mistakes were offset by landmark victories, including the confirmation of John Roberts and Samuel Alito, and expanding restrictions on abortion rights. "Oh, yeah, that's huge," said my brother, Allen. "That part I'm very happy about."

We were talking late at night on the telephone, after putting our boys to bed. Nearly two years had passed since those first debates in Wichita, before the 2004 election, and we were still arguing, still seeing things through radically different lenses.

"Don't you find it troubling that the Republicans can't seem to make things work?" I asked. "I mean, their budgets don't add up, and their agencies are in disarray. Important agencies like FEMA and the Department of Homeland Security."

After a pause, Allen said, "Yeah, I do worry about competence. One thing that really threw me for a loop was the whole Katrina business. I lost a lot of confidence in Bush over that. I thought he did such a great job bringing people together after 9/11, and I don't know what's happened since then."

"Has your opinion about him changed?"

"I still like George Bush. I like the fact that he's a Christian. But obviously that's not all that's important when running a country."

"Really? I thought those things — personal likability and Christianity — were pretty big deals for you."

"Sure, but give rural people some credit for reading the situation," Allen said. "George Bush's followers aren't a bunch of idiots. It's been a hard year. We know that he's made a lot of mistakes."

"Does that mean you're willing to give Democrats a second look?"

"I'm glad Bush isn't running again in 2008, let me put it that way. But it would take a remarkably bad candidate from the Republican Party and a remarkably good candidate from the Democratic Party for me to switch sides. Maybe if the Democrats were to run somebody who was pro-life and who just comes across as a competent leader."

"Do you think this brand of small-town conservatism has been discredited at all as a political philosophy? It seems like George Bush and the Republican Congress had the chance to demonstrate something the last six years. Ideology aside, they might have shown that traditional social and political values add up to an effective governing strategy. They work in the modern world."

"Whether it's fantasy or not, I still believe that traditional values *are* good. If anything, I'd like to move backward toward the way things were. I just don't think people who have a flexible view of morality have done much good for the country. Obviously, there are some things in the past that we wouldn't want to go back to, racial prejudice and all that, but that doesn't mean that we need to have an evolving sense of morality or believe in an evolving structure of society."

"But we're not a nation of small towns anymore. We live in cities. We're not a nation of white Anglo-Saxon Protestants. We're a melting pot. We don't work on farms, we work on computers. We don't all go to church. Don't we need a political culture that reflects all that churn and change?"

"Look, it's not something that I can point to and say that I have some philosophical reason for why I think my way is right. I'm just more comfortable in that vein. It's my nature, I guess."

"I'll be honest," I said. "After Bush, I think it'll be harder to convince people that you're right."

After a long pause, Allen said, "The last few years have been a huge missed opportunity, of course. What are the odds that we're going to have another time like this, with social conservatives holding so much control over the political process? I think my disappointment must be what liberals felt about Bill Clinton. I can't help wondering what could have happened with a stronger, better leader."

Allen believes that the right leader is out there. Another Barry Goldwater. Another Ronald Reagan. Another Newt Gingrich. Someone will take up the banner of his culture, perhaps someone a little smarter and a little more charismatic. He doesn't mind if it takes a while. Homelanders like to win, but they're also patient. In the meantime, rural Americans will continue to score victories. Their control of the GOP and their hard-wired advantages in our political system ensure that small towns will retain a prominent place at the center of our politics.

Indeed, even as their numbers dwindle, rural Americans are convinced that their renaissance has only just begun, that their culture will continue to make inroads into mainstream society, and that their vision of America will ultimately prevail. "God has called us to be His representatives in our nation and in our world," declared James Dobson, urging his followers to "select candidates who represent your views and work for their election."

Because metros appear certain to continue their long embrace of progressivism and liberalism (a trend that began a century ago), the divide between the two tribes will likely grow larger. Conflicts will intensify. If *Roe v. Wade* is overturned or substantially weakened, many rural parts of the country may ban abortions, while in urban states the practice will remain legal. More and more metro states are likely to offer same-sex couples broad legal and social equality, while in homelander states gay rights will continue to be deliberately proscribed.

We may find rural states where Christian religious symbols and rituals are incorporated into civic life, while urban Americans will maintain a strict separation between church and state. In rural-dominant communities, a significant percentage of our children may be educated in a creationist worldview, while in urban and suburban schools the teaching will remain secular and modernist.

This rift could reach the highest levels of our political culture as early as 2008. We may find Nancy Pelosi, a liberal urban Democrat from San Francisco, serving as House Speaker while New York's Hillary Rodham Clinton occupies the White House as our first female president. Meanwhile, a homelander archconservative such as Kansas's Sam Brownback could lead the U.S. Senate while Chief Justice John Roberts presides over the Supreme Court.

America's urban and rural cultures will have separate and mutually hostile chieftains. Our two tribes will look to different and often contradictory sources for their wisdom, their sense of right and wrong, and their understanding of our nation's future. Welcome to the homeland.

# Acknowledgments

Thanks to Howard Berkes, NPR's rural correspondent. The opinions in this book are my own, but his wisdom has shaped my views of small-town America. Also thanks to Al Cross at the Institute for Rural Journalism. The Institute's national conference in 2005, co-sponsored by the Knight Center for Specialized Journalism, was instrumental in informing *Welcome to the Homeland*. Finally, thanks to the staff of North Country Public Radio, who supported this project at every turn.

# Suggested Reading

In writing *Welcome to the Homeland,* I was influenced by a variety of books, articles, essays, broadcasts, and published papers. Here is a partial list of some of the texts that I found particularly challenging and illuminating.

Atwood, Margaret. *The Handmaid's Tale.* Toronto: McClelland and Stewart. 1985.

Bailyn, Bernard. *To Begin The World Anew: The Genius & Ambiguities of the American Founders.* New York: Alfred A. Knopf, 2003.

Bennett, William. *The Index of Leading Cultural Indicators: American Society at the End of the Twentieth Century.* New York: Broadway Books, 1999.

Biel, Steven. *American Gothic: A Life of America's Most Famous Painting.* New York: W.W. Norton, 2005.

Bokenkotter, Thomas. *A Concise History of the Catholic Church.* New York: Random House, 2004.

Brooks, David. *On Paradise Drive: How We Live Now (And Always Have) into the Future.* New York: Simon & Schuster, 2004.

Clinton, Hillary Rodham. *It Takes a Village: And Other Lessons Children Teach Us.* New York: Simon & Schuster, 1996.

Didion, Joan. *The Year of Magical Thinking.* New York: Alfred A. Knopf, 2005.

Frank, Thomas. *What's the Matter with Kansas? How Conservatives Won the Heart of America.* New York: Henry Holt, 2004.

Gingrich, Newt, Richard Armey, et al. "Contract with America." Washington, D.C.: Republican National Committee, 1994.

Goldwater, Barry. *The Conscience of a Conservative.* Sheperdsville, Ky.: Victor Publishing Company, 1960.

Hamilton, Alexander, James Madison, and John Jay. *Federalist Papers.* First published, 1788. New York: Penguin, 1987.

Jacoby, Susan. *Freethinkers: A History of American Secularism.* New York: Henry Holt, 2004.

Kurlansky, Mark. *1968: The Year That Rocked the World.* New York: Random House, 2004.

Lakoff, Goerge. *Don't Think of an Elephant: Know Your Values and Frame the Debate — The Essential Guide for Progressives.* White River Junction, Vt.: Chelsea Green Publishing, 2004

Least Heat-Moon, William. *Blue Highways: A Journey into America.* Boston: Little, Brown and Company, 1983.

Lemann, Nicholas. *The Promised Land: The Great Black Migration and How It Changed America.* New York: Vintage Books, 1991.

Lewis, Sinclair. *Main Street.* First published 1920. New York: Dover Thrift, 1999.

Menand, Louis. *The Metaphysical Club: A Story of Ideas in America.* New York: Farrar, Strauss, and Giroux, 2001.

Micklethwait, John, and Adrian Wooldridge. *The Right Nation: Conservative Power in America.* New York: Penguin Press, 2004.

Miller, Zell. *A National Party No More: The Conscience of a Conservative Democrat.* Macon, Ga.: Stroud & Hall, 2003.

Orwell, George. *1984.* New York: Harcourt Brace Jovanovich, 1949.

Packer, George. *Blood of the Liberals.* New York: Farrar, Strauss and Giroux, 2000.

Santorum, Rick. *It Takes a Family: Conservatism and the Common Good.* Wilmington, Del.: ISI Books, 2005.

Toffler, Alvin. *Future Shock.* New York: Random House, 1970.

Whitcomb, John C. and Henry Morris. *Genesis Flood: The Biblical Record and Its Scientific Implications.* Philadelphia: Presbyterian and Reformed Publishing, 1961.

Whitman, Christine Todd. *It's My Party Too: The Battle for the Heart of the Republican Party and the Future of America.* New York: Penguin, 2005.

Whitman, Walt. *Leaves of Grass.* First published 1855. New York: Bantam Classic, 1983.

Wilson, Woodrow. *A History of the American People.* New York: Harper & Brothers, 1902.

Zinn, Howard. *A People's History of the United States: 1492–Present.* New York: HarperCollins, 2003.